Treasury of

Big Game Animals

Treasury of

Big Game

An Outdoor Life Book

Animals

Text and Photos by Erwin A. Bauer

Outdoor Life • Harper & Row

New York, Evanston, San Francisco, London

Library of Congress Catalog Card Number: **72-90933**
SBN 06-010243-8

Designed by Jeff Fitschen

Manufactured in the United States of America

To all those with whom I have hunted big game with camera and gun ...

Charlie Abou, Blackie Amberson, Cully Anderson, Ken Anderson, Hank Andrews, Jack Antrim, Jim Baber, Columbus Bailey, Jim Barnes, Ollie Barney, Saloman Barragan, Bob Bauer, Parker Bauer, Peggy Bauer, Leo Beaumont, Julius Blair, Nick Blunt, Bud Brewster, Bill Browning, Stan Burrell, Willis Buttolph.

Also, Glen Childers, Ross Childers, Bob Cope, Howard Copenhaver, Keith Cormack, Joe Cross, Norman Deane, Sarel deJager, Denge, Domenico, Bill Dutton, Lew Eakin, Jim Feeley, Walt Findley, Bill Fisher, Nat Franklin, Ed Frecker, Simon Gamage, Bill Gambs, Bill Garnett, Earl Gibbs, Hassan Gul.

Also, C. L. Harris, Peter Hay, Bill Hendershot, Peter Herbert, Brian Herne, Joe Hodgson, Milton Hooker, Len Hughes, Clarence Johnson, Don Johnson, Charlie Kellenbarger, Cory Kilvert, Kimangut, Eric Kjos, Lou Klewer, Dick Kotis, Jim Koreski, Ram Krishna, Cy Kuefler, Elmer Lake, Sid Lantz.

Also, Glen Lau, George Laycock, David Laylin, Dale Lefferson, Joe Linduska, Cougar Long, Longollo, Philip Louie, Bob McArthur, Jim McLucas, Bob Machum, Mac Mackenzie, Lloyd Monning, Karl Maslowski, Neil Millar, Handy Miner, John Moxley, James Ngomane, Ivan Nyc, John Oney, Ed Osborn.

Also, Bovey Overholt, Clary Palmer-Wilson, Jon Parsons, Dave Phillips, Macedonio Polo, John Powell, Maynard Raasch, Tom Reynolds, Ian Ross, Rusty Russell, Saidi, Bill Sauer, John Sauer, Frank Sayers, Homer Sayers, Mike Sayers, Pete Sayers, Doc Schuckert, Lawrence Shelley, Austin Smith, George Smith.

Also, Jim Smith, Al Staffan, Bob Tate, Ken Tinley, Van Van Wagner, Gene Wade, John Walatka, Vern Walsh, Ron Warner, Jesse Weaver, Budge Wilcox, Don Wilcox, Waldo Wilcox, Wes Woodyard, Kentucky Yank, John Zalen, Mike Zenner.

Contents

North America

Whitetail Deer

DAYLIGHT was swiftly fading into dusk, into that strange, brief twilight of the northern winter when snow flurries begin to fall. Two hours of sitting motionless beside a frozen balsam swamp had left me almost too chilled to endure any longer the near-zero temperature. But a sixth sense kept nagging me to stay.

I flexed one numb leg and tried to stand on it, and at that instant I caught a flick of motion in the gloom. Next thing I knew, a buck deer of impossible size materialized from the swamp and stood facing me not forty yards away.

Even though the scene was blurred by snowflakes, the animal was outlined for one split second against a dark green background. That was long enough to know that its antlers were by far the most massive I'd ever seen. Then the animal vanished as suddenly as it appeared, as if erased by the curtain of falling snow.

Maybe it hadn't been there at all, I thought. The .270 still rested across my lap and normally I would have raised it. But the huge hoofprints etched in the snow verified that I had seen an extraordinary animal rather than a mirage. All at once I started shivering, and not from the cold alone.

The hike back to camp was long and bitter, most of it in silent, pitch-black Minnesota woods.

"You didn't score?" smiled Frank Sayers, my hunting partner, when I reached camp.

"No," I answered, "but I did see the most magnificent buck of my life." Then I described the animal's massive horns and the way it had evaporated into the twilight.

"If you saw a whitetail buck of any size," Frank said after I'd finished, "you saw the greatest game animal that walks the earth."

Tough and adaptable, the whitetail is considered by many to be the greatest game animal of all. The deer thrives in every type of terrain—farmland fringes, bottomlands and northern woods.

Greatest game animal? That is a very extravagant claim. But the more I thought about it that night deep in the North Woods, the more I realized it was true.

Frank and I have been lucky enough to wander widely around the world and have shared a good many hunting camps. I recall the tent we pitched deep in British Columbia's high Cassiars, where we stalked Stone sheep, the more luxurious elephant camp on the opposite side of the planet beside the Albert Nile, and half a hundred other camps in between. During those adventures we hunted most of the major big-game animals. Generally our luck has been good. But somehow the whitetail—the deer of America's southern swamps and bottomlands, the dweller of the fringes of mid-west farmlands and of the northern woods—stands out as the greatest challenge of all.

"Look at it this way," he continued. "Let's suppose you have unlimited time, and money is of no consequence. Your object is a collection of big-game animals, but only of trophy or record-book size. Go anywhere you like and never mind the price tag. Which would be the hardest to collect? Our own whitetail."

That point is well taken. Name almost any other game species—bighorn sheep, lion, brown bear, sable antelope—and if you can afford the time and money and possess a moderate amount of stamina and persistence, you can eventually bag a trophy with record-book measurements. But spend the rest of your autumns in the best whitetail habitats of North America looking for a Boone and Crockett head, and the odds will be against you.

The whitetail of today, *Odocoileus virginianus,* has been created by the stresses and pressures of 15 million years of evolution. It reached this continent that long ago, probably in the middle Miocene period, via an isthmus which existed between Siberia and Alaska. The species survived a later period of drought, the Pleistocene, followed by glaciers which covered much of the northern hemisphere. Countless other wildlife species such as the sabre-toothed tigers and mastodons were exterminated by the climatic changes. But the whitetail evolved into the tough, durable and beautiful animal which is still abundant after four centuries of intense market- and sport-hunting in America.

Tough? That may seem a strange adjective for a species so apparently frail and gentle. But "tough" is an understatement. And the toughening process begins the moment the deer is conceived.

All winter long (and winter is the Hunger Moon of the Indians in the North) a fetus is carried by the doe which lives on subsistence rations at best. Starvation is always a possibility, and it is compounded by intense cold and deep snows. Other animals hibernate or migrate, but deer fight it out. This is the season when natural predators are most active. So it is a tough doe that survives the winter ordeal, and her fawn will likely survive to be just as tough. By fall it will be able to jump cleanly over a six- or seven-foot barrier from a standing position. And it will be able to sprint thirty miles per hour through a woodland obstacle course.

Then, if it survives the first fall hunting season, it must face the same test of starvation and cold its mother faced.

Not many animals have been supplied by nature with so many escape mechanisms. The whitetail is a powerful jumper, and bounds of twenty-five to thirty feet are not uncommon from a running start. Few animals can be out of sight so quickly or so gracefully. The whitetail's close cousin, the mule deer, bunches its feet and bounces away somewhat awkwardly. But the whitetail gallops; its gallop sometimes merges with great bounds and is pure poetry of motion. When it is really under pressure, a deer becomes a horizontal cinnamon-gray blur. But no matter how fast it is traveling, a whitetail can abruptly brake to a stop and turn in another direction, a maneuver that would appear to break the animal's legs.

The deer's ball bearing anatomy makes this and other similar maneuvers easy. The front legs do not connect directly to the skeleton, but instead are separated by a tough rubbery tissue which acts as a shock absorber.

The whitetail is not merely a tenacious and remarkable athlete. It has good hearing, a phenomenal sense of smell and uncanny eyesight (even in semi-darkness and despite colorblindness) which some hunters swear is the equivalent of 8X vision or better. Although vision is difficult to measure in wild animals, one thing is true: a whitetail can spot the slightest unnatural motion from incredible distances. Whitetails may possess such keen hearing that they can distinguish the foot pad of a bear or another deer from that of a human without bothering to look up. When the wind and humidity are favorable, a deer can smell a hunter from as much as a mile away. A wise hunter keeps these things always in mind.

One evening in a Michigan deer camp,

Supplied by nature with a host of escape mechanisms, the whitetail is a powerful jumper and fleet runner. From a running start it can bound twenty-five feet; its gallop, sometimes merging with great bounds, is beautiful to behold.

Frank Sayers summed up a whitetail's ability to escape. "In any cover at all," he said, "an old buck can be as inconspicuous as a field mouse."

Most scientists who study animal behavior do not believe that wild creatures can think. Their reactions are considered to be based on instinct alone. And instinct is a combination of heredity, fear and perhaps the memory of past experience. In other words, a deer tries to avoid human beings because its ancestors have always been hunted, because as a fawn its mother ran away from people, and because the deer itself has been shot at.

But even the biggest, oldest bucks do not bolt blindly away at the sudden sight or sound of a human being. On the contrary, they may skulk nearby, completely hidden in brush from which they can keep the enemy in sight. Or, taking maximum advantage of cover, they may circle around to get behind him. Another buck may prefer to hide motionless, allowing a hunter to pass right by, maybe only yards away. There is much here to suggest that deer can reason.

Some years ago, Michigan conservation officials placed thirty-nine whitetails, nine of which were bucks, in an escape-proof enclosure of one square mile on the Cusino Wildlife Experiment Station. It was typical Michigan whitetail cover—hardwoods and pines mixed with swamplands. In good weather and with an ideal tracking snow, six experienced hunters were permitted to hunt inside the enclosure. At the time, a local newspaper columnist sneered that it didn't appear to be a very sporting proposition.

But four days passed before any of the hunters even saw antlers. In fact, it was difficult to glimpse any deer at all. And fifty-one total hours of pursuit were required to actually kill a buck, all this in a confined area from which the deer could not escape!

In another experiment in South Dakota, a radio transmitter and long orange ear streamers were fastened to a single mature buck which was then released in an open hunting area. The researchers were able to keep track of the deer's exact whereabouts by radio. A week passed and the hunters never saw the deer. They complained at the official checking station that no deer were in the area. Some of these same hunters were known to have passed within forty yards of the animal without seeing it or the orange streamers.

During the second week of the Dakota experiment, a team of expert hunters was dispatched into the exact area where the whitetail was lurking. But a careful search of all available cover, which was thin in that spot, revealed nothing. Then, by accident, one hunter practically stepped on the deer where it was hidden safely, orange streamers and all, in a thicket. Still, the deer raced away unhurt.

Whitetails have given me the slip so often that I go afield anticipating it. That is good advice to anyone. Then a hunter can concentrate on what he considers impossible, because that is precisely what an old buck will do.

In his efforts to avoid man, a big buck will not always bolt blindly away but may skulk nearby, hidden in brush from where he can keep an enemy in sight. Sometimes he may circle around to get behind the hunter. This is an extremely large deer, probably with a Boone and Crockett head.

Several years ago in late October, Bill Browning and I were hunting the Missouri River bottomlands of the Charles M. Russell National Wildlife Range in eastern Montana. This is mostly mule deer country, but a good herd of large and healthy whitetails had long been established in the riverine habitat. In fact, the whitetails may have grown too numerous there for their own good.

At the time of this hunt, the limit was two deer per person. Both could be whitetails, but at least one *had* to be a whitetail. Without this regulation, a conservation official explained to us, hunters would come into the area and shoot two muleys because it was so much easier.

Not long after daybreak one morning, Bill and I watched a splendid whitetail from a hillside far above, from a perfect vantage point, but a little too far away to risk a shot. The deer browsed for a while and then walked away into an isolated willow thicket tucked inside one narrow bend of the Missouri River and almost completely surrounded by water. Bill and I looked at each other in disbelief.

"We've got that buck trapped," Bill said.

"Unless he decides to jump off of a high bank and swim against a strong current," I answered.

The strategy we chose was to approach the thicket from opposite sides, Bill cutting through the willows upstream while I went downstream. The deer would be sandwiched in between us and somebody was certain to get

a shot. We would also be able to see if the deer escaped by swimming to the south bank.

But none of these things happened. The deer didn't swim, didn't make a break or give us a shot, and, in fact, we never saw him again. The buck just vanished—and that's all there is to it.

What qualities or characteristics make a big-game animal great? What factors must a sportsman consider?

The elusiveness or intelligence of the species is one. Its natural environment is another. Is it dangerous game? Is it available to many hunters? Is it a beautiful, handsome or rare animal?

Of course, beauty is in the eye of the beholder and the same sable antelope which thrills one hunter might not be as exciting as a leopard or a tiger to another. But few can dispute that our own whitetail is among the most graceful and striking animals ever to wander through the world's wildernesses. If we overlook or underrate the whitetail, it is probably because "familiarity breeds contempt."

As pointed out before, the whitetail is the opposite of rare; it is everyone's trophy, widely distributed and fair game almost everywhere it exists. Some of the mountain sheep of Asia, on the other hand, are only accessible to hunters with fortunes to invest. So abundance, too, is a factor in this evaluation.

Wild whitetails are by no means dangerous, not even during the autumn rut. They have not lured hunters to the grave as have bears and Cape buffalos, rhinos, elephants and the big cats. But more sportsmen die of heart attacks, freezing, and similar mishaps while hunting deer each year than through the hazards of all the others put together. Deer hunting, typical whitetail trophy hunting, requires far more

exertion than riding in an African safari car.

Now consider habitat. The steep, lung-busting climbs to the top of the world (often to no avail) are largely what makes bagging a mountain sheep anywhere such a challenge. The animal itself is not quite so elusive. The hunter who toils through a bamboo jungle in Kenya for a bongo will never forget the experience. Nor will the man who follows a pack of hounds in dense, humid jaguar country of Central America. But it's also pretty tough trudging through the country where the biggest whitetail bucks retreat in late autumn.

By the time a buck survives his first hunting season, he has known more hunting pressure than a kudu in Mozambique bush will experience in its entire life. By the time the whitetail reaches the fifth fall, it is shy and nervous almost beyond description. It is not far-fetched to believe that an old buck can sense the approach of opening day. The onset of autumn storms and lower temperatures is instinctively associated with the invasion of hunters and the bombardment which follows. So the biggest bucks drift away to the places least attractive to hunters, to dense alder thickets and balsam swamps, to the heaviest cover they can find. Add to this scene the deep, wet snows which are common during northern hunting seasons and rock-bottom temperatures, and you will see that the whitetails' domain is not easy to invade.

When elusiveness and the ability to evade hunters are considered, the old whitetail bucks rate the highest of all. One autumn recently furnished an excellent illustration of this.

There is a county near my home where the deer are of good size and very healthy, but are concentrated in a small area. There is never a shortage of hunters throughout the short Ohio season, however, and they comb every bit of this ground over and over again. It doesn't seem possible that any animal bigger than a cottontail could escape the pressure. During a season not long ago hunters were particularly unsuccessful, and some said there weren't enough bucks in the area to justify the hunting. They recommended that the season be kept closed.

But on the very next weekend after the season ended, the state game protector and state highway patrolmen were called out to investigate four deer killed at night on the highways in this same small area. Three of the four were very fine bucks—bragging size—and one was crowding the Boone & Crockett minimum. It is anybody's guess how they managed to remain inconspicuous as hunters crisscrossed back and forth through the woods, day after day. But they did. And no doubt other deer existed which hadn't wandered out to die on the road.

Every season, however, produces its share of incidents which suggest that big bucks are not so wise and wary after all. One of the finest bucks on record in Kentucky was shot by a hunter on his first deer hunt with a borrowed rifle he hadn't bothered to test-fire before. It was late in the day and the man was lost somewhere in the Daniel Boone National Forest, so he sat down to try to get his bearings. A few moments later a huge buck practically ran over the top of the hunter, and a lucky snap shot hit the deer. It ran another hundred yards before it fell. When the hunter walked up to the deer, he spotted the road—and his car—just beyond. Honest!

There is also the story carried by one of the wire services a year ago about the Montana hunter who was forced to take both his wife and mother-in-law on a deer-hunting trip along the same Missouri River bottoms which are full of whitetails with PhDs in making suckers out of sportsmen, as I have already noted.

All week long the man used every trick he knew to bag a good buck. He saw does aplenty and on the last day of the trip settled for a doe just to put venison in the freezer. If you guessed that both the ladies shot bucks without leaving the camp, in fact by pointing a rifle right through the tent flaps one morning, you are right. But the real heartbreaker is that the mother-in-law's deer is certain to be listed in the next revised edition of Boone & Crockett's prestige book.

But 999 of 1,000 jumbo bucks come the hard way.

I have already pointed out that there is no guaranteed method for reserving yourself a spot in the whitetail records. But there are some hints which any nimrod can use to tip a few factors at least slightly in his favor.

One way is to hunt in big-buck country. For such reasons as nutrition, hunting pressure, terrain and other unknown factors, deer grow bigger in some areas than in others, and often the area may be very small or restricted. Perhaps it is more applicable here to say that deer antlers grow bigger in some places than others.

An immensely serious trophy hunter might begin by checking the latest Boone & Crockett listings. Under whitetails he will find that an astonishing percentage of the biggest heads recorded have been taken in southern Saskatchewan, with southern Manitoba running a distant second. Good trophy states below the border are Minnesota, New York, Texas, Montana, South and North Dakota. States to avoid are all those in the Southeast where deer are very small, with one notable exception—Virginia. The Old Dominion happens to be among the best places to hunt in the entire country.

But two states really offer the big-buck specialist his best bet, and this is surprising because neither are known as good deer states. The kill in Ohio, for example, often is less than 2,000 total males and females per year (annually the road kill is greater than the hunter harvest), but the Buckeye State places as many bucks in the record books as either Minnesota or Texas, where the kill runs into six figures. In other words, a large percentage of Ohio deer have barroom betting-size racks.

However, Arkansas appears to be *the* state for trophy whitetail hunters. This state has more whitetails in the record book than any other two states (except Saskatchewan and Manitoba), although the total deer kill is small compared to many other states.

There are smaller areas in every state, and these might be less than a county in size, which annually produce the biggest racks. The way to locate these "islands" is to check the results of local big-buck contests over a period of several years or, better still, to contact your own state conservation department. Each department has a deer or big-game biologist, or specialist, who will have this information at his fingertips. He may even be able to explain why one bit of real estate grows heavier antlers on deer than another.

Another way to improve the odds of bagging a trophy is to sharpen your hunting skills. Chances at big bucks come far too seldom to be missed when they do come. This applies equally to any kind of big-game hunting. Practice shooting the year around and don't wait until opening day is at hand to pick up the rifle. Keep shooting until it is second nature and work especially toward a good, quick off-hand shot. Learn to read sign for freshness and become adept at walking quietly.

Did you ever consider jumping the gun— going hunting before opening day? I'm not suggesting that you break the law, poach or even

A young buck, about sixteen months old, with a pair of spikes. Normally, not until the buck is in his fourth or fifth year does he grow a rack that can be considered trophy size.

carry a rifle. But I *am* urging you to spend several days in the woods before the other hunters get there. If yours is to be a two-week hunt, why not set up camp a week ahead of time and spend that first week browsing through the woods, quietly, looking for deer and deer sign?

There are a number of sound reasons for this. To begin, deer are calmer and easier to approach before the first big bombardment. And while you're observing them, you're also getting acquainted with the woods, finding heavily used deer trails before other hunters find them, and beginning to feel at home in the bush. Try to do as much of this prospecting as possible just after daybreak and during the last hour before dusk; this offers the best chance to see what areas the big bucks are using.

If it is legal where you hunt, go out after dark before the season opens. Do your sleeping in the daytime and drive the backroads at night. Concentrate on the fire breaks and timber roads which are seldom traveled and see where you find the most deer activity. Again, if it is lawful, mount a spotlight on your car and go jacklighting, being certain not to have firearms of any kind in the car. This method is tremendously revealing, and you may find deer where you never dreamed they existed.

At least thirty different subspecies of whitetails have been identified, ranging from the northern woodland (*Odocoileus virginianus borealis*) and Dakota (*O. v. dakotensis*) varieties, which are largest, to the Florida Key

In late summer, the buck begins to shed the velvet from his antlers, hastening the process by rubbing them against trees and shrubs. Here a beautiful five-pointer, his antlers bare and polished for the rut, browses in fall foliage.

(*O. v. clavium*) and Coiba Island, Panama (*O. v. rothschildi*) whitetails, which are the smallest. A number of species are either disappearing, extinct or somewhere in between. Ranges of some are very small and may be confined to a single small island. Taken together, the whitetail subspecies range from the northern latitudes of James Bay southward to the Isthmus of Panama, from Puget Sound to Maine to the Florida Keys, in other words, across most of North America between the 10th and 53rd parallels.

It is very difficult for the layman to distinguish one subspecies from another. Males of all species shed their antlers annually, although in tropical Central America where the antlers are normally short, broad and gnarled, the time of shedding is not as regular as farther north. The slight seasonal changes in temperature may account for retaining antlers longer.

Extra tines on antlers, called non-typical heads, occur more often in Texas (*O. v. texanus*) deer than in others. There is a head taken near Brady, Texas, which has forty-nine points. On the other hand, the Acapulco buck (*O. v. acapulcenis*) seldom grows more than spikes. And the main beams of whitetail species south of the Isthmus of Tehuantepec in Mexico tend to grow upward or backward rather than forward.

I have done a good bit of photographing whitetails, at times in open hunting areas, but also on reserves and in sanctuaries where the animals are more confiding. No matter where, camera hunting is an excellent way to learn the changes in behavior of whitetails throughout the year.

In spring and summer they are most scattered. Bucks and does with fawns are likely to be anywhere. In the winter, whitetails are concentrated, with bucks and does grouped where the foraging is best. In between comes the rut. Because the rut normally coincides with most state hunting seasons, and because it's the most active period in a whitetail's lifetime, it is the time that most concerns hunters.

The rut, or annual breeding season, does not occur at exactly the same time every year, though very nearly so. In Ohio, for example, what might be termed the peak of the rut usually occurs in mid-November. North of Ohio it occurs somewhat earlier; south of Ohio, later.

Nor is the duration of the rut the same every fall. Occasionally most of the breeding activity will be concentrated in one week or so. More often it spreads out over a month or more. During the rut, short periods of great activity are interspersed with longer periods of relative inactivity. Cold weather seems to stimulate activity, while high temperatures slow it down.

Technically the rut probably begins in late summer when bucks begin to shed the velvet from their fully grown antlers. Though the velvet falls away naturally, bucks hasten the process by rubbing their antlers against trees, shrubs, and one another. I have even seen them rubbing against telephone poles, as well as against an old outhouse at a long-deserted Michigan logging camp. This rubbing gradually becomes an aggressive display—a duel against a sapling or another deer—and continues for months after all the velvet is gone. Thus, the presence of many slashed trees from which the bark has been peeled should be a sure sign that many bucks are in the area.

But is it? Not at all.

Two years ago in October, during a weekend scouting and photographing trip, I found an area of about ten acres where trees had been slashed and barked wholesale. I have never seen so much slash damage concentrated in any

Two young bucks engage in a sparring contest during the rutting season. This may lead to an all-out battle in which the bucks use their antlers, but fierce fights among whitetails occur less frequently than is believed, and usually at night.

other place. I decided to build blinds in the area and erected them in ideal places. Two weeks later most of the leaves had fallen from the trees, and I went hopefully into the woods.

I have always wanted to photograph whitetail bucks fighting. Actually, fighting occurs far less frequently than most sportsmen believe, and when it does it usually happens at night. In all my time in whitetail deer woods I have seen conflict only three times, and these incidents were merely brief pushing matches. Another time I saw two bucks with antlers locked; one was practically dead from the long struggle.

Now, as I entered my blind, I was hopeful from so much sign that I would see action. But I shouldn't have wasted my time. Not only did I fail to see bucks jousting; I didn't see any bucks at all. Only does. What happened?

We might find the explanation in a beautiful scene on an outdoor calendar I have, well done by the artist except for one thing. It shows a splendid whitetail buck with massive rack in a woodland opening. His swollen neck and his stance indicate that it is the rut. He is surrounded by three does. But the scene should be the other way around: during the peak of a whitetail rut it is far more likely that several bucks will surround a single doe. Elk and other male animals acquire harems; whitetails don't.

So where you find one good buck you are likely to find others nearby. And all will be where the does *in estrus* are, rather than where

16

most does are—or where they have been rubbing tree trucks recently.

This concentration of breeding bucks into groups accounts for the generally accepted belief among whitetail hunters that year after year certain areas are "big-buck places." From my own experience, I'd say that theory is no more true than the elephant-graveyard theory.

On a snowy, gusty evening last November I spotted eight bucks in the vicinity of one doe at the edge of a hardwood forest. There may have been other bucks and does nearby, but my count in the failing light was nine deer. Four of the bucks were huge old busters; the others had pretty good heads. Each was trying to outmaneuver the others, but no actual head-on clashes occurred. It was too dark for photography anyway, but I resolved to be on the spot first thing next morning. It was a very exciting prospect and, believe me, buck fever begins long before the hunting season opens.

In a whole year of Novembers there wouldn't be more than a few days as perfect for photography as the next morning. It was crisp and clear. Shortly after daybreak I drove out to the trysting spot, cameras ready, and found —nothing. Brush had been trampled, and leaves on the ground had been raked with sharp hoofs, but frost covered the evidence and the deer were gone. Soon, so were my high and hopeful spirits.

Luckily I located those deer again late in the afternoon. I'm almost certain it was the same group because there were eight bucks and one doe. They were about two and one-half miles as the crow flies from where I first saw them. My conclusion is that if there are big-buck areas, they are not necessarily in the same places day after day, let alone year after year. At least not during the time of the rut.

After the rut subsides, the bucks in an area might very well retreat into deep winter cover and concentrate there. And in traditional wintering areas, most often very remote, a serious deer hunter stands a good chance of getting a fine trophy if the season remains open late enough.

As I said, I have made many camera hunts in areas of both light and heavy hunting pressure. My experiences demonstrate that the heavier the pressure, the more nocturnal are the bigger bucks in all their activity, and of course the harder they are to see. About the only chance you have of seeing them in the open in heavily hunted areas is very early and very late in the day, right at the edge of the forest.

At the tag end of my whitetail-watching last fall, on the eve of open hunting season, I sat on a tree blind that a bowhunter had built several years before. It was flimsy, and I really didn't enjoy the precarious perch. But enough fascinating things happened on the ground to keep me up there for a while.

Around midafternoon a handsome buck appeared from the heart of the forest and strolled toward the edge of the woods. He didn't go out into the sunlight, but stayed in the shadows, moving quietly and scanning the forest all around. Eventually he vanished as silently as he had arrived.

Before dusk four more deer, including two bucks, passed below me within point-blank gun range. Again, none of them stepped beyond the forest shadows. Then and there I decided to spend opening day in that same tree, certain that I could collect my venison.

But I ended the first day without firing a shot. This time, however, I was tricked by other hunters. When I arrived on the scene opening day, five hunters were in the process of

At the peak of the rut, several bucks will surround a single doe. Elk and other male animals acquire harems; whitetails do not. Where you find one good buck, you are likely to find others nearby.

organizing a drive. Three of them were going on stand, one directly beneath my tree. The other two would make the drive from the opposite side of the woods. The stratcgy seemed to guarantee some shooting.

Later in the day I saw the leader of the hunt. I asked him if they had scored.

"Naw," he replied. "No deer in that woods. Scarce everywhere this year."

I wish I knew how the deer eluded those drivers. The next day I again saw deer from the tree stand, and I bagged one. It was so easy that I almost felt guilty. Because whitetails seldom look up, getting above them is one very effective game that hunters can play.

Today far too many of the world's big-game animals are endangered species and others are in such short supply that no hunting should be permitted. But the whitetail is not in this category. The number which can be harvested annually, safely and with no reduction in the herd, runs well into seven figures. A far greater hazard to northern woodland whitetails than hunters is the onset of winter. Then the weakened bucks (many having suffered a twenty-pound weight loss from the long lovemaking) and newly-pregnant does herd up and retreat to their wintering areas.

During the rut, only the bucks fight occasionally. But from Christmas through April the entire herd fights a desperate battle to survive. Winter may doom a larger portion of the herd than did the earlier shooting season.

Through much of the northern whitetail range, snow falls intermittently during December. There are occasional mild winters when it melts soon after falling, but normally it begins to stick and build up before the holidays. At the same time the temperature plunges downward. All through January and February there are unbroken periods of a week or more when the mercury is well below zero, particularly in the western part of the range. And the snow keeps accumulating, at times and in places to depths of three and four feet. It wouldn't seem that any quadrupeds could survive the bleak and deadly days of winter.

Trained wildlife experts believe that a whitetail's first and only instinct when winter arrives is to escape the intense cold. As soon as the first bitter winds blow and snow piles up, the deer desert the hardwood ridges and head for the best available dense covers. That is, they leave the protection of cedar and balsam swamps, now frozen and solid underfoot, for the heaviest stands of conifers. The deer thus maroon themselves in what are called "deer yards." According to Walter P. Taylor in his *The Deer of North America,* northern whitetails use only 10 percent of their total range in winter. Biol-

ogist John Madson compares this to a poor human family deserting the rest of the house to huddle around the warm stove in one room.

Until snows reach a depth of twenty inches or so, the deer will stray from the yards to forage, although never very far. An occasional whitetail may also travel short distances until it cannot or will not travel, and a sort of lethargy sets in. Trails outward from the yards gradually fill with snow and the animals are trapped in a small, trampled space. It isn't long before they eat all that is remotely edible within or near the yard. All trees are stripped bare as high as the largest deer can reach on hind legs.

Deer have been known to stand nearly motionless beneath the branches of a dense evergreen during a three-day snowstorm. Although some may bed down close to others in the snow, they apparently do not huddle together to share warmth. But when the temperature plunges much below zero, bedded deer must either get up and exercise or stiffen and freeze in their beds, which is not uncommon. Exercising uses up valuable energy that would be better saved for still harder times ahead.

Biologists have been bewildered by some facets of whitetail winter behavior. Often they have watched deer starve in overbrowsed yards rather than struggle through snowdrifts to an available food supply close by. Game biologists have even opened up trails and baited the trails with white cedar (a favorite whitetail food), but have had little luck getting the deer to move. As often as not, the animals starving in a yard prefer to stay there and keep starving.

During periods of high winds, and on occasional days warm enough to cause thawing, whitetails will not move at all for any reason. Of course they are most vulnerable to predation at these times. Wolves, coyotes, bobcats

As soon as the first bitter winds blow and the snow deepens, the deer leave the hardwood ridges for dense cover, seeking to escape the intense cold. They form "deer yards," from which they may stray, like these does, in search of forage.

and even packs of dogs gone wild (all of which also have problems getting about in deep snow) take a toll of the yarded deer. Conservation officers in northern deer country report that the wild dogs are by far the most destructive, and that the wolves and coyotes eat only those that are probably doomed to die anyhow. Modern snowmobiles also enter the picture. Although these devices have been used by wardens to carry emergency food to deer, too many have been used to chase and scatter yarded deer during the period when their resistance and energy reserves are at the lowest points. Chasing a deer for as little as a hundred feet could cause its end.

At the onset of winter, there is much fat on the bodies of most whitetails. This energy and heat reserve is located around the kidneys and heart, over the saddle and hips, on the brisket and covering the ribs. But this fat gradually is utilized, and by midwinter a deer's bones begin to show through its rough coat. Dull eyes and swollen jaws indicate acute malnutrition. For days on end a deer will stand humpbacked and shivering. Not even the sudden appearance of a forest ranger on snowshoes startles the animal.

Starvation can, in fact, eliminate all fear of men. Older, extremely hungry deer have actually learned to associate the buzz of a power saw with felling trees, and this has lured them to feed on the treetops. There are also on record pictures of deer browsing very near woods-men cutting pulpwood. Months earlier these same deer would not have come close to man for any reason.

Many people equate all deer with brown-eyed Bambi, perhaps because the deer that people see at parks and in Walt Disney films seem so trusting and gentle. But their opinions might change if they could see a November buck, neck swollen and red-eyed from the rut, looking for trouble. Even more vicious is a whitetail buck or doe competing for winter food. It happens like this.

Fawns are always the first to die because, being smaller, they cannot reach as high for food. Winter's grip tightens next on the does and last on the bucks, which get the best of whatever exists inside the yards. But it's when late winter thaws form a thick crust on the snow and deer begin to move about on top of the crust that the most vicious competition occurs. If there is plenty of new browse, the bucks may only bully the does, and the does bully the fawns away from it. But if the supply is limited, there is savage kicking and fighting for it.

A doe may drive her own fawn away from the nourishment it needs to survive one more day. Maternal love doesn't exist during these times. Severe northern winters have been known to kill more than half of that year's fawn crop. And during the worst winter on record, two million northern whitetail deer perished by starvation alone.

But springtime eventually comes. Longer days and sunshine produce a new crop of food for the deer, which have reached their lowest numbers for the year. There is no better illustration that the toughest and fittest of a species survive. And the survivors are the greatest game animals in the world.

Mule Deer

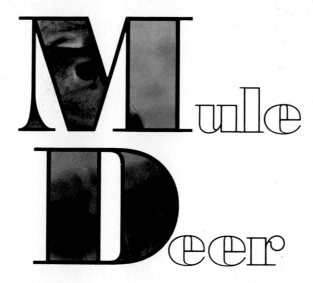

MANY OUTDOORSMEN may not agree that the American whitetail is the greatest game animal on earth, or even the greatest of the American deer. Bob McArthur, one of a vanishing breed of Montana ranchers, believes that the honor belongs to the mule deer.

Bob lives in the lonely headwater country of the Ruby River, and his modest ranch home stands where a dusty dirt road dead-ends in the shadow of the Ruby Mountains. The nearest town is thirty miles away. Bob still rides fences and trails his herd on horseback, rather than by four-wheel-drive Jeep or Piper Cub plane, because the country is too rough for any vehicle except a cow pony born in the mountains and of the mountain stock. Bob spends a good part of his life living in the saddle, amid some of the finest mule deer country of the West. Few have watched the species as long or as intimately as Bob.

"When I was growing up in this country," he told me, "the deer were more tame and trusting, even the big bucks. But today it's an entirely different matter."

All summer long of the year we hunted together, Bob noticed an uncommonly large number of very big bucks. Unlike the does and smaller bucks which were evenly distributed over the Rubys, the old males lived in the loftiest country they could find. They stayed on the highest ridges and just under the peaks, far from human intrusion but in other regions a habitat they would have shared with bighorn sheep.

As he rode far to keep track of his wandering livestock on their summer range, Bob watched the deer's velvet-covered nubbins grow into huge antlers with shiny ivory tips. The deer kept their distance, but aside from that paid less and less attention to the rider as summer passed. By early autumn when it was time to drive the cattle to lower altitudes, Bob estimated that there were at least two dozen mature bucks on his place and that nine or ten were of unusual size.

"Come on out for sure," he wrote, "because we'll have no trouble getting a big head for your wall."

I didn't make it to Montana until the tag end of the deer season. Others had already hunted on the ranch, but Bob reported that few had gone into the high country and none had bagged big bucks. The largest was a three-pointer or, if you live in the East, a six-pointer. Bob was still optimistic about getting a big rack and commented that we probably would have the choice of several.

We almost scored immediately. In the cold predawn we saddled a pair of reluctant horses, and by daylight we had already ridden two miles or more up Soldier Creek to a place where it tumbles down over a giant rock slide. Snow began to fall, adding to two or three inches already on the ground. Bob nudged his pony onto a thin trail which switchbacked steeply up a bare slope and I followed. Halfway to the top of a ridge, my companion slid off his mount and without a word pointed to a dark clump of evergreens ahead and above us. Standing, staring at us from the edge of the timber, was a fine buck deer.

Off of my horse, I eased my rifle from the saddle scabbard, sat down on the ground and used my knees as a shooting tripod. No time for buck fever and completely cool, I held the crosshairs on the deer's shoulder and squeezed off an unhurried shot.

For a moment, the deer stood motionless as if hard hit. Then it bounded away, apparently in no great hurry and completely untouched. There might have been an opportunity for a

second shot, but instead I sat in disbelief. I had to laugh at my own poor marksmanship because after all this was only the beginning of the hunt and we would see many other bucks.

Only it didn't work out that way. During the next week of hard riding and climbing over a good portion of the Rubys, during which we counted hundreds of mule deer, I saw only one other trophy buck, and that one was about 450 yards away and already increasing the distance.

Daily we found tracks of very large deer in the snow, and on a number of occasions these were probably only minutes old. But we never

Named for its big, black-fringed ears, the mule deer differs from the whitetail in the smaller, black-tipped tail (above) and in the conformation of its antlers. Each of the deer's antlers may branch in two beams, with each beam having several tines (left). A nontypical head (right) has multibranching beams with asymmetrical tines.

saw the kind of big mule deer antlers which deserve bragging about. The vanishing act would have done credit to whitetail bucks in the heavily hunted East.

There is more to the story. On the back of a card I received at Christmas was the following note: "The big bucks are showing up again. Saw four yesterday and this morning I could have shot two from the back of the corral. I think those muleys knew the exact day the hunting season closed. Let's try it again next year. Happy Holidays, Bob."

The mule deer, *Odocoileus hemionus*, is second to the whitetail in total population and distribution. "Muley" is a common name in the West, and sometimes "burro deer" is still heard in the Southwest. Slightly stockier in structure than the whitetail and averaging heavier weight, its name comes from its large, black-fringed ears. The mule deer differs further from the whitetail in its smaller tail, which is black or black-tipped, and in the antlers of the male. All points of the whitetail buck branch off the main antler beam, but the secondary beams (or points) of the muley are multi-forked as well.

Eleven races or subspecies of mule deer inhabit much of the western United States, from southeastern Alaska to northern Mexico and Baja California. This means the animal can exist in a variety of environments including wet Pacific rain forests and hot desert regions where water is scarce. Most abundant is the Rocky Mountain mule deer, *O. h. heminonus*, native of all ranges of the Rockies and most numerous in areas of open country mixed with forests. The whitetail is essentially a woodland species, while the muley prefers more open landscapes.

At one time both the Columbia blacktail, *O. h. columbianus*, and Sitka deer, *O. h. sitkensis*, of the Northwest were considered distinct species, but mammalogists now classify them as subspecies of the mule deer. Neither exceeds 150 pounds maximum weight, while Rocky Mountain bucks have occasionally been weighed at almost 400 pounds. A 200- to 250-pounder, however, is a very large one.

All mule deer live in magnificent surroundings. That's true whether it's Bob McArthur's Ruby Mountains or the Big Horns in Wyoming, the eroding Breaks of the Missouri River, the Mogollon Rim, the Kaibab, Sonora, Tonto Basin, or even Tiburon Island, Mexico, where the resident subspecies, *O. h. sheldoni*, may have already been hunted to extinction by commercial fishermen. You cannot go hunting for mule deer with gun or camera and not be thrilled by the scenery.

Any mule deer is highly suspicious, and if the species is less cautious than the whitetail, it is only because it has not been hunted so long and so intensively. A muley's eyesight is many times better than the best hunter's vision, and its powers of hearing and smell are extraordinary. Add the wisdom of old age—of an old buck—and the hunter finds he is dealing with a sensitive and canny animal.

Because of their sheer abundance at times and in places, mule deer are not too tough to shoot. In some areas where the bag limit is two per hunter, statewide hunter success sometimes exceeds 100 percent. But collecting an old male which has already survived several hunting seasons is a different proposition. It requires skill and persistence, as well as a knowledge of the animals' habits and behavior, or habitat, forage and weather. A successful hunt for a trophy head usually demands a good bit of physical stamina, too.

The mule deer of the western mountains is a greater vagabond than the whitetail. A particular canyon or mountain slope is saturated with animals one day and empty the next, for no obvious reason. When the hunting season opens, muleys travel even more. I know veteran hunters who firmly believe that the deer instinctively grow more restless before the first barrage of opening day. The restlessness may be stimulated by the oncoming of the rut. If there is any period of the year when the older bucks might abandon some caution, it is during the peak periods of estrus in does. Then there is much conflict among the males for breeding rights.

Once during a golden October, John Moxley and I were hunting in the mountains above Range Creek, Utah. There was enough fresh venison in camp to last us the whole trip, so now we were looking for very large heads or nothing at all. We found them very unexpectedly.

On foot and following a well-worn game trail, John and I had climbed from camp in the bottom of a canyon to the rimrock about 600 or 700 yards above. At the top was a gently sloping forest of tall pines. In an open glade— an arena bathed in the first rays of the morning sun—two large mule bucks faced each other. When we first saw them the deer were 200 yards distant, but the rattle of antlers as they smashed heads must have been audible much farther away. What followed was a savage wilderness duel which few outdoorsmen see.

The bucks were large and evenly matched. The aim of each appeared to be to drive the other back, or into the ground, and possibly to thrust antlers into the flank of the opponent. They would lunge, parry, momentarily lock together, snap apart and then lunge again. I have seen other wild animals in combat, but none so furiously and noisily as these. They were so occupied that John and I approached to less than fifty yards of the pair without being noticed, in fact until we could easily see the swollen necks, the red eyes and the slavering. Sadly this was a rare instance when I was not carrying a camera, a mistake I have tried never again to repeat.

The future of mule deer is bright compared to that of other deer and big game animals elsewhere. Scientific game censuses and techniques make it possible to harvest a huge number each year and still maintain the continental population at a high level, in truth as many mule deer as the range can now support. But it wasn't always that way.

Not long ago mule deer were involved in a terrible tragedy which has been an object lesson to conservationists ever since. In 1906 President Theodore Roosevelt created the Grand Canyon National Game Reserve in Arizona and thus, unintentionally, nearly destroyed the finest herd in America. The million-acre preserve included the entire Kaibab North Plateau. Government leaflets described Kaibab as a botanist's paradise, and it was the home of 3,000 Rocky Mountain muleys. These deer were known for their large size and for the massive antlers of the males.

Prior to 1906, unrestricted market hunting in the West reduced all big-game species to critically low levels. Elk and moose were rare, antelope nearly disappeared, and even mule deer were in very short supply. This explained Roosevelt's establishment of the Reserve and the banning of all hunting on it. In addition, war was declared on the deer's natural enemies: mountain lions, bobcats, coyotes and a few remaining gray wolves which had always lived in harmony with the Kaibab deer.

Violent battles between bucks occur during the rutting season, each trying to drive the other to the ground or thrust his antlers into his opponent's flank. Sometimes the rattle of clashing antlers can be heard from miles away.

For a few years, the Kaibab conservation project appeared to be a huge success. By 1918 the herd had increased by 600 percent to 15,000 animals. In 1923 the herd was estimated at 30,000 and still increasing, perhaps to a total of 100,000. But by then the tragedy was apparent. While their numbers increased under unnatural protection, the deer had almost completely destroyed their own range. The "botanist's paradise" had been eaten nearly to bedrock. Something had to be done—and fast.

The Forest Service tried to trap surplus deer and move them elsewhere, but as any game biologist knows, live trapping is expensive and impractical, especially in such a remote area. Next, the hunting season was opened to all. For a license of only five dollars, a sportsman could take three deer of any sex. But the remoteness and difficulty of access limited the kill to 675 animals, less than 10 percent of the number of fawns born during a single spring. A promising proposal to slaughter the animals with government hunters was attacked vigorously in national publications by Zane Grey, then very popular but a far better writer about the purple sage than an ecologist. He proposed that unemployed cowboys and Navajo Indians be hired to drive the deer to better range across the Colorado River.

What followed was one of the best publicized fiascos of the times. A local cattleman was contracted to drive "not less than 3,000, nor more than 8,000 deer" over the River, but 125 riders did not succeed in driving even one!

In the next decades, politicians, tourist promoters and other misinformed people became involved and prevented any reduction of the herd for its own good. At one point the Governor of Arizona threatened to call out the National Guard if foresters shot any deer in the Kaibab, but the governor himself was shot down by a Supreme Court ruling allowing foresters to protect the range from deer damage.

Altogether, tens of thousands of mule deer died of starvation, malnutrition and disease. Worse still, the environment has never really recovered from the ordeal.

There is a lesson, however bitter, in the Kaibab story. It is that inviolate refuges can become death traps for prolific big-game species when some method of population control —natural predators, hunting or probably both —does not exist to keep the herd within the refuge-carrying capacity. Under complete protection, populations of deer and other big-game species can explode, with tragic results.

I've hunted mule deer in three different ways: by driving, on foot and on horseback. All are good, but I like driving the least. Except when found in heavy spruce timber areas, mule deer can be driven. It's especially successful if they're in small islands of timber surrounded by open meadow. The best way to do it is to spot a couple of hunters at one end, and then drive or stillhunt from the other end. Somebody is going to get some shooting that way. But it's not much fun, and seldom do it.

It's important to remember that mule deer feed at night and sleep during the day. That's their normal routine. Generally around sundown the muleys get up from their beds and begin to meander toward feeding areas. They begin the return trip at daybreak. Virtually all movement is confined to early morning and late evening unless the animals are disturbed by other hunters or by natural enemies. My favorite technique is to be out and stillhunting first thing in the morning.

Proper stillhunting is a stop-and-go business. You stop, carefully study the entire landscape up ahead, and then go on fifty yards or so, depending on the terrain. It's surprising what you will see if you take your time in good deer country. And it's a kind of hunting which you can regulate to suit yourself. If you like to cover plenty of country, all right, get out and hike. If you suffer from spending too much time behind a desk all year, just take it easy.

Since mule deer country is also canyon country, another tactic is made to order for a pair of stillhunters working in cooperation. While one hunter moves slowly up the bottom or bed of a canyon, the other hunter travels a parallel course just beneath one rim of the canyon. The man on the rim will get most of the shots, because mule deer have a predictable tendency to run uphill when flushed, but the two men can change positions occasionally.

Another variation of stillhunting is to hunt on horseback. I have done quite a bit of this, but still cannot explain what happens. I'm convinced that on horseback it is sometimes possible to get much closer to deer before they flush. I've even had them pause and step forward to get a better look at me. Once a small buck slowly and cautiously walked to within a

Mule deer move toward lower altitude in the winter and climb higher as summer comes; but in any season, the biggest bucks are higher than the rest. Best advice for the hunter: climb high.

A mule deer doe, her big ears erect for any sound, displays the habit of curiosity which is characteristic of the species. When startled by danger, the deer will often pause to survey the situation.

hundred feet of me, and it was only when the wind shifted that he bounced away.

But more often than not, a man can do better stillhunting on foot than on horseback. He is better able to scan the country ahead, and he doesn't have to worry about jockeying a horse around. This much is certain: never try to shoot from a horse's back. One of my friends tried that once, and although he was on the laziest mare I've ever seen, he was immediately pitched six feet up into the mountain air.

You should also take account of a mule deer's natural curiosity, the one weakness, or failing, that the biggest bucks, as well as the yearling fawns, seem to have at certain times. If you flush deer and they move away at a walk rather than in wild flight, stay perfectly motionless for a minute. Many times such deer have stopped, turned and stared at me. That's the time to shoot.

Startled mule deer fit into three categories: those that only see you, those that smell you, and those that always head for the next county as fast as they can run. The second group almost always disappears as fast as possible. But a hunter has a chance with deer in the first category. They will not react as frantically as when they have a whiff of man-scent.

Though I lack scientific evidence, I don't believe muleys are alarmed by strange or bright colors. Hunters often ask me whether their red coats betray them. (Red coats and garments are required by law in some states.) What muleys *do* spot immediately is sudden motion. He's a smart hunter who sneaks slowly and without undue movement every second he's in the field.

Mule deer are somewhat migratory, moving toward lower altitudes in winter and then upward again with summer. Exactly when they move depends on snowfall and the availability of food. Most hunting seasons in the western states coincide with the mule deer's downward trek; the later in the season the lower the animals are likely to be. But no matter what the period, the biggest bucks are higher than the rest and the best advice for any trophy hunter is to hunt high.

Hunting the Sitka blacktail of Alaska and British Columbia may be a little different. As pointed out before, this is a subspecies of the dense evergreen forests, and hunting is more like eastern whitetail stalking than hunting for Rocky Mountain muleys. Even though a liberal five deer of either sex are usually permitted per hunter in Alaska—and between 10,000 and 15,000 are taken annually—these Sitka deer have such high reproductive potential that rigorous winters can cause heavy kills. An effective way to hunt blacktails is to cruise coastal areas by boat, a technique which might be used in other mule deer country.

The mule deer is a remarkably tough and tenacious animal and a dweller of the places I love best. Often overlooked is its great agility, and its ability to travel, at full speed, over some of the most precipitous terrain in the land. Only mountain goats are more surefooted. I have seen mountain sheep stumble and fall when running under pressure, but mule deer never make missteps; at least I have never seen them. They are extraordinary game animals.

Elk

Except for the National Park black bears, probably no big-game animal is more familiar to non-hunting Americans than the elk, or wapiti, *Cervus canadensis*. Visitors to Yellowstone and several other parks and wildlife refuges can easily view the species without leaving their cars. Elk are large enough and active enough to be very conspicuous. When offered sanctuary, the animals soon pay little attention to humans, and this often gives the impression that they are too tame to hunt.

But to sportsmen in the western mountains, the elk has an entirely different personality. In spite of their size (an adult Rocky Mountain bull may exceed 900 pounds, an average cow weighs 350–400 pounds) and sometimes ponderous appearance, trophy bulls can be bewildering and frustrating to hunt. Even in good elk country, the percentage of hunting success can be very low because the elk is a wily game animal.

When Europeans first waded ashore on this continent, the elk was the most widely distributed of all North American deer. Its range extended from the Pacific eastward almost to the Atlantic, right to the water's edge in some areas. Elk ranged widely through southern Canada and almost as far south as Mexico. There are only seven states which have never contained elk: Maine, New Hampshire, Vermont, Massachusetts, Connecticut, Delaware and Florida. Today the elk's greatly narrowed range includes only most mountain ranges west of the Mississippi River. The one eastern exception is a herd of about 600 animals in Michigan's Pigeon River State Forest region, and these are endangered by the major discovery of oil thereabouts.

Five separate subspecies of elk are recognized in North America, all close kin to the red deer and other larger deer of Eurasia. Most important and abundant in the New World

35

is the Rocky Mountain elk, *C. c. nelsoni*, ranging from Colorado northward through Yellowstone Park to the Canadian Rockies. The Roosevelt elk, *C. c. roosevelti*, of Washington's Olympic Peninsula, has also been introduced onto Afognak and Rassberry Islands, Alaska, where it now exists in huntable numbers. The rarest and smallest of the wapitis, the tule or California valley elk, *Cervus nannodes*, was once very abundant in lowland southern California, but is now an endangered species. Only a few hundred individuals survive in an Owens Valley reserve and in a fenced preserve near Bakersfield. Merriam's elk, which once occupied isolated (by desert) mountain ranges in Arizona and New Mexico, has been extinct for a long time.

I have done a good bit of elk hunting and elk watching. Some of the most memorable trips have been with Malcolm "Mac" Mackenzie, an extraordinarily capable guide and outfitter of Cochrane, Alberta, during the last half of September in the southern Canadian Rockies. This is an exquisite time and place, not only because the aspen and tamarack are aflame with color, but because it is the lovesick moon—the rut—of all elk. That is an exciting and dramatic season.

Early one morning Mac and I departed the Kananaskis Highway. Trailing two pack horses loaded with our gear, we rode into the highest country of that area and chose a campsite which I will always remember for its beauty.

A lush alpine meadow, divided by a brook fed from lingering snows, was almost completely surrounded by steep rock walls and slides. At one end of the meadow stood a mixed clump of spruce and golden tamarack, and in the shadow of these trees we pitched a single wall tent and hobbled the horses. At dusk, just

As the breeding season gets underway, the silent mountains suddenly resound with the piercing call of bugling bulls challenging one another over territories and the available cows. Imitating the bugle call of a bull elk may entice an animal into camera or rifle range.

as Mac was getting ready to cook dinner, we heard a sound which made the bristles stand on the back of my neck.

The first notes were low and soft, but they quickly swelled to a shrill and eerie whistle which sounded much closer than it was. Next followed a hoarse grunting; then all was silent again.

I didn't sleep as well as usual after a long ride in the western mountains, perhaps because I kept thinking about that bull. I have been lucky enough to hear many of the great sounds of the wild—timber wolves running at night, the claxon honking of wild geese, lions roaring in Kenya's Northern Frontier—but none are more exciting, more haunting than the calliope bugle of a herd bull elk. I finally fell asleep, but it seemed that only seconds later Mac was waking me for breakfast.

Mac had trouble catching one of the hobbled ponies, so we rode out onto a rocky ridge north of camp, in the direction of the bugler, later than we planned. When the going became too rough for the animals, we tied them heads to tails and out of sight in a depression before we continued on foot. At the end of the ridge we hunkered down and through glasses studied the blue shadows below. We did not wait long before a wilderness drama began.

The herd of nine cows and calves was easy to spot at the edge of an area burned years ago. Charred and crisscrossed deadfalls covered the new browse on which the animals were feeding. We heard the herd bull before we saw it.

From a hidden draw came the same penetrating, ascending whistle we'd heard at dusk the day before. A moment later the splendid six-pointer emerged with head held high, neck swollen and antlers carried parallel to his back. As I focused my glasses for a sharper picture, the bull bugled again. And a moment later the challenge was answered by another bull.

However, a duel never really developed. The second bull soon came into view, but was not as big or as old as the harem bull and was not really a serious challenger. He loitered around the fringe of the cows, prancing back and forth, but retreated when the sultan raced suddenly in his direction. That ended the skirmishing until Mac produced a length of copper tubing from inside his shirt and carefully imitated the elk's call. Now bull number one looked upward in our direction.

For what seemed a very long time, the bull appeared puzzled. Then it bugled in defiance once more and hurried directly toward us. It was as thrilling a spectacle as a wanderer in the Rockies is ever likely to witness.

Most elk seasons are fairly long, and hunting is possibly more productive toward the end of the season, after snows have driven the animals to lower elevations and the herds are concentrated where forage is more available. But it is never more exciting or fascinating than very early and during the rut.

Biologists disagree on exactly what precipitates the rut each year, since there is some variation (in the same region) in when it begins, when it peaks and how long the activity lasts. A number of factors including the amount of sunlight, rainfall, and temperature fluctuation probably contribute. Activity is apparently stimulated by the sudden oncoming of storm fronts or very cold weather. Over most of their range, bulls show symptoms of uneasiness as early as late August.

The first sign occurs when bulls rub their antlers against anything to scrape off the velvet covering of summertime. The largest animals may have grown main beams measuring from fifty to fifty-five inches long, in the short period since May. Only moose acquire more massive antlers in the same span of time. Next, elk bulls begin to act aggressively toward other bulls of the bachelor groups in which they've spent the summer. The sparring becomes more and more heated until the bachelors part company to search for female companionship. The largest and most dominant males collect harems of cows and spend most of early autumn trying to defend or isolate them from other bulls. A harem can consist of one or two females, or ten to twelve.

A lovesick bull, with cows or only coveting them, is a savage and ludicrous beast to watch. He is also so evil-smelling that his presence can be detected from far away. He stomps and excavates the earth with antlers, throwing up large chunks of sod, while slavering, urinating and bugling. I once watched a bull along Yellowstone's Gibbon River so beside himself with passion—and with no other bull in sight to challenge—that he fought with and uprooted a twelve-foot high spruce. Then he stepped back and bugled over the fallen tree. On another occasion in Montana, I photographed a wapiti bull wearing twenty-five or thirty yards of barbed wire in his antlers, probably a result of his dueling with a fence.

Wapiti bulls produce a variety of strange sounds, some not unlike the barking of hounds in the distance. But the usual bugle is more of a piercing whistle which rises and falls and is followed by gasping to reinflate the animal's lungs. Hear the flute-like sound once and you never forget it.

Rutting bulls engage in violent combat with rivals, though not as frequently or for as long as some literature has suggested. Bulls have been engaged for up to an hour and battles can result in serious injury (possibly fatal according to some reports) to one or both animals. More often than not, several short, sharp rounds of antler-rattling establish supremacy and send the loser skulking away.

Imitating the bugle call of a bull is not difficult, and it is a sure way to entice an animal into rifle or camera range. On occasion Mac Mackenzie has called bulls to within less than fifteen yards of a hunter in very dense woods; that can be a chilling experience, even though the bull would not be likely to press home a charge on a human. There are few reliable reports of rutting animals attacking people, though there are a number of accounts of bulls attacking pack animals and dogs. My photographer friend Bill Browning was once treed when he tried to take close-ups of a hot-and-bothered bull. The unlikely scene of this incident was the golf course of Banff Springs Hotel in Banff National Park.

Many good calls are on the market, along with instructional records on how to use them. Bulls respond best to calling early or late in the day, and the caller should always remain unseen. I have used calls to gain the attention or curiosity of bulls in national parks for more interesting photos. In the process, I learned that the worst mistake is to call too often in any situation—or too soon after a bull responds.

When Columbus reached the New World, there were an estimated 10 million elk on the continent. But the last elk in the east were eliminated during the 1840s. By 1910, the big deer had vanished from ninety percent of its original range and a mere 50,000 survived in seven western states. The causes for the decline are worth describing because of the valuable conservation message.

Clearing land for agriculture was the first factor; elk are incompatible with people raising crops. Although elk ran in herds of as many as 1,500 individuals in the "Old West," market hunting to feed miners, railroad building crews and proliferating frontier communities took a huge toll. For example, one professional hunter based in Leadville, Colorado, marketed at least 35,000 pounds of elk meat during a three-month period. For this he received about $3,000, or about eight cents per pound. More to be deplored was the wholesale killing of elk during the early 1900s, just to obtain charms and watch fobs for members of the Fraternal Order of Elks. Unlike all other American deer, elk have unique canine teeth of ivory-like material in the upper jaw. Tens of thousands of elk were killed just for this "ivory" and the carcasses left to rot. Ivory poachers in the Jackson Hole country fastened elk hooves to the soles of their boots to confuse game wardens. And in the winter of 1915, 500 elk of the Yellowstone area were killed for the tusks alone.

Things are better today, and the wapiti population is holding fairly well, probably near the maximum which remaining elk range can support. The species has been reintroduced to a few areas from which it had been erased long ago. Still, there is considerable opposition to the presence of elk in many areas because the large wintering herds can be destructive to ranchers' haystacks. To maintain a good population of elk, it will be necessary to purchase more and suitable large wintering areas. Although elk prefer to stay in high country as long as food is available and before the land is

The rutting battles of the bulls are sometimes fierce and deadly, but more often a few short rounds of antler rattling to establish supremacy. The loser slinks away, the winner begins to collect his harem.

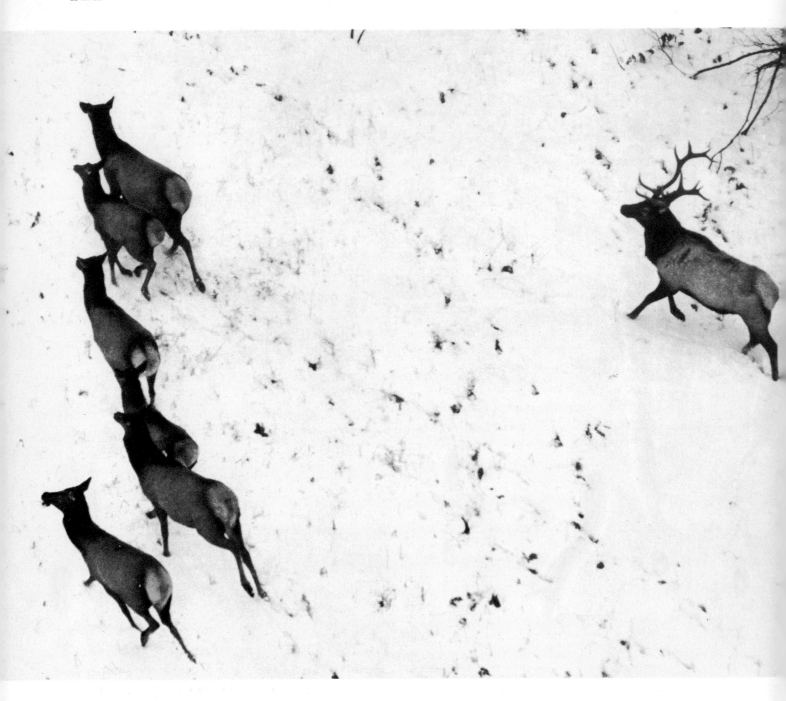

A bull with his harem heads toward lower country as snow comes to the mountains. In their downward migrations in search of food, the elk often come into conflict with ranching and agriculture. Elk concentrate in large numbers in wintering areas. Occasionally they must be fed artificially to assure their survival.

covered by deep snow, the seasonal snows eventually drive them lower and lower until they conflict with ranching and agriculture.

Most of the best elk hunting exists in the western National Forests or in Canadian provincial forests. It is rarely within easy access of paved roads, and the average sportsman will need guidance to enjoy a successful trip.

A beginner's best bet is to obtain the services of a guide or outfitter to take him into good wapiti country, most likely on horseback and hopefully by pack-tripping. A pack trip can be any outdoorsman's most rewarding experience and consists of travel-camping, of being entirely self-sufficient, while riding out and hunting in roadless high country. As often as not, you will see some of the most beautiful country on this continent, and the hunting may be for other species of big game as well as elk. Hunters and guides ride on saddle horses and all their gear is carried behind on pack animals.

On a pack trip, the outfitter furnishes everything except the hunter's guns and personal items. That includes horses or mules, all camping and cooking gear, food, wrangling and guide service. It does not include the hunter's firearms, sleeping bag, clothing and personal necessities. If hunting prospects are good enough, the outfitter may set up camp in only one or two places during a pack trip. Or he may be constantly moving. Either way it is the highest adventure and a rare wilderness experience, whether the pack-tripper is a wildlife watcher, cameraman, or hunter.

Outfitters advertise in the where-to-go sections of the outdoor magazines. Fish and Game or Conservation Departments in the western states where there is elk hunting have available lists of licensed guides. It is wisest to write to several guides, rather than one, and to ask for references, all of whom should be contacted. There are a few bad apples among the outfitters, and they might as well be culled out in the beginning.

There are two prime periods to schedule an elk hunt. I have already described the first, my favorite, which is during the bugling period. The other comes after October storms have driven the herds downward to lower levels. Chances of success are highest then because the animals are more concentrated, and there may be tracking snow on the ground. The hunter also must cope with lower temperatures and less benevolent weather. Hunting may not be as pleasant in the teeth of a blizzard, but will be no less challenging because the rut is finished and bulls have regained their normal wariness.

Cervus canadensis is an amazing animal. Its sight and hearing may not be as good as some other big game; with a steady wind in my own face, I have had elk stare toward me from fairly close range and never see me. But the species' nostrils are always tuned in—a sort of nasal radar—and not many animals have a keener sense of smell.

When an elk confronts danger—and elk may detect danger from far away, without the hunter's ever seeing it—it reacts instantly and instinctively. If the animal happens to be in the open, it breaks hell-bent in the opposite direction and may not stop running for several miles. If it is in dense timber, which is more likely, the animal slinks away as quietly as a cat, leaving only a trail of hoofprints behind. Either way, the wapiti is the winner.

Moose

IT WAS NOT an easy portage in the predawn, over the rock spine which created Rabbit Falls. The trail was steep and boulder-strewn so that I was sweating when we reached the pool of Rabbit River at the base of the white water. There, Ira Bloodbrother relaunched the canoe.

"It's still early," the old Iroquois guide said, "so let's take time for a pot of tea."

Exactly what followed isn't clear anymore because it happened too unexpectedly to really comprehend. A sudden grunting and crashing resounded in the brushy thicket just behind us. Next thing we knew, a bull moose was standing close enough to be identified in the yellow light of the campfire. I distinctly saw the large moist nose, the dewlap and the faint outline of antlers against the gray sky. The animal was huge.

The moose looked at us. And we looked back. Nobody moved.

Finally Ira whispered: "Go slow to the canoe and get your rifle."

I had been kneeling beside the fire and started to stand erect, but that one movement was like pushing a button: at the same moment, the moose turned and was gone.

That happened in 1947, almost twenty-five years ago, on my first moose hunt. It was the first moose I ever saw in the wild and the only bull Ira and I encountered on that week long trip in northern Ontario, during which we covered plenty of excellent moose country. Since that time I have seen hundreds of moose, but that very first encounter still stands vividly in my memory.

If it is done correctly, hunting the largest deer that walks the face of the earth could hardly be anything but exciting. And fascinating. And perhaps hard work as well. It is quite unlike any other hunting on this continent today.

Consider the animal itself, *Alces alces*. Its natural range is in northern evergreen and willow forests around the world, although in Europe the species is called elk. By any name, the moose's dimensions are king-size. He's big and may look even bigger than he is. A mature bull stands seven and one-half feet at the shoulder and weighs over a half ton. Full-grown cows measure only slightly less. Calves weigh 25 pounds at birth and average 500 pounds when only a year old.

Four subspecies of moose are native to North America. The eastern moose (*A. a. americana*) ranges from Maine northward to Labrador and extreme eastern Canada. The Canadian moose (*A. a. andersoni*) occupies the region from Ontario westward through Saskatchewan. The subspecies of the Rocky Mountains from Colorado northward through Alberta is the Shiras moose (*A. a. shirasi*). The largest of all both in body size and antler dimensions is the Alaska-Yukon moose (*A. a. gigas*). The palmated antlers of this one can actually exceed six feet from tip to tip and may weigh more than eighty-five pounds, making it the most massive head trophy a hunter can obtain anywhere.

A bull moose is ponderous or magnificent, ungainly or handsome, depending on the viewpoint of the beholder. Its drooping nose is too big, the dewlap or "bell" under the chin is useless, and the body is too short for the legs. It completely lacks the elegance and grace of its cousin, the whitetail, and even of the American elk, which comes closest to matching its size. But every prospective hunter should keep one point in mind: the moose's humped back, long legs and seemingly clumsy gait are deceiving. The species is not only tough, but can travel as quietly as a cat through a dense forest.

It can also move suddenly and swiftly—and is a master of the vanishing act.

Hunting seasons across the land are normally scheduled for the period just before, during or just after the autumn rut. Depending on the latitude, the elevation and possibly on the weather, the peak of the rut occurs anytime between early September and the end of October. The closer a hunting trip coincides with this peak, the better the chances of success. Bulls are simply more active, more visible and more vulnerable when they're in love. Normally very placid and peaceful animals, bulls can become belligerent during the rut, but they are not really dangerous to man.

Both bulls and cows can be very vocal, especially during fall's lovemaking moon. Bulls grunt, moo or bellow, to establish a territory, as a challenge, and to make contact with cows. Cows may or may not answer the calls of bulls with grunts which are softer and more difficult to hear.

Particularly in the eastern half of North America, artificial calls are used to lure a moose to within range of a hunter, or just to make a moose betray his own location so that the hunter can stalk closer. Most calls are megaphone-shaped and fashioned of anything from birchbark (which northern Indians have used for ages) to rolled-up roof shingles from an abandoned trapper's cabin. A few Indian guides in eastern Canada still use vocal chords alone, but calling this way has generally become a lost art.

The most effective hunting tactic in many portions of northeastern America is to hunt by canoe, paddling quietly on small shallow rivers or parallel to lake shores. To do so on a misty September or October morning in Ontario, when the birch and maple trees are in

Docile as the cow moose may appear, she will vigorously defend her calves in the event of danger. These are Canadian moose, a species which ranges from Ontario westward through Saskatchewan.

full color, is an extraordinary experience. It is a time when wild waterfowl are migrating southward and huge flocks flush suddenly out of the wild rice at the approach of a canoe. More startling still is when without warning a lovesick bull answers the guide's bugling and splashes out into full view, ready to fight. It is an awesome spectacle.

Hunting by watercraft is not often possible or practical in the western half of North America. There the animals are hunted in a manner similar to elk or mule deer, although moose occupy a slightly different range. They like moister places than do elk or mule deer, and that is where to concentrate your hunting.

The moose of the Rockies, Alaska and the Yukon are especially fond of willows, which form a bulk of their diet the year round. But they also consume large amounts of other succulent browse. A good place to search is in the dense willow flats which usually parallel many western waterways. Another good method is to climb a vantage point high above the flats and then to glass them thoroughly.

Many hunters in the western mountains are surprised to find moose in improbable, unmooselike places. I have found them at times in high grassy basins better suited for sheep. The only sound explanation is that they are trying to escape insects at lower elevations.

Although some experienced moose hunters may disagree, I believe moose have very good hearing, an acute sense of smell, and poor vision. In other words, all moose-hunting strategy should be based on hunting upwind as quietly as possible.

Say a moose is feeding in dense willows, which is a typical situation. You can see the broad palmate antlers, and you have decided that this is the bull you want for your trophy room. But the body, with its vital target areas, is too well screened by willow to try to connect and you must get much, much closer for a killing shot. Stay cool and you will score.

First make your approach from downwind, or at least into a crosswind. Then move slowly: watch where you step. Avoid getting mired in muck because this can be very noisy. At the same time, always keep an eye on the animal if possible. Remain motionless whenever the animal is facing you. Move closer only when it is facing away. A moose may look directly at you and still never see you if you do not move.

With experience, a hunter soon learns to tell whether or not moose are in the country he is hunting. The presence of fresh dung pellets is one obvious indication. These are larger than the droppings of elk, and many more are deposited at any one time in one place. The hoofprints are large (as large as six or seven inches), double-teardrop-shaped with some space between the sharp points, or more space than in an elk print. Moose dewclaws also are imprinted if the earth is soft enough.

Look also for evidence of browsing: soft willow tips nipped off, or twigs of maple, birch, aspen, balsam or mountain ash eaten off as high as a moose can easily reach. Wallows in wet places are good signs. So are saplings rubbed smooth by antlers (to scrape off the velvet) and strips of bark eaten away from aspens. At a quick glance the latter might be mistaken for beaver gnawing. And keep in mind that all of this same sign might also be made by elk.

Except when many animals are concentrated in a given area by weather, deep snow or the rut, a moose hunter is not likely to see as much game as a deer hunter or even an elk hunter. Moose are not herd animals, and not very gregarious. Even in the best habitat, one moose per square mile is high density.

Still, a sportsman's odds today for bagging a bull are good and perhaps much better than they were a generation ago. Scientific management and the setting of open seasons is one reason. In addition, certain timber-cutting practices all across the North have proven beneficial to moose because of the tender young browse which results.

Nowhere do moose grow to such enormous dimensions as in Alaska, where an estimated 150,000 animals live in suitable habitat from the Stikine River of the southeastern panhandle north to the Colville River on the Arctic Slope. The greatest numbers are concentrated along rivers in the willow bottoms and upward to second-growth birch forests to timberline plateaus. In most of Alaska, timberline is not very high. In this environment bull moose attain weights from 1,000 to 1,600 pounds and cows from 800 to 1,200, which is impressive size any way you view it. Only the males grow antlers, and although an occasional bull may live twice as long, maximum antler size is attained during the sixth or seventh autumn of his life. Trophy-size bulls can occur anywhere in Alaska, but the biggest come from three areas: the Alaska Peninsula, the lower Susitna Valley and the Kenai Peninsula.

Even though moose is an important game species and well known to sportsmen, much of its life history is hazy. Moose, for example, are often regarded as purely sedentary animals, but that is far from true. Over most of their range (and particularly in Alaska, Yukon and the Northwest Territories) the animals embark on seasonal migrations associated with breeding and move from one good forage area to another. Breeding causes the greatest movements of all, and these treks can cover forty or fifty miles. One tagged moose was known to have wandered sixty miles from point of release.

It is difficult to explain how it happens, but during the early rut (early fall) all or most of the largest bulls in a vast area seem to concentrate in one much smaller locality. Experienced Alaskan guides know that to find one trophy bull in September is to have found an area where others are likely to be.

In 1967, Jack Antrim, Frank and Homer Sayers and I made a pioneer hunt by floatplane and by backpacking into the Mackenzie Mountains of the Northwest Territories. We flew camping gear into several remote lakes where a small aircraft could safely land and from there hunted out to spike camps on foot. It was an extraordinary adventure because at the time, the country had not been hunted at all since a construction project had been started and abandoned during World War II. White sheep were our main objectives, but we watched carefully for all other game as well.

During the first week or more of the hunt, we saw no moose at all, even though we were passing through ideal moose country. But after establishing a new camp on a new lake, we suddenly found ourselves in country similar to the rest but saturated with moose and especially with large bulls. Every morning they bugled back and forth around the lake shore. One paused while walking past our tents to sniff at salted lake trout hung on racks to dry. We estimated that there were seven or eight bulls in a two-square-mile area, and that figure may have been low. In another month or so they probably would have dispersed, having lost the desire for feminine companionship. And soon after that the huge palmate antlers would fall to the ground.

Moose are strong swimmers, aided by their coat of hollow hair, which helps to buoy them in the water, and their broad hoofs. In the summer the animals take to the water to avoid insects and eat aquatic plants (right).

Shiras moose plod through deep Montana snow in search of food. Deep or prolonged crusted snow, on range that is already overbrowsed, causes malnutrition and death among the herds every year.

It is true that *Alces alces* has been eliminated from some areas where it once abounded, especially in our eastern border states. But the immediate future of the species is bright and moose populations are holding steady almost everywhere from the Canadian border northward. Moose have a fairly high reproductive potential and quickly fill any suitable range to its capacity. Nature rather than hunting pressure is the major factor in the abundance of moose.

Deep or prolonged crusted snows, particularly when combined with over-browsed range, can lead to malnutrition and even to the death of many moose in a given area. At the very least, extreme bad weather greatly decreases the survival rate of the next year's calves. Weather takes a greater toll than predators.

It seems that such a huge and powerful animal has little to fear from other animals. But wolves do kill some moose, especially young or winter-weakened individuals in springtime and even full-grown moose bogged down in winter snows. Brown and black bears also kill an occasional calf. When moose populations grow too large or exceed the carrying capacity of the range, parasites can function as a limiting factor.

I have had more than my share of strange encounters with moose. On a summertime pack trip for trout fishing in Assiniboine Provincial Park, British Columbia, Bill Browning, my son Bob and I had pitched a camp in an area known as Policeman's Meadow. That was a mistake, because a young bull moose made himself at home and practically moved in with us. When Bob would collect firewood or drinking water from the creek, the moose would go along. He stood nearby and watched while we cooked dinner. After dark he tripped over and entangled himself in tent ropes, ending everyone's sound slumber for the night.

Once when photographing in Jasper National Park, I saw a grizzly grazing on a mountainside in perfect position for pictures. To get closer to the bruin, I had to pass through a dense willow thicket. Halfway through it I encountered a cow moose with very young twin calves. Without hesitation the cow moose came after me, and failing to find a tree big enough to climb, I retreated to my car. Perhaps the three moose had bedded in the willows as they normally do during daytime—or maybe they were hiding from the grizzly. No matter though, because I didn't get my pictures, not even of the moose. Docile and dumb-looking as they may seem, cows will invariably and vigorously defend calves. Cameramen take note.

Many people hunt moose more for the delicious meat than for a trophy. In Alaska alone the harvest is about 10,000 animals, or about 5 million pounds of protein. No matter how strenuous the actual hunt, it is usually more strenuous to butcher the animal and transfer the meat from field to food locker.

Hard work or not, a moose hunt can be the major event of any autumn. The animal makes an impressive trophy. And there is no more exquisite month to be afield than September, moose-hunting time.

Mountain Sheep

I HAVE SELDOM met a sheep hunter who for various reasons does not consider the sheep the greatest game animal he has ever encountered. Sheep hunting is an addiction cured only by advancing age. For almost anyone who loves challenge and lofty places, to stalk the first sheep is to be hooked forever.

Other kinds of hunting are more dangerous and for many, danger is the most important ingredient. But the odds for success in sheep hunting are not very great, and that makes the game more worthwhile. In addition, the sheep hunter suffers. He scales lung-busting mountains and toils along thin, icy ridges using handholds as often as footholds. He finds himself soaked with sweat in biting cold, and at times he wonders at his decision to go sheep hunting in the first place. But when a hunter bags a sheep, he wears the accomplishment as if it were a badge of honor. From then on, any

other kind of hunt is a mere warm-up for the next sheep hunt.

There is fine insight into the sheep hunter's philosophy in *Great Arc of the Wild Sheep,* an excellent reference for any sheep hunter. Author James L. Clark, late of the American Museum of Natural History, dedicates his work to "those hardy sportsmen of the world who prefer to meet the challenge of the climb and secure one fine sheep head, rather than to hunt at lower levels for easier game. Some hunters believe that sheep are the *only* game animals.

The true wild sheep of the world populate a series of awesome mountain ranges that span three continents, from the Mediterranean islands across central Asia to North America. These sheep have the generic name *Ovis.* There are five species of *Ovis* and, depending on which scientific authority you recognize, up to fifty subspecies distributed around the

Rocky Mountain bighorns, largest of the North American wild sheep, make their home above timberline from Colorado north into Alberta and British Columbia. Massive three-quarter-curl horns on these rams will continue to grow through their lifetime, but may "broom" off at the ends.

globe. About twenty-five subspecies of *Ovis canadensis,* the bighorn, and *Ovis dalli,* the Dall sheep, inhabit or once inhabited North America. Several subspecies including the Audubon sheep are extinct.

For purposes of record-keeping and trophy measurement, hunters divide North American sheep into four classifications: Rocky Mountain bighorn, desert bighorn, Dall and Stone. The desert is one of many bighorn subspecies and the Stone, *O. c. stonei,* is a subspecies of the Dall. The aim of every serious sheep hunter is to collect a trophy head of each, a feat known as a Grand Slam. But because of the rarity and inaccessibility of the desert sheep, this goal is seldom accomplished. Those few sportsmen who claim all four heads consider themselves the royalty of the outdoor fraternity, and their pride is easy to understand.

Considerable disagreement exists over the origin of wild sheep in the New World. They probably arrived via some prehistoric land bridge which once connected Alaska and Siberia. In any case our sheep have an astonishing similarity to their Siberian cousins. It is believed that any variations between the two are simply a result of evolution, an adjustment to a particular environment. But the enigma remains of how and why such a completely nonmigratory animal ever traveled so far.

The first European to describe (and perhaps

to see) wild sheep in America was Francisco Coronado, the Spanish explorer. During his search for the Seven Cities of Cibola in 1540, he wrote of a "large, curl-horned animal" which was undoubtedly an Arizona desert bighorn. After that there is little record of sheep for almost three centuries until 1800 when one Duncan McGillivray, a Canadian fur trader, shot a bighorn on the Bow River in Alberta. The 1806 journals of Lewis and Clark noted the "animals of immense agility," bighorns, found at Gates of the Mountains on the Missouri River in Montana.

Before the winning (or losing) of our West, sheep were very abundant. And then they were not confined only to the highest, loneliest mountain pastures as they are today. It wasn't until exposed to firearms that they became so super-sophisticated and so difficult to hunt in their final mountain sanctuaries.

One point should be made very clear: Trophy hunting by sportsmen had (and has) nothing whatever to do with the present limited numbers of sheep. Blame instead our expanding civilization, the need of available pasture for livestock, and disease contracted from domestic sheep. The fact that as many as 100,000 wild sheep remain in the continent today can be in part credited to sportsmen's conservation agencies, which alone have financed sheep studies and research projects.

The most marvelous of all American sheep is the Rocky Mountain bighorn. Rams may exceed 300 pounds and they have been credited with the equivalent of 8X vision. That may not be an exaggeration. The home of the bighorn is above timberline in most ranges of the Rockies from Colorado northward into Alberta and British Columbia.

The entire existence of the northern big-horn, *Ovis canadensis canadensis,* climaxes in late fall. The previous winter in a bitter and bleak environment of long sub-zero nights is a survival test during which starvation, disease and predators eliminate all but the fittest ewes and rams. In late spring the ewes which survived the ordeal slip away to remote sheltered ledges to give birth, usually to single lambs, which, though very wobbly at first, are soon playfully butting heads with other lambs. New green grasses which sprout behind melting snows provide easy living in summertime. Then the rams segregate themselves from the other sheep, usually loafing leisurely in higher meadows. But beginning with the first autumn storms, summer friendships are forgotten and the rams become rivals for breeding the ewes, which are now conveniently assembled in herds for that purpose.

Bighorn ram combat is a violent spectacle which I have never been able to see at close enough range. After prancing and squaring off, the rams back apart, sometimes as far as thirty-five or forty feet, then suddenly on stiff hind legs launch into a head-on charge at one another. The pile-driver impact of horns can be heard a mile away and is repeated over and over again. From a distance, the impact has an anvil sound.

Slow-motion pictures have revealed how the shock of the impact ripples through each ram's body, how dust and splinters fly from the horns. Though blood drains from noses and ears, and both animals reel drunkenly from the furious pounding, the fight will continue until one is clearly the strongest—at least strong enough to stroll away with the females and until another challenger comes along. Then the duel is repeated.

I learned the force of the blows when I once watched a young desert ram with barely

Smaller and leaner than their Rocky Mountain cousins, the desert bighorns survive in harsh regions where temperatures reach both extremes and forage and water are sparse. The thin-horned sheep with the ram in photo at right is a ewe. These sheep were all photographed at the Desert Game Range, near Las Vegas.

three-quarter curl horns snap in two the ten-inch pine post of an enclosure at the National Desert Game Range in just four attempts.

The smaller, leaner desert bighorn is now found only in localized portions of its original range of the dry Southwest. Most zoologists recognize four important desert subspecies as follows: the Mexican bighorn, *O. c. mexicana*, of Sonora, Chihuahua, southern New Mexico and Arizona, and southwestern Texas beyond the Pecos River; the Nelson bighorn, *O. c. nelsoni*, of southern Nevada and Utah, northern Arizona and south and east of the Sierras in California; *O. c. cremnobates* of extreme southern California; and *O. c. weemsi* of Baja California. None is really abundant anywhere and the latter two are so increasingly rare that they should be given complete protection.

The future of desert sheep is today vastly brighter in the United States than in Mexico because healthy herds are established and living in security on several National Monuments, national and state wildlife ranges. To thrive, sheep need some small source of water and must be free of competition from domestic stock for existing water and forage. In Mexico they have neither, and continual poaching is an extra factor threatening survival.

Few other large animals can share the harsh habitat of the desert sheep where temperatures reach both extremes, where the forage is sparse and unsucculent, and where water exists only in widely scattered sources. Only the occasional mountain lion or mule deer might adapt to such scarcity. So desperate does the need for a drink become that once within two years, thirty-four bighorns fell into a single spring hole trying to reach the water which seeped only intermittently deep inside. This death trap containing the bleached skulls and carcasses was discovered by biologists in the Choc-olate Mountains of eastern Imperial County in California.

Due to its conspicuous color, the Dall sheep is the easiest of the family to spot far off on a mountainside. Except, however, in McKinley National Park, where it has long been protected, it is everywhere difficult to approach. The Dall sheep inhabits Alaska, the Yukon and the Mackenzie Mountains of Canada's Northwest Territories.

With increasing age, Dall rams grow massive curling horns (as do all *Ovis* rams), while ewes and young rams have short, thinner and slightly curled horns. Like claws, hooves and fingernails, these sheep horns grow from skin of a substance called keratin. Entirely different from the bony, annually-shed antlers of all deer, horns continue to grow in size throughout the life of the animal, most of the growth occurring during spring and summer when more nutrition is available. By the time a Dall ram is five years old, he has a three-quarter curl, and the curl becomes full between seven and eleven years. A trophy head has at least a full curl. Maximum age of a sheep is about fourteen years.

Dalls feed primarily on grasses, leafy ground plants, some mosses and lichens found on alpine slopes and ridges. Some willow browsing occurs in winter. They can ordinarily dig down through snow for food, but exceptionally deep snow or icing can prevent them from reaching food and eventually cause starvation. In spring, sheep seek out fresh, new vegetation in snow-free areas. As the snow line retreats during the summer, they follow it to the highest meadows and ridges. All sheep require certain minerals in their diet and habitually seek out places—salt licks—where these minerals are accessible at the surface.

Dall sheep live in relatively dry country and prefer a special combination of open alpine ridges, meadows, and steep slopes with precipitous, extremely rugged escape terrain in the immediate vicinity. Thus, they have areas for feeding and loafing; yet if danger approaches, they can flee to the rocks and crags.

Today Dall sheep in Alaska and northwest Canada are generally in good supply throughout their range, but they were not always so plentiful. At various times since 1900, severe winters and market hunting reduced numbers drastically. The chief natural predators are wolves. Usually sheep can easily outdistance their pursuers in rugged cliffs and steep "escape" terrain, but when deep snow, malnutrition, or disease prevents or slows the escape, predators can exact some toll. Although lynx, coyotes, wolverines, and grizzly bears are known to take sheep, they are not important predators. During early prospecting and mining days in Alaska, market hunters depleted populations to a greater extent than other animals ever could.

The blue-black Stone, which is the color of polished gun metal in a bright sun, is a subspecies of the white Dall. The main chunk of its natural range is in northern British Columbia. An intergrade between the white and Stone races which occurs where their ranges overlap is called Fannin sheep. Like the Stone and white, Fannin rams reach a maximum weight of about 200 pounds.

Another wild sheep, the Barbary or aoudad from North Africa, not of the genus *Ovis*, has been established in the Canadian River Rim region of New Mexico and on some Texas ranches. It is multiplying sufficiently to provide limited hunting on a quota basis. But most serious sheep hunters would prefer to see native sheep reestablished.

Sheep-hunting success, whether with gun or telephoto lens, depends on a combination of determination, good physical condition, sufficient money, and a knowledge of sheep country. There isn't any substitute for the first three. The high-altitude hunting is costly in time, energy and money, but a sheep hunter can get by, as most beginners must do, by relying on a guide or outfitter to interpret the country.

During most open hunting seasons, rams will still be segregated into small bands. The all-male groups may have one or two old monarchs bigger than the rest, perhaps having an inch or two longer horns, and this difference separates the once-in-a-lifetime trophy from an average head of horns. Not even the most massive elk or moose racks, however, can be considered with just the average sheep, or so a serious sheep hunter will assure you.

When ram hunting, you must constantly look upward toward high-hanging basins and to green glades just below or on the edge of rimrock, usually facing to the south. An ideal place is where water seepage from a glacier or from snowfield ice has combined with sunlight to grow enough succulent grasses to keep the animals from wandering far away in search of forage. But do not expect to find many rams on single, postcard-picture peaks from which there would be no escape from danger. Instead, look for a conglomeration of peaks connected by ridges and divided by deep canyons, all of them difficult to traverse.

There are few dull moments in mountain sheep hunting. Discomfort, yes. Cold, chills and muscle spasms, of course. But never any boredom. A hunter rides or hikes out across naturally spectacular terrain, from which the view is always spectacularly vast, and he never stops looking. If he does not always spot sheep,

Dall sheep, snow-white spots against rocks and alpine grass, are easily seen on the rugged crags of Alaska, the Yukon, and the Northwest Territories.

he may see a grizzly, a herd of caribou, wolves or a wolverine, all animals which sometimes share the same high real estate. Then, eventually, there is the day—and the moment—when a good ram is spotted and the long, upward stalk begins.

There isn't much point in trying to describe a stalk for sheep. All stalks are different; most are slow, tedious and even agonizing. You wind up with lungs on fire and legs feeling like worn-out inner tubes. And chances are good that when you finally reach the destination, the spot within rifle range of the target, the rams will have evacuated to another mountain far in the distance. So you sit and try to decide whether the situation is worth following up.

I do not agree with some sportsmen that North American sheep are substantially more wary than other big game. It's only that the bighorn and his clan live in a dizzying world which is more challenging than the animal itself. Nor is a ram ever as fleeting a target as the faster whitetail, say, staying out in the open even though the range is long. Sheep are not swift afoot, and their agility is lacking compared to other mountain big game such as the goat in particular, the mule deer, and possibly the elk.

Nor do many other big-game species become tame so soon when given complete protection as any of the sheep. In McKinley Park, Alaska, for instance, Dalls pay little attention to those photographers who bother to climb up onto the lonely ridges where they spend the summer. I've passed many days in this thin environment among bands of rams, sitting to rest when they bedded down and traveling along at a discreet distance when they traveled. The longer I spent with the sheep, the more they seemed to trust me.

With my son Bob on one occasion, I spotted a band of sheep in a distant basin above the only road through McKinley Park. Viewed in a spotting scope, the animals proved to be rams, so we loaded as much photo equipment as we could carry easily into rucksacks and began the slow, laborious climb to reach the same altitude.

At the time Bob was eighteen, in superb physical condition even for a young man. No wonder that at fifty I needed twice as long to reach the same elevation as the sheep, although Bob ended up by lugging all our equipment. The rams were bedded down and it wasn't until we were fifty or sixty yards away that one or two became slightly uneasy and stood up. While I focused through the telephoto, all but the largest were on their feet, stretching and moving unalarmed to the next bench just above.

But one big ram only stared dully at us as we approached cautiously, careful never to climb directly toward the animal which was and still remains the most magnificent sheep I've ever seen anywhere. I wondered why it did not arise and follow the others—and mentioned this in soft voice to Bob. Then when we were only fifteen yards away, the sheep stood up on very unsteady legs and painfully—very, very slowly—began to struggle up the slope.

Then I realized the reason for the lack of fear; it was agony to stand up and move. The ram was too old for much exertion and ob-viously was living its last days. It was a miracle that the great white sheep had ever survived the winter.

A sheep hunt is rarely an inexpensive undertaking. Before starting out, there is the matter of a license. The minimum non-resident fee anywhere in the United States or Canada is $150. Baja California desert sheep permits have been scalped at $1,000 a copy.

Next, an outfitter must be engaged, and because the trip by pack and saddle horses covers very remote mountains, this also is expensive. In most good northern sheep country a sheep hunt shouldn't be scheduled for less than ten days or two weeks, and some outfitters are reluctant to go afield for so short a period.

The pack train carries the hunters into sheep country where camp is pitched. Then from camp the hunters ride out looking for sheep. When these are located, hunting continues on foot. For this type of expedition, the hunter needs suitable equipment.

Put a warm sleeping bag and foam mattress at the top of the list; a good night's sleep between hunting days is extremely important. All hunting clothing should be soft, warm and light in weight. Don't forget long underwear, plenty of warm socks and a suit for foul weather which will not tear or rip easily despite hard use. A couple of extra pairs of gloves come in handy.

Every experienced mountain hunter has his own preferred footgear. My favorites are eight-inch or ten-inch leather bird-shooter boots with knobby composition soles. If it is wet, I wear rubber-bottomed pacs of the same height, also with vibram soles. No matter what the shoes, they should be well broken in before any hunt anywhere.

The rifle is of the utmost importance. So is knowing how to shoot it. It makes little sense to travel a thousand miles for just one shot—and not be prepared to make it count. A flat trajectory is important, both to reach far out (although the average shot will probably be between 150 and 250 yards) if that is necessary, and to compensate for the shooter's error in estimating the range. The bullet should be heavy enough to down the animal if the shot does not hit a vital spot.

Not many shots at sheep are made under ideal conditions. You may be trembling with excitement, nearly dead from exhaustion or altitude, or, more likely, experiencing both of these conditions. Add such factors as wind and running animals, and you have all the ingredients for missing. That's why sheep hunters claim there is no other kind of hunting.

I have shot several sheep with a .270 and 7mm Remington magnum calibres using bullet weights of 150 grains. This combination has been adequate, although some hunters may prefer something slightly heavier because grizzlies are occasionally encountered in mountain sheep country. That is only one bonus among many for the man who hunts on top of America.

Grizzly Bear

IN SEPTEMBER, 1959 I hunted white sheep and bears in the Cassiar Mountains of British Columbia. One of the guides was an Indian, Charlie Abou, who was an extraordinary woodsman. In December, 1960 he wrote me the following letter.

Dear frien,

Writing you this just to tell you all about trouble we had this winter with grizly bear. First my son Jim and I went up Scotty Creek to see our traps there the big bear met us and go after us he never give us chance to pull my gun out which tie down sleigh he came right up to where we stand with our dog team. Its only about six feet away from us and open his mouth already thats when I throw my mitts and cap to him. That back him up a little so I had chance to get my gun out. The big bear ran away. . . . On December 26 the same bear met us not far away from here. (Hyland Post). We saw him first so I shot the grizzly with 30.06 I gave him nine shot before he die. I tell you frien hes real tough bear ever die. After this I went up to Cold Fish Lake when I arrived there late one evening everythings spoiled all one side Charles house no roof all the timbers tear down and there nothing left no even a grain of tea left so I look over Alex's place the doors open like there nothing there too. So I got so scare I dont think I stay there 40 minutes I just turn right back same evening when I going down lake I seen in your living room all windows broken in I never even go near that place. Beside I never had a wink of sleep until I got down here. . . . I believe that is the same bear which I shot cause theres big cut in his paw. So long frien a very happy new year and my best regards to you.

Sincerely yers.
Charlie Abou.

O ne morning the following spring in a lonely valley of northern British Columbia, far from the same Cold Fish Lake, another Indian trapper was splitting firewood beside a crude log shack when his world came to a sudden end. Maybe his dog, a huge malemute bitch, gave him a brief warning. Maybe not. But nobody will ever know.

When another Indian passed the spot several days later, he found man and dog side by side and dead. The shack was destroyed almost as completely as if a bomb had exploded inside. Even tin cans were ripped apart. It was a scene to turn anyone away in horror. And all around it were the unmistakable pawprints of a medium-size grizzly bear.

The year before, a grizzly had surprised two Yukon trappers while they skinned a wolf, fatally mauling one of them. In Alaska a grizzly just out of hibernation killed both the hunter and the guide who tracked it to its den. Not long ago a grizzly sow attacked a man and wife hiking in Glacier National Park. The tale of grizzlies tearing three trail campers from their sleeping bags during one nightmarish night at Glacier is well known everywhere. Almost anyone who has lived very long in grizzly country can describe similar grim incidents, some true and some not so true.

W hat kind of creature causes such incidents? Where does it live, and what makes it tick?

North American history has been vastly affected by certain wild animals. Much of the

The grizzly is potentially among the most dangerous of all animals, for it possesses enormous strength and, when provoked, a fierce and aggressive spirit. Since early settlers first encountered the huge bear, it has excited men's fears and stirred their imagination.

continent was first explored by beaver trappers and fur traders. And everyone knows about the economic importance of the buffalo to the Indians—and the near elimination of the species. Later, market hunting for waterfowl and passenger pigeons became a great industry. But no animal has excited men's fears and imaginations more than the grizzly bear. No native animal has ever been surrounded by more legend and colorful lore. And maybe no beast is more misunderstood.

The grizzly, *Ursus horribilis,* or more recently *Ursus arctos* to some authorities, is one of the largest carnivores on earth. Only the Alaskan brown bear (if indeed it isn't only a bigger grizzly) and the polar bear are larger. Potentially, the grizzly is the most dangerous and formidable creature to walk on four feet. It is unpredictable and when full grown is as magnificent a brute as any outdoorsman will ever encounter. I have met lions and rhinos, jaguars and elephants at close range, but a large grizzly always seems more awesome.

No wonder it is considered such a great game animal and such a highly coveted trophy. And, sadly, no wonder it isn't very abundant anymore. The grizzly is bordering on oblivion in the United States, except in Alaska, where a fair number of the bears remain. Canada also contains a sizable population. But nowhere is the grizzly more than a fraction as plentiful as during primitive time.

Once this amazing bruin was abundant al-

most everywhere in the West. There isn't any way to determine accurately the number of grizzlies in existence more than a century ago, but in certain areas they were numerous enough to be a nuisance to ranchers and farmers. One area, believe it or not, where grizzlies were especially plentiful is the one now occupied by the city of Los Angeles.

The Indians of our West learned to live in semi-compatibility with grizzlies, and vice versa. Most tribes attributed great wisdom, strength, and even magical powers to the bears. Some thought grizzlies were brave ancestors reincarnated. Occasionally Indians would hunt grizzlies, but with their primitive weapons it wasn't a very healthful pastime. A necklace of claws could be proudly worn.

Nobody will ever know who was the first European to meet the grizzly, but almost certainly it was either Cabeza de Vaca or Francisco Coronado (or a member of their parties), explorers who wandered about the Southwest during the first half of the sixteenth century. It's likely that the first grizzly killed by a non-Indian was shot with a Spanish crossbow. The first clear reference to grizzlies was made by a Jesuit missionary, Claude Allouez. In his *Mission to Kilistinouc,* written in 1666 about the Assiniboine River region of western Canada, he notes, "Indians are eaten by bears of frightful size, with prodigiously long claws."

The early explorers found it hard not to encounter grizzlies, and there are many quaint and interesting accounts of these meetings. In 1805 Lewis and Clark met this "tremendiously looking anamal," [*sic*] and it wasn't exactly a cordial contact. The bruin chased Lewis back into the Missouri River. Lewis later wrote: "There was no place by means of which I could conceal myself from the monster until I could charge my rifle. In this situation I thought of retreating in a brisk walk until I could reach a tree about 300 yards below me, but I had no sooner terned myself about but he pitched at me, open mouthed and full speed. I ran into the water to such debth that I could stand and he would be obliged to swim, and that I could in that situation defend myself with my espontoon."

Luckily for Captain Lewis, he didn't have to use his espontoon, which is a short pike. But some frontiersmen who followed weren't so fortunate. Kit Carson was treed like a possum a number of times, and old Jim Bridger regarded the bears with great respect. "Grizzlies," he told a friend, "is nothing but devils in fur coats."

Another of the greatest mountain men, Hugh Glass, survived a brush with a grizzly that seems incredible. In 1825 Glass shot a bear but only wounded it, and the bear dragged Glass from a tree into which he tried to escape. The animal proceeded to maul and mutilate Glass beyond recognition, breaking bones and tearing most of his scalp away. His condition appeared so hopeless that his companions (including Jim Bridger) abandoned him for dead.

But somehow, unattended, and after lying in a coma for days, Glass survived and crawled more than one hundred miles on his belly down the Missouri to Fort Pierre, South Dakota. There he continued his recovery, and he later went back to trapping and exploring in the Rockies.

An entire library could be filled with grizzly-hunting stories. Ben Lilly of New Mexico, the most famous bear hunter of all, once tracked a giant grizzly for five years. An eastern industrialist, who said he wanted the trophy, paid the bearded old man a salary to carry on the relentless tracking project. But he never found time to join Lilly for the kill.

I t is hard to say how the grizzly first received its name. Earliest accounts used the terms "gray bear" or "white bear," both of which were probably translations of Indian names for the animal. But more than likely, grizzly is derived from one of two sources: from *grisel*, and old French word meaning "gray"; or from the Old English *grislic*, which meant "horrible" or "demonlike." Some early writers called the brute a "grisly" rather than "grizzly" bear. Later on, during the era of Jim Bridger and the Mountain Men, a grizzly was called Ephraim, or Old Ephraim, or Old Eph. A common term today is "silvertip," a name that describes the animal when the sun backlights the long guard hairs on its back.

Actually, grizzlies come in various colors, from almost black through all shades of brown to almost light blond. Occasionally younger bears are bicolored: dark brown underneath with a blond or near-yellow saddle.

An adult grizzly is truly impressive and remarkable. He can run with startling speed, and an actual charge must be a chilling, fearsome thing. I have watched a female grizzly negotiate a rimrock that appeared difficult even for a bighorn sheep. Still more remarkable, a pair of small cubs followed her.

It isn't easy to confuse grizzlies with the black bears that often share the same range. The wide dished-in face and shoulder hump of the grizzly are highly distinctive. And to me at least, a grizzly has a bolder, more confident and rolling gait. Even the pawprints are distinctive from a black bear's, because the long claws of a grizzly's front feet are etched in soft earth. A black bear's claws do not show unless he is scratching or is injured.

Ask a hunter how big grizzlies grow, and his answer will invariably be exaggerated, because his trophy is such an impressive beast. But reports of grizzlies far exceeding a half-ton in weight must fall into the category of legend. Zoo bears have attained extraordinary size (one up to 1,350 pounds), and it is even remotely possible that some grizzlies reach that size in the wild. But few bears bagged by hunters can ever be weighed, a fact that adds to the lore and mystery of the critter. A 500-pound male is a good one, rest assured, and so is a 400-pound female.

G rizzlies figured prominently in the early days of southern California's settlement, both as a nuisance and as they furnished strange kinds of sport. If ranching wasn't always profitable, it was because the bears found fat cattle easy to catch and even better to eat. Hunting the bears was at first a serious business, but it evolved into a dangerous and harmful game.

Those Spanish settlers, it seems, missed the excitement and spectacle of the bullfights and cockfights they had enjoyed at home. Maybe it was inevitable when one bright day somebody suggested lassoing a grizzly. The "vaqueros" were skillful riders, recklessly brave, whose horsemanship was a matter of immense pride. Roping (or trying to rope) bears with oxhide reatas became an important pastime hard to match for pure thrills. Every fiesta was an excuse to go out and rope some bears—and every roped bear was an excuse for a fiesta. Life, we suspect, was lively in old California.

One day somebody suggested putting a captive bear into an arena with a bull to see what would happen. The result was a savage bear-bull fight, the first of thousands held on every feast day or birthday of a saint for almost half

71

Distinctive features of the grizzly are the wide dished-in face and large shoulder hump. Paw-prints can be distinguished from those of the black bear by presence of claw marks in soft earth, as shown in photo of forefoot track (below).

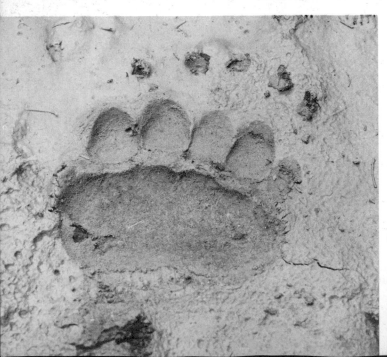

a century thereafter. Both bulls and bears were handled and treated as were valuable gladiators in ancient Rome or prizefighters today. The fiercer they were, the more famous they became. All over California the most ferocious bears became highly valuable properties.

As late as 1857 a bull-bear fight was held at the mission of Los Angeles, and others were held at the San Fernando mission after 1860. The spectacle caught on briefly elsewhere in the West, and on October 8, 1868, a fight was staged in Helena, Montana. The bear was a huge male captured along the Sun River nearby, but no account remains of how it fared against a bull or bulls. Fortunately, that seems to have been the last of a bloody, deplorable sport. But the incredible strength and ferocity of grizzlies in those battle pits contributed much to grizzly legend today.

It's curious how little is known about grizzlies today, in this era of science. It is believed by many, for example, that these bruins are purely flesh eaters, but that isn't true: they're really omnivorous. Perhaps the largest portion of a typical western grizzly's diet is obtained by grazing on grass and berries. I have watched a grizzly eat not only the blueberries he found on an Alberta hillside, but entire berry bushes as well.

As a result of their scientific and exhaustive study spanning seven years in Yellowstone Park, biologists John and Frank Craighead have become the best authorities on grizzly bears today. Using baited traps made of sections of culvert pipe with falling trap doors, the brothers captured alive 391 bruins. Next the animals were drugged and, after investigation for age, sex, health and other biological data, were released. From the results, the Craigheads learned a good bit about the species.

The Craigheads found, for example, that the average grizzly in the Park lives to be only six years old, and that four of every ten cubs perish before a year and a half (which is weaning age). Causes of death include a forty percent loss to hunting when the bears wander outside the Park onto National Forest lands. Problem bears which must be eliminated to protect people in the Park account for another eighteen percent loss. Still, the Yellowstone population appears to hold at a level of between 250 and 300 animals.

Late in 1961 the Craigheads trapped and drugged a female grizzly which was destined to make history. On regaining consciousness, the sow found a bright new two-pound collar around her neck. The collar contained a two-ounce radio transmitter complete with batteries and antenna. By using radio receivers, the biologist-brothers became the first men ever to maintain contact with bears as they traveled about and the first researchers to learn much about a bear's wandering habits. Eventually transmitters were attached to twenty-nine bears and their itineraries charted on maps of the Park.

To date the Craighead investigation remains as one of the most worthwhile and dramatic wildlife studies ever completed. It may help save the species from extinction. But apparently nothing can save a close cousin, the Mexican grizzly, *Ursus nelsoni*. This animal was fairly abundant throughout the northern Sierra Madre until about 1850. But since then unregulated hunting and, worse still, in recent times the indiscriminate use of sodium fluoroacetate poison (1080) have virtually wiped out the largest and most majestic animal native to

Mexico. If any remain, they are concentrated in the Cerro Campana about fifty miles north of Chihuahua City. As elsewhere, Mexicans in bear country developed an unreasonable fear of the animals, and mothers warned children that a bear would hug them to death if they were naughty.

One thing is certain in Mexico or anywhere else: grizzlies do not attack by grasping and hugging a victim to death—the old bear hug. A grizzly's attack (which, luckily, I've never seen) is a head-on frontal onslaught in which the brute bites and slashes with its forepaws at anything that moves. Persons who have survived attacks by grizzlies agree that the mauling usually stops when the victim is still.

Will a grizzly attack without provocation?

Probably there are more opinions on this than there are grizzly bears, but the wisest answer might be "No—not ordinarily." A lot depends on how you define provocation.

Is it provocation when a cub wanders into your path and cries out in surprise? Next thing you know, Mama may be on your back. Is it provocation if you unknowingly stumble on a bear's meat cache? Or if you meet a grizzly that has just been stung by a whole hive of hornets and is furious with the world? Or how about the big old sow I shot in British Columbia several years ago—the one with abscessed, almost completely hollow teeth? My dentist examined the skull and reported that the bear must have been suffering incredible pain. If that bear had attacked out of pure desperation, would it have been provoked or not?

Because grizzlies are potentially dangerous to men and even more so to livestock, they have always been relentlessly hunted and persecuted. And probably—tragically—this will continue until all are gone. Everything has been used from helicopters to poison cartridges and electronics. Some people will not mourn the passing, those who shudder every time they hear of a rare grizzly incident and then remark that such a dangerous beast doesn't have a place in the civilized world.

Well, airplane and car crashes kill human beings wholesale, and no one suggests that we save the civilized world from flying and driving. In addition, many times more humans are killed or injured every year by domestic cattle —and even by bumblebees—than have been injured by bears in the last half-century. Like plane crashes, bears simply make headlines. They always have.

In diminished numbers members of the bear family, Ursidae, still exist almost everywhere on earth. But nowhere in the world do so many bears or such a vast assortment of them survive as in North America—in just one state, Alaska, where all North American species are found. This includes the very common black as well as the rare blue (a color phase of the black) glacier bears of Cape St. Elias and Glacier Bay, the blond Toklat grizzlies of McKinley Park, and the polar bears of the Arctic Ocean. But in a narrow belt which closely coincides with the coastal salmon spawning grounds lives the greatest grizzly of all: the brown or Alaskan brown bear. It's the largest living carnivore.

Everything about the brownie is the most. It is a most impressive brute to meet anywhere anytime, and a prime pelt which squares at ten feet is a most coveted trophy. Brown bears may be the most unpredictable of an unpredictable family: only seconds after scratching its flanks and gamboling clownlike in a stream, I once saw a half-ton male become insanely aggressive when another bruin invaded his pool. There is also the most confusion and

Followed by her cubs, a grizzly sow nimbly climbs a ridge on a food-hunting expedition. Young are born in January, when the mother is in her winter den. By April, the cubs are strong enough to accompany their mother into the world. Perhaps the most dangerous grizzly of all is a female who believes her young cubs are threatened.

disagreement over this bruin's scientific name.

Some consider it only a large race of *Ursus arctos* or *horribilis,* the grizzly grown to great size because of better nutrition. In other current literature it is a separate *Ursus middendorffi* or *Ursus gyas.* Whatever the correct nomenclature, the big bear's natural range includes the entire Alaska Peninsula and all the islands of Alaska *except* those in the southeast, south of Frederick Sound, those west of Unimak in the Aleutians, and the islands in the Bering Sea. There may be as many as nine different races, with those of Kodiak Island and the Alaska Peninsula the largest.

Except for those of Admiralty, Baranof and Chichagof islands, browns are bears of the normally inhospitable barrens. They prefer a mixture of rock slides, snowfields and tundra, interspersed with evergreen forest and thickets of alder and devil's club, often shrouded in mist or a cold drizzle. This type of terrain, laced with salmon rivers, furnishes enough forage for a living and suitable places to hibernate. Brown bears hibernate for at least half of the year, and therefore half of their lives. They do not get along especially well with human beings, and particularly not around human settlements where conflict-of-interest is likely to develop.

I have seen a good many brownies but have not had the slightest trouble with them. Once when fishing the Brooks River of Alaska's

Grizzlies sometimes hiberate in dens near timberline, emerge in spring and prowl the mountainsides, gorging on the fresh vegetation. Grizzly tracks have been found on bare summits at altitudes up to 5,000 feet.

Katmai National Monument during the peak of the sockeye salmon run, a steady procession of bears passed me as I cast just below Brooks Falls. Most appeared not to notice me at all, although several strolled much less than a hundred feet away. But that didn't prevent the weak, uncertain feeling in my knees.

During the night of the same day, one or more bears broke into a shack beside my cabin which anglers used to dress fish, apparently undeterred by the electric fence which had been erected around the structure to keep them away. That night bears passed through the Park Service campground without waking a tent full of campers. And in the morning two young bruins staged a wrestling match on the gravel beach near the Brooks Ranger Station

at exactly the same time an amphibious plane-load of fishermen and more campers arrived.

The Brooks and Kulik river camps of Katmai probably provide the best opportunity to see brown bears, as well as other Alaskan wildlife. But the most spectacular show occurs each year on the nearby McNeil River, which is extremely inaccessible. During one day on the McNeil when salmon were running, biologist Lee Miller of Alaska's Department of Game and Fish counted sixty different bears. And there is in existence a photograph of the Mc-Neil rapids in which there are twenty-eight bruins.

Brown bears are not all that plentiful elsewhere nowadays and may be in trouble. Illegal hunting by aircraft, shootings by oil exploration and logging crews, undisciplined military personnel and commercial fishermen all have contributed to a considerable unnecessary slaughter in recent times. The fact that the average size of trophy bears killed legally each year is growing smaller and smaller is good evidence that this bruin is now neither reaching maximum age nor holding its own.

The size of brown bears has been grossly exaggerated, mostly because few have ever been weighed. In addition, the weight of any one brownie varies greatly throughout the year. The animals are thinnest in springtime after emerging from hibernation and fattest in late fall just before denning up to sleep. At this time mature males weigh between 500 and 900 pounds with an occasional giant reaching 1,400. Females average between one-half to three-quarters as much.

A very large male may have a skull measuring eighteen inches long and will be about nine feet tall when standing on hind legs. Browns have been known to survive thirty years in captivity, but a wild one would be fortunate to live half that span.

Most mating takes place in June with male and female not consorting together for very long. But it is a period when the species appears more than normally irritable (perhaps also because hunger and scarcity of food are more acute at this time), and when a high percentage of the incidents with humans occur. Cubs, which are hairless and weigh less than a pound, are born in January or February during hibernation. Females have been observed with as many as four young, but one or two cubs are far more common. Female bears at times adopt orphan cubs in addition to their own, and all accompany the mother through the second year of their lives. Females breed every two or three years, but probably at three-year intervals.

Brown bears will eat almost anything—from berries, grass, sedges, roots, wild parsnip, to great amounts of fish when available and meat, no matter whether it is of a wild or domestic animal, fresh or carrion. The species cannot be considered an important predator although in springtime it may try to catch very young animals or very old ones weakened by the winter. Instances of cannibalism in brown bears have been recorded.

When a bear kills a large animal or finds a dead carcass, he will cover it with earth and debris, perhaps to lay claim or to hide it. The animal keeps returning until all is consumed. Some bears remain by the carcass, possibly sleeping on it until every putrid bit is eaten.

The long winter sleep which in all North American bears (except the polar and the southern black bear) is dormancy rather than complete hibernation, lasts from November until April or May. The duration is longest in areas with the most severe climate. The den is a natural shelter in a rock cave or in the depression left in the earth when a tree is uprooted. A brown bear sometimes digs its own shelter, most often above timberline.

There are no better symbols of the American wilderness, which is too rapidly vanishing, than the brown and grizzly bears. Hopefully, we will always have both the bears and the wilderness. But to save the bears, the time may be here when we must declare a moratorium on hunting them.

Black Bear

OF ALL North American wildlife, few animals are more misunderstood than *Ursus americanus,* the black bear. It is never a fearsome natural enemy of humans, which is one common misconception. Nor is it the overfed Gentle Ben, Smoky the genial firefighter, or the panhandling clown it might appear to be along the highways through Yellowstone. Instead, it is a shy and retiring native of deep forests which few people have ever seen outside of roadside zoos, television and the national parks.

When the first Europeans waded ashore at Plymouth Rock, black bears dwelled in all the forests of the continent. Today the range is restricted to the hardwood highlands of the Appalachian Mountains, to swamp forests of the deep South, to wooded New England, the northern Midwest, the Rockies and Cascades, and all of Canada and Alaska except the Arctic.

In other words, the species has fared better against the spread of civilization than some other wildlife. It is fairly abundant today, perhaps because of its near-human intelligence and the ability to cope with man's ugly devices, when that becomes necessary. Consider the following sad but incredible incident which occurred in May, 1959, almost within sight of the nation's Capitol.

Andrews Air Force Base is an important military post twelve miles southeast of Washington, D.C., surrounded by a high wire fence and a heavily guarded perimeter. Still, a black bear wandered out of a nearby woods and somehow got onto the base unseen—and without proper security clearance. The discovery of the bruin strolling between nurses' quarters and the North Atlantic Communications Center caused great consternation. Air police were alerted and rode out with weapons, dogs, and high-powered searchlights; airmen drove their wives and children to see the great bear hunt. But in all the confusion, the bear escaped.

By now familiar with civilization, the bear soon turned up again in southeast Washington, in sight of the Capitol dome. Strollers in Fort Dupont Park saw the bear and their report started the biggest wild-animal search since Indians roamed the district. Police from Maryland, the District of Columbia, the National Park Service, and the U. S. Air Force joined Dr. Theodore Reed and other animal experts from the Washington zoo in the pursuit.

They saw the bear here, there, everywhere, leaping over cans, strolling down a street. The trouble was catching him. The climax came on Memorial Day, when more than 1,000 people —many armed with rifles and shotguns— tramped about the Fort Dupont golf course and picnic grounds looking for the bear. He was spotted at least eight times, but got away, making tracks with astonishing bursts of speed estimated at thirty-five mph. In the course of the day the bear broke up a baseball game in the park, stopped traffic on East Capitol Street, and generally played havoc with the organized ways of city dwellers.

After being hunted all over Washington, the bear began trudging along the thirty-three-mile expressway to Baltimore. He was spotted near Friendship Airport, south of the city, and later at the old Auburn Cemetery, in southwest Baltimore. When police sped to the scene, the bear clambered over a six-foot fence and was gone again.

The hunt continued all through the night; about one hundred Baltimore policemen were combing downtown streets in twenty-five squad cars, their dogs sitting in the back seats. Finally, about four a.m., the bear was spotted on a West Baltimore street; the cruisers had him cornered.

The lead car of the pack rammed the bear and knocked him down. The bear staggered to his feet and tried to get away. Twice more the driver smashed into the bear while his comrade blazed away with his revolver. Then one patrolman took careful aim and fired a single shot into his head. The luckless bear fell heavily in the middle of the street.

"Toward the end," said Dr. Reed, "I imagine he developed a pretty low opinion of mankind." He should have.

At almost the same time, at another air force installation (Edwards Air Force Base in California), a 125-pound black bear was strapped into an aluminum ejection capsule of a B58 bomber to be tested. Later the animal was ejected while traveling at 1,060 mph, eight and one-half miles above the desert bombing range where it parachuted safely to earth. The bear had not volunteered to serve as a flying guinea pig, but was used (before risking a man's life) because its spinal column and internal organs are so similar to a man's. In fact the similarity between a human and a skinned bear has startled more than one outdoorsman.

The black bear's name is very misleading. Some are actually black in color and predominantly so in the South and East. But they are also brown, tan, cinnamon and every shade in between. There is even a bluish race at Glacier Bay, Alaska. As often as not, cubs of different colors are born in the same litter. But in any color, there is always a triangular patch of white or cream on the upper chest.

Color alone does not distinguish blacks from the larger grizzly bears, however, which may share the same range in the West. Grizzlies have noticeable humps over the front shoulder;

blacks do not. Grizzlies also have wider, dish-faced profiles; blacks have thinner Roman noses. Black bears of all ages can climb trees, while grizzlies are land-bound.

Two characteristics of the black bear are invariably exaggerated: size, and ferocity or aggressiveness. Hunters especially are prone to overestimate any bruin's dimensions. Although an odd black may reach 500 pounds, the average for a full-grown bear, which may be five to six feet long and stand thirty inches at the shoulder, is much closer to 250.

The heaviest black bear ever authentically weighed and recorded was a 605-pounder captured alive in 1957 at a garbage dump near Tupper Lake in the New York Adirondacks. Department of Conservation researchers estimated the male's age at between five and ten years. Incidentally, the Adirondack region is a very good one for big black bears, many over 400 pounds and a few above 500 having been taken there.

Although blacks can at times be very destructive to livestock and to apiaries, there are almost no authenticated records of this species of wild bear attacking humans. Each year as many as one hundred bear "incidents" occur in the National Parks, but these are instigated by tourists who feed them, unlawfully, and who believe the bruins to be tame and cuddly. They treat the animals as pets and even try to ride on them. That is a costly mistake. I have spent a good deal of time photographing the bears of Yellowstone, but even with my vast background of dealing with animals would never consider taking the chances with park bears that many tourists who are entirely unfamiliar with wildlife behavior take.

Although black bears will indeed eat meat, fresh-killed or carrion, they never get enough and really are omnivorous. Of necessity, the species thrives mostly on grass, nuts, berries, bulbs, roots and more plant foods than can be catalogued. Few other animals relish such a vast variety of woodland edibles, which includes small reptiles and amphibians, insects and insect larvae, probably mushrooms.

There are a good many hunting techniques for black bears, and these vary with the region. In the South and the western mountains, where it is legal, the bruins are hunted with packs of hound dogs which follow the fresh tracks. Sometimes a younger bear seeks refuge in a tree or den after a fairly short and easy chase. But most of the time the quarry leads dogs and hunters into the most impenetrable swamps or thickets it can find to make good its escape. The older the bear, the more difficult to bring it to bay.

One of the most grueling hunts I can recall involved a black bear big enough to make the Boone and Crockett record books. It began during a mule deer hunt with Ray "Budge" Wilcox on his Range Valley Ranch in Utah's West Tavaputs country, some of which ranks with the most rugged real estate in the United States. It is a relatively dry region where 9,000-foot plateaus are slashed by vertical-walled chasms and deep box canyons which have known few human footprints. On the ranch next to Range Creek, a large black bear had begun to kill sheep, just a few at first, but later in wholesale numbers. When the rancher could not cope himself, he called upon Willis But-

Black bears vary in color from black through shades of brown to cinnamon, plus a bluish race found at Glacier Bay, Alaska. Tan specimen at left shows traces of black in its pelage. All bears have a triangular patch of white on the upper chest.

tolph, a government hunter who owned a motley pack of hounds for dealing with lion and bear renegades.

On the eve of the opening of the deer season, a heavy snow fell on the Tavaputs high country. And the following daybreak Buttolph picked up fresh tracks of a very large bear, most probably the sheep-eater. The tracks pointed downward toward a dense strip of timber not far from Wilcox cow camp, where the bruin would probably sleep off the heavy meal of mutton. Before starting his dogs on the trail, Buttolph asked us if we cared to join the hunt. We did, and I will never forget it.

The track, or rather tracks, because two bears rather than one had streaked for the timber, were smoking hot. Somehow Buttolph got his pack to concentrate on the bigger bear, and after that they were away in full cry down a dizzying slope. That's when our troubles began.

Although the chase was quickly out of hearing, the three of us continued down the canyon wall inches at a time, clinging to handholds to keep from pitching into space. The rock wall was so steep that at times it appeared we couldn't descend any farther. But since it was just as scary to climb back out, we continued. It wasn't until midafternoon that we reached fairly level ground at the bottom of the canyon, through which flowed a cold, clear brook. We slumped down for a drink—having carried no water or food at all—and listened for the dogs. But the canyon was silent and there were no tracks to follow since whatever snow had fallen was now melted at this lower elevation.

"I'm guessing," Buttolph said, "that the bear turned downstream, so let's head that way."

The going was no longer precipitous, but the dense tangle was almost impossible to hike through. Sometimes we had to drop to hands

By clawing bark from trees, the black bear marks the limits of its territory. This bruin, photographed after an early snowfall, is sleek and fat after a summer and fall of hearty eating in preparation for winter dormancy.

and knees. What made it worse was not knowing if we were headed in the right direction, until we came upon a place where the brush was flattened and where a bear-dog fight had taken place. One hound was left behind, dead, its belly ripped from end to end. A half-mile farther and we finally, very faintly heard the baying of the hounds.

"They've treed the bear," Buttolph said. That put new life into old legs which were complaining terribly.

It was another mile to the action and a large cottonwood, from whose crown the biggest black bear I had ever seen stared down at the dogs which encircled the tree, baying. One dog had a badly bloodied head but didn't seem seriously hurt. When the dogs saw us approach, their baying became a constant din.

Buttolph carried a pistol, and that was the only firearm among us. He did not have a clear shot through the yellow foliage and his shot did not hit a vital spot. Quickly, snarling, the bear came back down the tree to confront the dogs again.

What followed isn't—and wasn't—clear. The animals fought in the middle of the creek and somehow Buttolph, who also waded in, made a killing shot at point blank range and thereby may have saved the rest of his dogs. Then while the hounds worried the carcass all of us sat down to unwind.

The rest of the adventure was both anticlimactic and nightmarish. Because it was too dark to begin the ascent out of the canyon, we spent a cold and hungry night beside a bonfire after skinning the bear. My leg muscles were in knots and I couldn't sleep because of the pain. At daybreak we began the long climb upward. Although we found a slightly less dangerous route, the way to the top was still an almost vertical obstacle course.

One final point is worth making about that hunt. Through several decades in the mountains Willis Buttolph has followed more black bear and mountain lion tracks than he can possibly recall. The bears, he declared, are twice as intelligent, twice as long-winded and invariably twice as difficult to bring to bay. They are also more destructive to valuable hound dogs.

The black bear has one great weakness which originates in the stomach. The animals can never pass up a free meal, and the habit of visiting garbage dumps has encouraged some hunters to build blinds nearby where they wait for a bear to come and refuel. It's a good way to obtain a bear rug, but not very exciting sport. Elsewhere guides or hunters deliberately place out baits of scrap foods, rancid fats or fish entrials to attract by smell any bears in the vicinity. In some states baiting is perfectly legal; in others it's forbidden. Where it is legal, ninety-five percent or more of all bears taken are attracted in this manner.

Most black bears nationwide are bagged by accident—by hunters out after deer, elk or another species. During a normal day's prowling through the woods or maybe during a pack trip, a hunter may chance across a black bear, stalk it and hopefully end up with his trophy. A good many bears are shot by deer hunters waiting motionless and silently on stand, perhaps overhead in a tree blind. In the northern states, bears often follow the same game trails made and used by deer.

The most challenging way to collect a black bear trophy is without benefit of bait or dogs; going afield alone with a bear and nothing else in mind. The fact that very, very few rugs are acquired this way is evidence of the great challenge. It is also evidence of the bear's extreme

A black bear sow with her cub suns herself in a meadow of lush grass. Born in late January or February, cubs lead a secure life for the first year under their mother's protection. After emerging from the den the following spring, the family may split up and the cubs are on their own.

shyness and highly developed senses. It is a great game species—make no mistake about it.

A bruin scents danger at least as readily as a nearby garbage dump, which means that a sportsman must take every advantage of the wind. A black's hearing is also extremely keen, so keen that a hunter must always move quietly through a forest, even when the forest floor is littered with crisp dry leaves. A bear's eyesight may not be quite as good as a whitetail deer's, for example, but it is good enough to spot careless movement on the part of any hunter.

The wise bear hunter can tip the odds slightly in his favor by concentrating his efforts in those places where bears are most likely to be during the fall shooting season. As soon as deep snows and temperatures fall, bears go into a winter-long dormancy (except in the South). To prepare for this, the black bear spends autumn on a feeding binge to store up fat for the long sleep. That means the hunter must seek out places where ripened berries, fruits (abandoned apple orchards), acorns, and other mast are abundant, because that is where the bears will also be.

Another excellent way to locate black bears is to keep in touch with beekeepers in bear country. The average black bear absolutely cannot walk away from a hive and will suffer terrible pain from multiple bee stings while raiding one hive after another. Bears have even been electrocuted when the buzz of high tension wires was mistaken for bees swarming around a hive. This taste for honey causes no

trouble if the bees are wild, but it does not endear bruins to apiarists, who wage outright war on them. Electric fences do not discourage many bears, but traps and poisons take a toll. In parts of Florida, beekeepers may have discovered a solution in placing their hives on overhead bearproof platforms. Let's hope so, anyway.

Researchers in many states have learned much about black bears by live trapping and immobilizing the animals long enough for scientific study. Tagging or marking the bears has revealed much about their movements, for example that most have a strong homing instinct to return to the place of capture. Problem bears which are causing trouble around campgrounds, resorts or garbage dumps invariably come back to old haunts even after they've been transported as far as fifty miles away across large rivers and into different watersheds.

This type of research in Yellowstone Park has also revealed more of the black bear's intelligence. Very quickly one summer, the bears learned to completely avoid camp and picnic areas at which bearproof trash cans had been installed. But they kept making regular visits to areas where refuse was more easily available.

Outside park sanctuaries, away from the temptations of free food and in open hunting areas, the black bear has an entirely different personality. Except perhaps for the mountain lion or jaguar, no North American game animal is more difficult to bag in fair chase. That means without dogs, bait, vehicles or any other devices except a gun, camera or bow. A hunter alone is no match for *Ursus americanus*.

Polar Bear

THE FIRST EXPLORERS of the polar regions of the world found far more than bewildering expanses of ice and snow. They also found wildlife in astounding variety and numbers, because the Arctic is far from being just a hostile, frozen wasteland.

Its open waters are rich enough in plankton to support vast schools of shrimp, oily fishes and pods of whales. There exist large clam beds on which the herds of walrus can grow to tremendous size. Late in springtime endless flights of eider ducks, shore and marine birds arrive to nest. This is also the year-round home of Arctic foxes and hair seals, but most conspicuous and more often mentioned in the journals of the explorers were the large numbers of white bears encountered. As late as 1820 there are accounts of seeing polar bears roaming over the ice floes "like sheep on a commons."

Today the best authorities on *Thalarctos*

maritimus believe that no more than 10,000 survive, and the IUCN (International Union for Conservation of Nature and Natural Resources) has placed the polar bear on its list of rare and endangered species.

The species is truly international, living both on the edges and often far out in all the polar seas which surround the North Pole. Specifically, it is a resident of the United States, Canada, Greenland, Norway and the Soviet Union. Many bears spend their entire lives far out beyond claimed international boundaries. Although the animals still occur and are still hunted in the Bering Sea, in Arctic Canada and Hudson Bay, the greatest numbers occur outside of North America. Probably they are most abundant around Russian-owned Wrangell Island, Novaya Zemlya, Franz Josef Land, and off the northern cape of Spitzbergen, which belongs to Norway.

Because of its remote and lonely environment, not much is really known about the white bear, and until recently no studies had been made to find out. Eskimos and other dwellers of the Arctic have always hunted the bear as a subsistence item, and the polar bear had no other enemy (except occasionally for the orca or killer whale). Until the European exploration of the Arctic began in earnest, the polar bear got along with the primitive people who shared its habitat just as other large animals prospered among other primitive societies around the world—until the balance was tipped by newly arrived civilization.

Let's examine the fragmentary information we have on polar bears. Life begins inside an ice pressure ridge or in a cave beneath windswept snow where, during midwinter, a female secludes herself to bear one or two cubs, and rarely three. These are naked, blind, and weigh less than a pound apiece. Through the almost total darkness of winter in the Arctic, the cubs burrow into the thick warm fur of the mother and nurse until they grow hair of their own and reach the size of beagle dogs. Then sometime during April or May when the days are suddenly very long, mother and cubs emerge from the den. That must be a terrible transition for all. For the old female drained of fat and energy there is the immediate and absolute necessity to find food for all. And for the cubs, it means staggering from total warm black into a dazzling, cold, white world.

From this point, there is a great gap in our knowledge of polar bears. Of course the next year or so must be spent entirely in hunting (mostly hair seals) to survive. We assume that if food is plentiful enough, and the female strong enough to hunt it, the cubs will grow rapidly. But exactly how rapidly? How about cub mortality? Does the family remain in one general

territory and become familiar with it, or does it begin a nomadic existence of wandering wherever ocean currents and ice floes lead to available food? And do other unknown factors motivate these bears?

Some authorities believe that the bears are territorial—that Bering Sea bears are Bering Sea bears and do not go anywhere else. Other scientists suppose that polar bear populations are fluid and that the animals move about the globe without detectable pattern. Maybe there is a small clue in that bears found inland, or on or near shorelines, are most likely to be females. At the same time, bears found far out at sea on the ice packs are most often males. This could indicate that males tend to wander at will, while females remain close to familiar haunts because of the need to den every second or third winter. How frequently a female can breed is another unknown fact. So is whether she uses the same den over and over, or seeks a new one.

Polar bears have been known to live thirty years in captivity. But figuring that a normal life span in the wild would be only one-half or one-third of that, say ten to twelve years, a male might very easily travel around the world during his lifetime. The ice floes on which bears live are constantly moving, and these could ferry them for thousands of miles and from one continent to another. No one knows for sure.

What is evident is that the adult white bear is a magnificent beast which can reach 1,000 pounds and which is perfectly suited for life on top of the globe. Here is a land mammal buoyant enough to swim long distances without great effort. Although other mammals swim well enough, they will sink if unable to paddle vigorously. Polar bears can also dive and apparently can remain underwater for a

In a lifetime a white bear may completely travel around the world on floating ice floes. Seals are its main prey.

Polar bears travel and hunt together across arctic ice only during the breeding period. Otherwise they are solitary.

minute or two. There are reports that they catch everything from ducks and seals to various kinds of fish underwater, but these are hard to believe.

A polar bear's vision is excellent in daylight or darkness, because it must keep hunting to survive during the perpetual darkness of December as well as in the blinding brightness of June. There is disagreement about the animals' hearing, and the consensus among Eskimos, who are the most experienced hunters, is that it is only fair. However, there is no question at all about a polar bear's sense of smell.

No matter whether it is the aroma of a prey species, of a female bear in estrus or a cache of blubber in an Eskimo camp, a polar bear's nose will pick it up from far away—possibly for many miles when wind and atmospheric conditions are favorable. Among the most effective ways to kill bears was to cook whale or fish oils and to allow the odor to drift away on currents of air. It was learned that one bear thus lured had traveled eight miles in a straight line following the scent. That cost the bear its life, as it has many others.

Hunters—primitive Eskimos as well as modern sportsmen—have naturally looked upon the polar bear as a great game animal. Killing a bear meant status and acclaim around the igloo and the huge white pelt was worth much conversation (bragging?) in anyone's trophy room. Hunting this immensely handsome animal from the greatest wilderness left on the earth, the distant Arctic, just *had* to mean challenge and high adventure. Of course,

it was—until the arrival of the internal combustion engine and particularly the ski-equipped aircraft. According to most accounts, the early Arctic explorers probably bagged more bears than was necessary, but the polar bear population didn't start plunging downward until large numbers of people invaded the Arctic with airplanes, after everything from oil and military maneuvering to trophies.

It is very important to consider how polar bears have been hunted. The traditional way is to travel by dog team out across the ice pack in late winter or early spring looking for bears or their fresh tracks. This necessitates covering great distances in severe climate, often over difficult and possibly dangerous terrain. The hunter is likely to suffer before he is finished. Considering also that the chances of success are poor, this method has never been very popular, and in fact very few non-Eskimos have ever hunted this way. Most of the bears in trophy collections today were taken in Alaska during a hunt which required aircraft or a boat out of Norway or Spitzbergen.

The hunting in Alaska is done with guide-pilots who operate in pairs during early spring and fly their sportsmen-customers out of such coastal villages as Kotzebue and Barrow. Whenever the weather is good enough, they cruise far out over the ice fields of the Bering Sea and that way cooperate in searching for animals. The two-plane buddy system is a precaution in case one is forced down, which is not unusual. By flying, more territory can be covered in a few hours than man and a dog team could explore in weeks. When a bear is sighted, one plane lands as near as possible so that guide and hunter can attempt a stalk. The success ratio has hovered close to one hundred percent, and a hunter does not have to endure great hardship or spend much time in Alaska to score.

This is not a high quality hunt, although there is an element of danger. But the danger comes from crashing on the ice rather than from the bears. The Alaska Fish and Game Commission has attempted to regulate the annual harvest of bears in this manner by setting a fairly small quota. Some pilot guides have not only found ways to circumvent the law and to take out illegal trophies, but also can drive the bears by buzzing with one plane toward the hunter waiting beside the other. That makes the kill even easier. There is almost no way that a small staff of game wardens can police Alaskan polar bear hunting. Neither the Boone and Crockett Club nor the American Rifle Association considers any such use of aircraft as taking a bear by fair chase, but still this type of hunting flourishes.

Perhaps it is even worse in Norway. There the hunters cruise the edges and channels among the ice floes in a heavy-hulled seagoing boat. When they come upon a bear, usually swimming, they shoot it from the deck. Females as well as males are taken (whereas Alaska kill is generally confined to males), because it is impossible to determine sex in the water. A single cruise might produce several bears per person.

As many as 400 additional bears per year are killed by market hunters and commercial fishermen in the Svalbard Islands of the Barents Sea alone. These are caught in traps, poisoned or shot with set guns when they wander ashore. These methods are not legal in Norway, but with pelts selling for $500 in Oslo and Hammerfest shops, and with no enforcement in the remote regions, the slaughter continues.

Most recently the polar bear has been confronted with another of man's inventions—the

96

same snowmobile which now shatters the beautiful stillness of winter wherever there is snow. During 1970, in an effort to give employment to Eskimos as guides in remote outposts, the Canadian government made available a number of permits to take polar bears. The hunter got his trophy pelt; the guides got the meat and a pretty substantial payday. But these hunts were also of low quality.

To save themselves as much work as possible, the Eskimos used sled dogs (no longer needed to pull sleds) to chase and bay bears to the limit of their endurance which, surprisingly, proved very small on solid ground. Then the guides hurried their clients to the encircled bears by snowmobiles—and that was that.

The polar bear's future on this earth is certainly not bright. Only the Soviet Union offers the animal complete official protection, but there is no way to know if it is enforced. The species is almost gone from Greenland, once an area with a high population, and the polar bear is becoming more and more scarce around Spitzbergen. It is even possible that nature is against the white bear, because a warming trend in Arctic waters is reducing its ice floe habitat. Add also the fact that significant quantities of DDT and toxic mercury are being found in seals, whales and other dwellers of the polar regions on which the bruins feed. Since they are at the top of the food chain, the passing of these poisons ends with—and accumulates in—the great ice bear.

To stop hunting everywhere may only delay the polar bear's departure from the roster of living things. But the seasons must be kept closed, until there is sound scientific evidence that a harvest is still safely possible.

Mountain Lion

AMONG THE HAPPIEST, most successful hunting adventures I can recall was a September pack trip into the Hummingbird and Oyster Creek headwaters of the Alberta Rockies, the region where Martin Bovey obtained the world-record bighorn ram in 1924. My companions were the Sayers brothers, Frank, Homer and Pete, all warm friends, plus guides Bob Machum and Mac Mackenzie. We did not find any record-book rams, but had collected two uncommonly large bull elk. However, neither the trophy heads, the warm companionship, nor the exquisite alpine country were the highlights of the trip.

Toward the tag end of our hunting, on a morning following a fresh snowfall during the night, Bob and I rode from camp toward a certain lofty meadow where previously we had found much elk sign but had seen no elk. Bob gambled that following the snow, the elk might be easier to track and to spot—and he was

right. Near timberline we came across very fresh tracks of a herd of eight or nine which we followed on foot after tying up the horses inside the cover of evergreens.

"There is a large bull in the bunch," Bob whispered after checking the size of one set of tracks and the manner in which the animal had urinated.

The herd was traveling slowly and leisurely on a meandering course in and out of the broken timber. We came upon the animals standing unalarmed on the opposite side of a clearing only 125 yards away, but only six of the elk were in sight and among the missing was the herd bull. Our best bet was to stand motionless—to watch and wait. That's when I noticed movement slightly to the right, and the movement was an animal.

Because it was brown in color, I at first thought it was another elk. But elk do not creep onto the trunks of deadfalls as this one

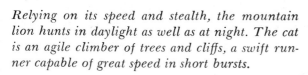

Relying on its speed and stealth, the mountain lion hunts in daylight as well as at night. The cat is an agile climber of trees and cliffs, a swift runner capable of great speed in short bursts.

Cougar caught in the act of stalking a raccoon. Cat dropped from a rock in front of the startled raccoon, which retreated to the jutting branch of a blowdown. Outcome of the contest was never in doubt; the cougar killed its prey in the next instant.

was doing. For another instant its identity didn't register, but then I realized that we were watching a mountain lion stalking an elk.

The next few moments were unadulterated agony. I wanted to see what would happen next, but was afraid to move for fear of spooking either the elk or the cat. Suddenly something else alarmed the elk, and in an instant all had evaporated from the scene. Only the pulse pounding remained.

Two days later, on departing the wilderness en route toward the Kananaskis Highway, the riders at the head of our pack string saw a second lion dart across the trail about fifty yards ahead of them. The odds against seeing two on a trip are impossible to calculate.

I did not bag an elk on that trip and maybe I can blame it on the lion. But I wouldn't have traded that fleeting glimpse of a crouched cat for the biggest bull in Canada. Seeing a mountain lion in the wild is a very, very rare experience. Few humans have ever done so, even among those who have lived in lion country all their lives.

Mostly because it is so elusive and now confined to the loneliest wilderness regions, *Felis concolor*—the puma, cougar, painter, catamount, leon (in Spanish America) or mountain lion—is another of the great game animals about which we still know too little. It

103

is as well a species which could vanish before we understand its importance to man.

When Columbus was exploring the Americas, the mountain lion was the most widely distributed large carnivore in the New World. Of all the big cats, only the leopard had a greater range on earth. Living from northern British Columbia southward all the way to Patagonia near the tip of South America, it thrived in every conceivable type of environment: in mountains, deserts, both coastal and sub-alpine forests, in swamps and on prairies. Authentic records show that the cats existed in forty-eight of the fifty states, the District of Columbia, and all Canadian provinces. What remains of that range today is the most remote mountain fastnesses of the West and Southwest, where an estimated 4,000 to 6,500 still roam. Twenty or thirty of the Florida cougar, *Felis concolor coryi,* may yet survive in southern Florida thanks to establishment of Everglades National Park. A very small population of *F. c. Couguar,* the eastern cougar, may exist in New Brunswick. And the range of the species today in Latin America is unclear.

Beginning in 1964, biologist Dr. Maurice Hornocker conducted the most exhaustive study of lions so far attempted. In addition to the scientific aspects of the five-year study, physical stamina and determination were put to the test.

As an assistant to the Craighead brothers during much of their investigations of Yellowstone grizzlies, Hornocker gained valuable experience in dealing with large animals. He selected the Big Creek drainage, an area of about 200 square miles in the Salmon River Mountains of central Idaho (Idaho Primitive Area) for his investigations. He had just three assistants: Wilbur Wyles, an excellent woods-

man well known in the state as a lion hunter, and Wyles' pair of redbone hounds, Red and Ranger.

The men and dogs trekked more than 5,000 miles, much of it on snowshoes, and captured alive forty-six different lions, many of them over and over again. All travel to catch lions was done on foot during the extreme temperatures of midwinter, in terrain so steep and rugged that it was difficult even for the dogs. There were no roads in the region. Each treed lion had to be tranquilized, examined, weighed, marked (tattooed and tagged) and released unharmed—all this with the minimal equipment they could carry on their backs and in areas where the only trails are thin game trails. But the information obtained was considerable.

Hornocker and Wyles found that the average adult female weighed 100 pounds and the average male 150. The largest male encountered was 181; the lightest scaled 130 pounds. Lions may weigh slightly more elsewhere on the continent, but the rumors of 300-plus-pounders are only rumors. The Big Creek area contained a stable resident population of only ten lions (or one per twenty square miles). Occasionally transients moved across or touched on edges of the area, but never lingered. Each year two or three litters with two or three kittens were born, but the area population always remained at about ten.

All of the resident adults—male and female —had firmly established territories, the boundaries of which were marked with mounds of brush or pine needles scraped together and urine-scented. The average winter home range for females was from five to about twenty-five square miles and males utilized generally larger areas from fifteen to thirty square miles. Lions avoided invading the territories of others, a behavior which Hornocker termed "mutual avoidance." It may well be that solitary predatory animals elsewhere on the globe exhibit similar behavior as a survival mechanism. Animals which live in packs can share food killed by others of the group, but each mountain lion is its own means of survival.

The mountain lion is easily the most solitary of all the world's big cats. A male and female may consort together briefly during mating. Kittens also remain with the mother for nearly two years of training. But that is all.

Mating can take place at any time of the year, and gestation is ninety days. As many as six kittens (but an average of 2.5) are born in a cave or den. There competition among them develops very early and the survival rate is not high. The father never participates in protecting, feeding or training the young. Young cougars become self-sufficient at eighteen to twenty months and then strike out on their own.

In much of the West, the lion's undeserved reputation as an enemy of man and a threat to the livestock industry refuses to die. Even Teddy Roosevelt, who was a pioneer wildlife conservationist, wrote of the lion: ". . . the big horse-killing cat, the destroyer of the deer, the lord of stealthy murder, facing his doom with a heart both craven and cruel." That passage was composed early in this century, but was read as recently as 1969 during a stockman's meeting in Montana when federal assistance was requested to deal with a current cattle killer.

Lions do occasionally kill and eat livestock, and these individuals can soon be eliminated. But the cougar never has been a threat to man anywhere, anyhow. Brushes with man are rare and even harder to authenticate.

The main prey of the lion is the mule deer and, in such areas as the Hornocker study, elk as well. During the five-year examination of lion-killed carcasses and bones, it was evident that old and young animals, the easiest prey, composed most of the kill. Specifically, seventy-five percent of the elk and sixty-two percent of the deer killed were less than one and a half or more than nine and a half years old. Lions also eat whatever else they can easily catch: hares, rats and mice, squirrels, raccoons, coyotes, even grasshoppers.

Apparently lions hunt as much or more in daylight as during darkness. A healthy adult is a splendid, lithe creature, capable of great speed in short bursts, an excellent climber either of trees or rock cliffs, a swimmer when it is necessary. All of the senses are well developed, which explains why lions are so seldom seen by man. In other words, the cougar is an efficient stalker and killer. But driven by hunger, it may at times take on more than it can handle.

Once in 1967, Wilbur Wyles came upon a female which had been injured when attacking a small bull of a herd of four or five elk. It was clearly evident in the snow how the two had rolled down a steep slope, crashing into a tree and permitting the elk to get away. Wyles treed the cat which, though bloodied around the mouth, appeared well. Three weeks later, Wyles recaptured the same female, now very thin and hardly able to climb, about four miles away. Quick examination revealed a broken jaw, canine teeth torn out, antler punctures in the shoulder and hind legs. The lion had been suffering horribly, slowly starving to death, and Wyles shot her.

Far too many lions are still destroyed every year by the indiscriminate use of 1080 poison and steel traps, both methods used (in

Most solitary of the big cats, the cougar is rarely seen with mate or cubs. Hunters use dogs to follow a cougar's trail until the cat is cornered or treed. Unlike other cats, the cougar won't face up to a barking dog—and this trait is usually its undoing.

1971) by government predator control agents. This is a deplorable waste of a beautiful and valuable animal. But probably ninety-five percent of all lions killed are taken by hunters using packs of hounds.

One well-known weakness in the character of every lion is its undoing: A cougar will not face up to a barking dog, not even to a yipping mongrel which it could easily destroy, let alone a whole pack in hot pursuit. All of the world's other big cats will sometimes turn on dogs, and the leopard is particularly prone to do this. But a mountain lion will come to bay rather than try to discourage its pursuers. Large males, as well as females with cubs, have been treed by terriers which weigh little more than jackrabbits.

If good, experienced lion dogs can be introduced to a fresh track, the conclusion is foregone. They will follow the track at good speed until the cat is either cornered or treed. The older the track and the rougher the country, the more difficult is the chase. But long or short, through badlands, brush or rarely through easy terrain, it is no problem to shoot the treed mountain lion out of its perch.

Because lions have not been plentiful anywhere for a long time, a hunt even with capable dogs and an inexperienced guidehunter may still consume much time and cause terrible blisters on a dude rider's behind. You really must love to hunt, ride hard, and suffer to enjoy a genuine average lion hunt. Not too many people nowadays want to suffer that much—and hence the so-called "guaranteed" hunt has originated.

In states where the lion is not a game animal by law, or where any number can be taken by any means, some professional hunters will use drugs or roping to capture lions alive and cage them until a client is located. Kittens are often taken and raised to full size in captivity for the purpose. After a day or so, when the hunter has just about reached the limit of his endurance (and this may be very soon on a hard saddle), without his knowledge, one of the captive lions is released out of sight and just ahead of the hounds. In weakened physical condition and befuddled by strange new territory, it is quickly treed and after a short ride by the client, converted into a handsome tawny rug.

That is a sad end for a splendid animal. But recently an encouraging amount of sentiment to save the mountain lion has developed. Bounties have all but disappeared on the species, which now has full game animal status in a number of states. Several of the old-time lion hunters who in the past counted for vast numbers of the cats have quietly dropped out of the game or have sold their dogs. A few have retained their hounds and still go chasing lions because it gets into the blood. But when the quarry is treed, they take pictures of it, leash the dogs and go home again. On these terms, one cougar can furnish a lot of hunting and excitement to many outdoorsmen—and be no worse the wear for it.

Recently I talked to George Hightower of Red Rock, New Mexico, one of the most famous of the old cat hunters who now manages a state wildlife research station. "Sometimes," he admits, "I get an awful yearning to go follow the hounds again. But I don't believe I could ever shoot another one. They're too scarce nowadays where they used to be too many."

Ollie Barney of Tucson is another veteran lion man who still goes hunting. But today it is mostly to train young dogs, and it provides an excuse to wander about in the lonely, haunting ranges of Arizona. "This country," Barney told me, "wouldn't be the same without lions. When they're gone I guess I'll go, too."

The cougar is truly a biological barometer. Not long ago it was considered only as an unwelcome predator of other game species. Now we know that its presence is a sure indication that deer or elk are abundant in the area, and in great enough abundance to feed the cat or cats. Otherwise, the lion couldn't exist there at all.

Maurice Hornocker made an important observation concerning the deer-lion relationship. Whenever the lion kills a deer, the rest of the herd immediately leaves the vicinity and usually travels far away until it is again molested and forced to shift once more. This way the deer (or elk) do not overbrowse certain areas, which they might otherwise do, causing long-lasting damage to their own food supply. That makes for healthier deer.

Mankind has a habit of viewing all wildlife as either good or bad—valuable or menacing. Large predators such as the mountain lion have invariably been considered to be bad and to be feared. The result is persecution, of which *Felis concolor* has had its share. Hopefully, attitudes will change with the times so that the cougar will be assured of survival.

Pronghorn Antelope

IN 1843 during a trip on the Missouri River, the painter-naturalist Audubon saw the American antelope for the first time. His description of the animal has never been matched.

"Hurra," Audubon wrote, "for the prairies and the swift antelope. They fleet by the hunter like flashes or meteors. They pass along, up or down hills, or along the level plain with the same apparent ease, while so rapidly do their legs perform their graceful movements . . . that like the spokes of a fast turning wheel we can hardly see them, but instead, observe a gauzy or film-like appearance."

Almost anyone who has ever hunted or studied the species *Antilocapra americana* has been equally impressed with the antelope, which is not a true antelope at all. Rather it is the sole member of the family Antilocapridae, which is unique to western North America and has no counterpart elsewhere on earth. Its dis-tinctive category aside, it is among the fastest animals anywhere on four feet and in appearance at least is the most striking quadruped on this continent.

The antelope is our only big-game animal with branched horns (deer have antlers, not horns), hence the common and probably more appropriate name pronghorn. It is also unusual in being the only hollow-horned ruminant which annually sheds its horn sheaths. The black outer horns drop off in late fall each year and new larger horns grow on the bony cores.

At the beginning of the nineteenth century, the antelope was the most abundant large mam-mal in America. In the numerous early ac-counts of travelers over the Great Plains, the bison is most often mentioned because it was far more visible and because it was such a huge and impressive beast. But Seton estimated that in 1800 the antelope population was about forty million. In 1971 between 250,000 and

111

300,000 survived in fifteen states and Canada, making it our fourth most abundant big-game animal, after the whitetail, mule deer and caribou. More than half of today's population exist in two states, Wyoming and Montana. There was a period when the future of the antelope was in great doubt and only a serious conservation effort brought it back to the present status.

Originally the pronghorn ranged across all of two million square miles of the prairie lands from Iowa and western Minnesota to Washington and Oregon and from Alberta to Mexico. At times the animals gathered in such great herds that the rolling plains seemed to undulate as they wandered about. One cross-country traveler thought the foothills were shimmering in noonday heat until he identified the movement as a vast herd of pronghorns. But by 1920 as few as 15,000 remained in scattered small bands.

The sharp, disastrous decline was caused by a number of factors. One was the natural curiosity or lack of wariness in the species, which it no longer has. This made the antelope vulnerable to comparatively short-range rifles of the 1800s. Disease introduced by domestic sheep also took a toll, but mostly it was a matter of overgunning. After bison became scarce, the market hunters turned to pronghorns. In such frontier communities as Denver, wagonloads of antelope were daily hauled into town where the hog-dressed carcasses sold at a dollar a dozen. Antelope meat was the only kind served in many railroad construction camps and sometimes only the tenderloin portions were used. In addition, ranchers were beginning to build fences all over the West. They looked upon pronghorns in their pastures as competition to their cattle for the existing grass, almost exactly as they looked upon wolves and coyotes as being enemies. For a period the antelope was a very endangered species.

Fortunately after World War I, Americans (especially American sportsmen) began to realize that saving the antelope was a national obligation. Various state laws passed earlier were either too late or too ineffective and besides, antelope were migratory. They paid no attention to state boundaries. As early as 1877, just after Colorado became a state, the first session of the General Assembly voted to classify the pronghorn as a protected species. Coursing with dogs was prohibited and only bona fide butchers could hunt the animals. But no penalties were provided for violations and there was no money for enforcement. Antelope all but disappeared in Colorado as elsewhere.

The first step to save *Antilocapra* was the establishment of three federal refuges: 1.5-million-acre Charles Sheldon Range in high plateau country along the Nevada-Oregon border, the Hart Mountain Refuge in Oregon, and the National Game Range (also meant to protect bison) in Montana. All have proven very valuable, but in 1971 the federal government came under great pressure to relinquish the Hart Mountain area to cattle interests. That would be a great step backward.

More important than the refuges, however, were the scientific studies by qualified biologists of the antelope's life habits, and later of restocking the animals back to favorable range where they had been eliminated. Everywhere the studies revealed that antelope in no way competed with livestock and could in fact get along well with cattle. Not only were they browsers, rather than grazers, depending largely on sagebrush, but they ate a good many other plants which were either injurious or deadly to domestic animals. Some notable examples are prickly pear (eaten spines and all with no ill effects), loco weeds, larkspurs, rubberweed, rayless goldenrod, cockleburs, soapweed, needle and thread grass. In some areas antelope were found to thrive on range plants which ranchers consider undesirable. When that point became known, persecution practically ended.

Today the antelope provides the only plains shooting for big game on this continent. When pursued by fair chase, without motor cars, walkie-talkies and similar devices, the antelope provides hunting of the highest quality. The pronghorn has extraordinary eyesight and depends on this even more than fleetness afoot for protection. And the older a buck becomes, the more difficult it is to approach even within very long range. A pronghorn's eyes are extremely large (larger than a horse's) for its size and arc deep-set as a protection when browsing on sage or other brittle plants.

The speed of the antelope is great enough that there is no need to exaggerate, which is often done by a rifleman after missing a series of running shots. The species has been actually timed in excess of fifty mph, covering the ground in seemingly effortless bounds of ten to twenty feet. Whereas many of the world's very swift animals can only maintain their maximum speeds for short sprints, pronghorns have been known to maintain fifty mph for more than a mile and to average thirty mph over seven miles. Occasionally antelope seem to run at high speed for the fun of it. Several times I have had them race parallel to my jeep for no apparent reason, and one of these times my speedometer was registering forty-five mph when three animals suddenly darted across the road in front of the jeep, only to stop on the other side and stare as I passed on.

Depending on the predominant color of the landscape—whether the green of springtime or the cinnamon of autumn—the beautiful antelope may be very easy to see, or so well blended into its background that detection is difficult. Most often and especially when standing (rather than bedded down), the white rump or cream-colored belly is what betrays the pronghorn. Both males and females are brown along the backs, but bucks also develop black collars and muzzles. The older they grow, the more the black areas spread.

It is easy to tell when an antelope is alarmed, aroused or uncertain about something. Particularly when it is frightened, the animal will leap away, at the same time erecting and flashing the long and shiny white hairs on its rump. This is almost certainly a warning (perhaps in lieu of vocal warning?) to all other antelope nearby. On one occasion in Montana when trying to stalk a buck surrounded by a dozen does, I saw one white rump flash and this quickly spread from the first among all of them. Moments later all were out of sight and running. That is a typical hunter-antelope encounter.

Many hunters are astonished at the pronghorn's small size on the first close inspection. A buck stands only 3 feet or so at the shoulder and when full grown seldom weighs more than 100 to 115 pounds. Does average smaller than that. Under ideal conditions in the wild an antelope might reach nine or ten years, but average longevity, according to all studies made to date, is much less than that.

Several years ago during a hunt near Jordan, Montana, I had unusual opportunities to observe antelope off guard. Whenever possible on a big-game hunt, I try to arrive on the scene several days prior to the opening of the season. That is good advice to anyone because this time can be used to get acquainted with the country, to find out which portions of it contain the most game, and even to locate good trophies.

One thing I soon learned was that pronghorns are diurnal; they do not seem to be active after dark. If I could keep a herd in sight until nightfall, they would be in exactly that same spot at daybreak, no doubt having bedded right there. One evening I spotted a herd of fifteen animals from about one-half mile away, and I kept the glasses on them until it was no longer light enough to see and until nearly all

had bedded in a two- or three-acre area. I realized while driving back to the ranch that here was a perfect opportunity for getting really close to the animals.

Perhaps because of the protection it offered from a cold northeast wind, the herd had

Trio of pronghorn bucks (above), *their white rump hairs lying flat, amble complacently along a ridge. Alerted herd* (below) *gallops away with rump hairs flared, the signal to the unwary that danger is near.*

Depending largely on sagebrush for its food, the pronghorn also eats many other plants that are either injurious or deadly to domestic cattle. Persecution of the pronghorn ended when studies showed that the animal was a browser that did not compete with livestock on the same range.

bedded just beneath and on the west side of a low ridge. I figured that before daybreak next morning I could crawl onto the ridge unseen and look directly down on the animals. The rising sun would be in my favor because it would be at my back and directly in the eyes of the antelope.

The strategy worked perfectly. Although chilled to the bone from lying prone on the frosty ground, I had a ringside seat for the awakening of an antelope herd.

At first I couldn't see the animals at all and feared they had wandered away during the night. But as soon as the first red rays of the sun cleared the ridge, the action began. One by one the animals stood up, stretching in the manner of hound dogs tired from a long chase, and defecating. Then as the does and yearlings began to drift toward the north, in the direction of a small stock tank, the only two males in the herd faced each other and stood head to head, hooking horns and shoving. The skirmish was very brief and no visible damage was done, but at the end only one buck followed the herd after escorting the loser for a short distance in the opposite direction.

Often the competition is more spirited than that. In Yellowstone Park I have seen a buck attempt to isolate one doe away from the herd, all the time harassed by other bucks. Fighting among bucks continues throughout the rut, which normally occurs in September and October.

In springtime the does retreat to the same fawning grounds favored year after year, where one or two young weighing from five to nine pounds are born. The fawns are very pale in color and when motionless blend perfectly into a sagebrush background. Once in Wyoming I nearly stepped on a very young fawn before seeing it, although it wasn't very well concealed by brush.

Young pronghorns grow rapidly and are precocious. When only three days old they are difficult for an agile man to catch. At six days they can outrun an average dog and week-old fawns have been known to run as far as a mile along with their mothers. The weight at birth is doubled or even tripled by the end of two months, and seven-month fawns will average sixty pounds.

Pronghorn mothers stoutly defend fawns in danger. They have been observed charging such common predators as coyotes, foxes, golden eagles and might drive all three away. They have also upset and bruised wildlife biologists in the course of catching and tagging fawns for scientific purposes. Such tagging helps to set open seasons and to manage the species for its own good. Next to hunting, deep prolonged snow is the most significant factor regulating pronghorn numbers. Natural predators are relatively unimportant.

Far too much of today's antelope hunting is done by chasing them with pickups or four-wheel-drive vehicles, no matter whether the local law frowns on the practice. That is an efficient way to get meat but cannot be of great satisfaction to the hunter. Bagging a good trophy male by finding and stalking it alone on foot is an entirely different matter.

Most antelope country is fairly flat, gently rolling at the most, and well-suited to an animal equipped with telescopic vision. Especially after the first firing on opening day, it becomes increasingly difficult to find a buck which can be approached within close range. That bucks can survive several hunting seasons and flat trajectory rifles is testimony to their wariness.

Late in the season the best hunting strategy is to venture afield well before daybreak in good antelope country and wait on some high prominence at sunrise. Atop a rimrock, hay or straw stack, you can spot animals and where they are moving before they spot you.

It has often been written that pronghorns can be attracted by tying a white handkerchief or streamer onto a stick and allowing it to flutter in the breeze where the animals can see it. The theory is that curiosity lures the buck into easy gun range. Well, I've tried the trick a number of times and the result has always been the same. The pronghorns spooked immediately, and I never saw them again. The stunt might have worked a couple of generations ago, but nowadays antelope are far too sophisticated to be fooled so easily.

And that is a lucky thing for a great game animal.

Mountain Goat

IN CONTRAST to most of our big-game animals, mountain goats today occupy virtually the same ranges where they were found by the first explorers of the West. Except in a few areas, *Oreamnos americanus* may be almost as abundant today as ever before, and that reveals a great deal about the species. The goat's natural habitat is confined to the least accessible mountain fastnesses which human beings avoid. That habitat explains why the goat has never been among the most sought after of big-game species. It is no fun to hunt.

The earliest observers of the goat could not agree upon its identification. Captain Cook never saw one alive but after examining skins brought to him by Indians, remarked: "There is here the White Bear." The early explorer Alexander MacKenzie concluded that it was a white buffalo, and Lewis and Clark believed it was a kind of sheep. None of these and not even a true goat, the mountain goat is actually an antelope, or perhaps a goat antelope, more closely related to the chamois of Europe than anything else. It is the only member of its genus *Oreamnos*.

Physically the mountain goat is bearded, thick-set and not unlike a small buffalo in structure. The heavy shoulders and long white hair make it appear heavier and more ponderous than it really is. In many animals outward appearances are very deceiving, and in this instance the goat is by far the most dexterous, most sure-footed of all native big game. Goats are at home in places where only other goats and birds can go.

On a hunting pack trip in the British Columbia Cassiars several years ago, Rusty Russell and I had spotted three white objects on a steep green meadow at the base of a nearly vertical cliff. A hasty look through binoculars revealed that they were goats rather than patches of snow and so we set up a spotting scope to see if there was a good billy in the trip. Secretly I hoped there would be no billy because I did not relish climbing into that particular spot. Luckily, the scope revealed only a large nanny with yearling kids sleeping in the pale autumn sun. Just as Rusty was about to put away the scope, he noticed a movement just beneath the goats, which appeared to be unconscious of anything nearby.

"There's a pack of wolves," he said after a moment, "stalking those goats."

The goats remained bedded until the wolves were only one hundred yards or so below them. Only then did the three stand up and begin an almost leisurely walk—not run—toward the cliff, the steep face of which they scaled as easily as if it were a gentle slope. The wolves sat down to watch them because there was nothing else to do. To this day it doesn't seem possible that anything at all could have climbed that cliff, which out of curiosity Rusty and I examined at closer range later on.

"The Stone sheep, which share these same mountains," Rusty told me, "are like cripples compared to the goats."

The species is marvelously equipped to survive in its cold, craggy, upside-down world. The animal is heavily muscled and square-set to assure balance. The shaggy outer coat (guard hairs), which is shed annually in early summer, covers a thick fleecy undercoat which compares with the finest cashmere wool. This combination is protection against the bitterest winds and subzero temperatures. But most remarkable are the unusual black hooves.

Instead of a concave surface within the horny shell of the hoof, as all deer have, the mountain goat has pliable pads which are

Nimble-footed mountain goat goes up, up, up a sheer cliffside to a lofty perch where it feels secure. Equipped with convex, pliable hoof pads which protrude beyond the outer shell covering to supply grip, the goat relies on its agility and its inaccessible habitat to escape wolves or hunters.

slightly convexed to protrude beyond the outer shell covering. These provide the traction— the grip—which enables a goat to travel over the smoothest surfaces of rock inclines in such a sure-footed manner. The square shape of the goat track differs from tracks of sheep and mule deer which are most likely to be found in lower goat areas.

Hunting goats with gun or camera and telephoto lens can prove a very easy or very harrowing, frightening experience. It all depends on where the goats are located and if they have previously been hunted or not. Given protection for a long enough period, they soon become tolerant of humans and allow them to come very near.

Even in open hunting territory, an occasional goat is easy to approach, usually by climbing the opposite or back side of the mountain and coming upon it from above. Goats tend to look for danger from below and seem only dully surprised when a man appears up above. They also seem to consider their own agility and inaccessible retreat as protection enough, thereby allowing riflemen to come much too near.

Far more often than not, goat hunting is a dizzying, lung-busting chore better left to professional mountaineers. You spot a billy which looks huge, start climbing toward it and eventually wonder why you did. According to an old Alberta mountain guide, "Goat hunting is the easiest game to swear off of in the middle of the hunt."

The original and present range of the goat included most major mountain ranges of the Rockies of northwestern Montana and northern Idaho; the Cascades and Olympics of Washington; the Alberta Rockies; most mountain ranges of British Columbia and southern Yukon; and the coastal mountains of south-

In the summer, the mountain goat sheds its shaggy outer coat of hair, which covers a thick fleecy undercoat that compares with the finest cashmere wool. This double layer protects the animal against bitter winds and subzero temperatures.

east Alaska. The species has been established around Harney Peak and Mt. Rushmore in South Dakota's Black Hills, where it is very easy to see.

An adult goat will stand between thirty-six and forty-two inches at the shoulder and weigh from about one hundred pounds as a yearling to more than two hundred as a full-grown billy. Older billies in good goat range may reach between 250 to 300 pounds with pointed black horns measuring over ten inches long. The world record horns from an animal taken in 1949 in the Babine Mountains of British Columbia measured twelve inches on each side. Any pair over ten inches qualifies for the record books.

Not many animals give the impression of being so content, so compatible with what to humans is a very hostile environment. Even when under duress, goats never seem to be in a hurry. It is easy to get the impression that they are stupid. A normal day is divided between feeding, usually early and late, and bedding during midday. The animals are diurnal, and most studies have revealed that they do not travel very far. An entire herd might live out its span on just one or two mountains, migrating only up and down between summer and winter range. A single nanny (easy to identify because of only one horn) was known to spend an entire summer on one 200-acre mountainside.

Only during the late autumn rut is there much lively activity, but even then billies do

not vigorously try to acquire harems, as do elk, and combat between males is confined to bluffing and pushing. Serious injury because of these encounters is practically unknown. The animals do not breed until two and one-half years old.

Nannies bear single kids, occasionally twins, in springtime, during May and June in Idaho and Montana. Birth takes place within the roughest portions of the local goat range. Nevertheless the kids are able to follow the mothers over very difficult terrain within a few days. There is one record of a kid being able to walk a short distance within ten minutes after birth. It is absolutely astounding what difficult terrain the average kid can negotiate easily when only a week or two old. By six weeks the young goats are weaned and go feeding at the nanny's side.

One summer in Glacier Park, while fishing for trout in a remote alpine lake, I watched the antics of a small herd of females with kids which always seemed to be scuffling with other kids and getting lost. Upon discovering it was lost, the kid would bawl and begin searching for a friend, but be rebuffed by all strange mothers until it found its own. It appeared that all the nannies were intolerant both of other kids and other females. They remained together in a loose herd but beyond that did not seem to notice the others.

Because it seldom reacts as quickly or as dramatically to sights and sounds as some other animals, a goat's senses are too often considered very poor. When a loose rock is dislodged by a hunter, a bedded billy may give no sign of hearing it. The goat may not even show recognition when a person comes within view below. But the animal both saw and heard what was going on and in fact has excellent eyesight, hearing and an especially keen sense of smell on which it greatly depends.

When very *suddenly* startled, a goat invariably reacts by erecting its tail, at first ever so slightly. Next it may squat or brush the ground with a forefoot. Just before running it may stamp the ground with both front feet. When the goat finally does make its break, it will invariably run upward and there are few rock formations it cannot climb.

In recent years there have been numerous attempts to trap and stock goats into new ranges and to restock the species in a few areas where their number has been depleted. The animals are fairly easy to trap because they willingly enter enclosures which are baited with salt and mineral blocks. According to Jim McLucas, Montana Fish and Game Department big-game trapper, they do not even show fear when the trap is sprung, but usually go on licking the salt. It is only when humans ap-proach the trap that the goats become very nervous and bunch up in the farthest corner of the enclosure.

Goats inside a trap must be approached with the greatest caution, because they then do not hesitate to use their sharp horns on one another or on anyone who tries to handle them. An upward thrust of the horns can disembowel a careless person. It takes at least two very strong men to throw an adult goat, to hold and hog-tie it. Unless the animal is to be released immediately, sections of rubber garden hose are forced onto the horns to render them less dangerous and the goats may be blindfolded or tranquilized if they are to be moved any distance. Blindfolding seems to calm them and to stop resistance to handling.

The mountain goat may not be anybody's candidate for greatest game animal. But it certainly is among the most challenging, thriving as it does in an alpine environment where nothing else except a few small mountain birds can live. For me at least, hunting goats has been the toughest climbing—the greatest physical test—of any hunting I've ever done, anywhere.

Caribou

T HE CARIBOU is a deer of the family Cervidae, which is generally associated with the arctic and mountain tundra and the lonely northern evergreen forest which encircles the Northern Hemisphere. It is a handsome game animal, still very abundant and economically very important to human dwellers of the Arctic regions.

No less than twelve different races of two species of caribou exist in North America, and there are a number of others in Scandinavia and Russia, where the caribou is called reindeer. Some scientists consider all caribou and reindeer to be of the same species *Rangifer tarandus*. But probably to most authorities the woodland caribou is *Rangifer caribou* and the Barren Ground caribou is *Rangifer arcticus*. For the purposes of trophy record-keeping, the Boone and Crockett Club has confused the matter further by adding a mountain caribou to the two categories.

The woodland caribou exists across forested Canada from Newfoundland and Labrador to the Rockies, but nowhere in large concentrations. Once its range also included the boundary states from Minnesota to Maine, but it has since been eliminated there. It is a difficult animal to hunt because during fall it usually inhabits heavy timber or swamp forests.

The typical and most abundant Barren Ground caribou, *R. a. arcticus*, ranges from Labrador north of the treeline to the Mackenzie River in the Northwest Territories. Next most important is *R. a. stonei*, the most common big-game species of Alaska, inhabiting most of that state except the southeast panhandle, the islands and the Alaska Peninsula. The latter place (and Unimak Island) is home of *R. a. granti*. Mountainous British Columbia contains *R. a. montanus*, a splendid animal of the high country. On Ellesmere and other Canadian islands and in extreme northern

Greenland as far as eighty-three-degree north latitude is an all-white caribou, *R. a. pearyi.* A small race native to Queen Charlotte Island, Canada, became extinct early in the twentieth century.

All caribou have a number of characteristics in common. They are the only members of the deer family in which both sexes grow antlers. The antlers of mature bulls are large, massive, and reach this size in an astonishingly short growing season. Caribou bulls grow on the average a larger antler mass compared to the size of the body than any other animal. The antlers of females are much shorter than those of males, are more slender, and are usually irregular in shape. A good male caribou rack is often the most striking head in a trophy room.

Caribou may lack the grace and beauty of their smaller cousins, the whitetails and mule deer of warmer latitudes. At first encounter neither does the lumbering bull caribou provide as majestic a countenance as a bull elk. But the caribou's environment has dictated its appearance, and it is perfectly adapted to live under harsh conditions.

The most conspicuous features of the caribou are its large, concave hooves which spread widely to support the animal when it travels over soft snow, muskeg and tundra. The enlarged hooves also serve well as paddles for swimming, and caribou readily cross large bodies of water which happen to be in their migration path.

Nothing in North American wildlife matches the caribou migration. A century ago, vast bison herds still stirred plumes of dust as they wandered across the Great Plains, and farther east flocks of passenger pigeons darkened the skies during passage. But today the various caribou herds provide the only mass spectacle which humans can see on this continent.

Barren Ground caribou grazing on the tundra of northern Alaska.

Once in early summer I spent an entire day at Polychrome Pass in Mount McKinley National Park watching thousands of caribou passing far below as well as close beside. They walked in ones and twos, small groups and large ones, spread out over the flat below as far as I could see in either direction. Some were loping; others seemed to take their time, stopping to graze or bite at a deer fly on the rump.

I could hear the grunting of the closest caribou, some of which gave me a wide berth as soon as they spotted me. Others paid no attention at all and walked so close to me that I could hear the clicking of heel bones and the crunch of heavy hooves in the carpet of gray lichens on the ground. Lingering long after the animals passed was the distinctive, slightly rank odor unlike that of any other deer.

Caribou are never in any way dangerous to hunt, but they are very unpredictable, and this unpredictability gave me one of the greatest frights I've ever had. It also happened in McKinley Park when I spotted a band of white sheep in good photographic position a day or so after the caribou migration passed.

Early in the morning I started a stalk to get within close range of the rams, but turned back less than halfway to the goal. A large blonde grizzly with two young cubs was digging for marmots in the same mountainside. Instead of retreating when she saw me, the sow whoofed and turned, bluffing a rush. I got out of there fast—and wisely.

Male caribou's antlers are larger in comparison with its body than those of any other animal. This bull carries a massive rack with typical forward-thrusting palms called "shovels." The caribou is one of two members of the deer family in which both sexes grow antlers.

Next day the sheep were bedded in virtually the same place and the bears were not in sight, so I shouldered cameras and headed up the mountain again. It was a rare sunny day for McKinley and so I hurried my ascent and gave no thought to plunging into a draw dense with willows on the way.

Halfway through it, a large animal whoofed and nearly ran over the top of me.

I was lucky that the animal was a female caribou rather than a grizzly, but not until much later did enough strength return to my knees to allow me to climb out of the draw.

For the record, the cow had gone into the willows to give birth to a calf. I saw the calf when it was less than an hour old, before it could stand. I hurried away as fast as weak legs would travel, hoping the cow would return. It was a very unusual encounter in another way: this was not a normal calving area for the caribou in that region.

In Alaska most calves are dropped in the same area year after year, after a migration to the spot by pregnant females. Newborn calves, which weigh about thirteen pounds, are up and walking in a couple of hours. After a few days they can easily outdistance a man or swim across a cold river. Average weight of a calf is about twenty-five pounds, only ten days to two weeks after birth. However, it is at this time that they are most vulnerable to wolves (which also have young to raise) and occasionally to grizzly bears, coyotes and wolverines. According to most observers, cows do not defend their young from predators as vigorously as other mothers, and in fact sometimes abandon them without apparent reason.

It is necessary for all types of herd animals to keep moving continually to find adequate food. If they did not, serious overgrazing would result. After calving, the caribou tend to scatter to summering areas, remaining in loose herds. All summer they thrive on a wide variety of plants, favoring the new leaves of willow and dwarf birch, grasses, sedges and other succulent plants.

Although summer means abundant food, the season can be an ordeal for caribou. The animals are constantly harassed by warble flies and nose flies and followed by hordes of mosquitoes. Caribou have been observed running about aimlessly—even in a frenzy—and one explanation is that they are trying to escape the torment of the insects. Windy places to feed are preferred, because this keeps down the number of mosquitoes. At times wading neck-deep in water gives temporary relief. I once saw several male caribou scuffling for position atop a lingering icefield which seemed to deliver them from flies. The largest bulls won the best positions and bedded down in the center of the ice, where they spent several hours.

Autumn and the heavy frosts kill not only the insects, but also the succulent plants of summer. Now the caribou shift to a diet of lichens ("reindeer moss") and dried sedges. After a normal summer, caribou enter fall in prime condition, sometimes with two or three

→

Mass migrations of caribou, on their way to better feeding grounds, provide the only remaining spectacle of this kind in North America since the passing of the bison and the passenger pigeon.

Woodland caribou, an inhabitant of the Canadian forests, pokes the snow for sparse winter food—usually lichens and dried sedges.

inches of fat on the saddle and rump. Velvet peels from the antlers in late August. By early September, when the tundra is aflame with color that resembles an oriental tapestry, both the annual rut and the hunting season begin.

The bulls stop feeding and start fighting, although seldom seriously enough to cause great injury. The preoccupation with fighting and love, plus wide-open country, adds up to an animal which is fairly easy to hunt. The migratory routes are very well known, and for the trophy hunter it is usually a matter of studying many heads before selecting the best one.

A caribou bull in hunting season is particularly handsome. The whitish or cream-colored cape, rump and legs emphasize the brown body, grown sleek for the bitter winter ahead. A good adult male will weigh 350 to 400 pounds, and there is a record of a 700-pounder from Unimak Island in the Aleutians. Mature females average from 175 to 225 pounds.

The finest Barren Ground heads come from central Alaska. All but twenty-three of the best 469 heads on record according to Boone and Crockett 1964 listings were collected in the forty-ninth state. The largest Barren Ground head was bagged in northern Labrador by an Indian guide, Zack Elbow, in 1931. The finest woodland racks are taken in Newfoundland, and the Cassiar region of British Columbia has ac-

counted for most of the best mountain caribou.

An estimated 600,000 caribou divided in thirteen more or less distinct herds live in Alaska. That is probably only a fraction of the population of pre-gold rush days, when herds migrating across the Yukon River were big enough to delay paddle-wheel steamers for hours.

Some of Alaska's caribou herds have been diluted with reindeer blood which once was introduced through senseless government projects to try to make herdsmen out of Eskimos. These reindeer introductions from Europe did no one any good, and that includes the native caribou.

As this is written in 1971, the caribou herds of Alaska's North Slope and all points between there and Valdez on the coast are being threatened by a giant petroleum pipeline. At the beginning of this century about two million Barren Ground caribou wandered across arctic Canada and the polar islands, but a federal census in 1959 placed the number at about 200,000. The population appears to have leveled off at that figure.

For many natives of Alaska and northern Canada the caribou is essential food for themselves and their sled dogs. Since the dogs have been replaced with snowmobiles, some of the pressure is off. For sportsmen, that is a rare bit of good news.

Walrus

ONE OF THE MOST exciting wildlife spectacles I have ever seen occurs in summertime on a bleak and lonely island in Bristol Bay in the Bering Sea off of Togiak, Alaska. This island, one of the Walrus Island group, is actually a volcanic pinnacle which protrudes for 500 feet or so out of the cold green sea. It is constantly lashed by storms and is usually enveloped in mist or clinging fog. Separated by twenty miles of treacherous, angry water from the nearest mainland coast, it is uninhabited by humans, and in fact only an occasional party of Eskimos have ever stepped foot there. John Moxley and I made a trip there in July 1970, and while I would not now trade the experience for anything, I am reluctant to return—at least by the same means of transportation.

We had spent several weeks fishing with Bob Curtis in the Wood River-Tikchik Wilderness.

Bob, a veteran bush pilot, had often flown over the walrus island, but never got any closer than that. A landing on the surging seas all around, he assured us, was impractical, and most of the time so was the trip by small boat. After leaving Bob in Dillingham, a small coastal village at the head of Bristol Bay, we had several days of calm weather and met a bush pilot who thought he could land his amphibian close enough to the island to wade ashore. He also had flown over the place several times, but had never seen it from ground level. John and I decided to risk the trip, figuring we could turn back if the water was too wild to land.

It is an hour's flight from Dillingham to the pinnacle island. Looming through the gray mists in the distance, the first sight of the island suggests an eerie scene on some lost planet. The peak was dissolved in fog and the middle

Air view of island in the Bering Sea where I photographed walruses on the beach. This tiny piece of land, actually a volcanic pinnacle jutting from the sea, is constantly lashed by wind and waves—a treacherous place to land a seaplane.

part seemed to hover in space. Viewed much closer, the black island was here and there dotted with dark green vegetation and frosted with the white of hundreds of thousands of sea birds nesting there. The sea appeared smooth, without a chop on it, and so we prepared to land directly toward the east side of the island.

The next few minutes were among the longest I've ever experienced. The sea's glassy smooth surface was deceptive. What we could *not* see from above were the huge swells which surged around the island. Descending, we struck the crest of the first swell, and when that fell away beneath us we went hurtling ahead and were almost buried under the next swell. Somehow the pilot held on and we eventually skidded onto the gravel beach, somewhat older for the experience.

What a primitive spectacle greeted us there! Every ledge in the steep rock, no matter how narrow, was filled with as many noisy nesting murres and kittiwakes as it could hold. An eagle glided above and its course was followed by screaming from the nearest nesters. But birds were not the only island dwellers; on the steeper rock cliffs several hundred yards to the south was a herd of Steller's sea lions. And on a very narrow gravel beach to the north were jammed several hundred walruses. They were so close together that they seemed to be piled on top of one another.

"Finish your filming as fast as possible," the pilot advised, "I don't like the looks of this place or the weather which is coming in."

Nor did I, because a fresh wind was beginning to blow.

We spent an hour or so photographing the walruses, all of which were bulls and many of which had extraordinary tusks. The animals were not afraid of us and would grudgingly give a little ground or scramble toward water's edge when we came too close. Only one bluffed a pass at me. Altogether I ran twenty rolls of film through a pair of Hasselblads, and no telephoto lenses were necessary. I'm sorry I didn't shoot more, even in the gathering gloom, because that was my first, only and perhaps last experience with walruses. If we hadn't left the place when we did—in a takeoff which produced a cold sweat all over—John Moxley and I might have been on the island a long, long time.

It could be debated whether walruses are game animals or not and whether they deserve a place in this book. Either way, they have been hunted and are most interesting mammals, being of the order Pinnepedia. This is the world's family of pinnipeds—or finfeet. It includes thirty-one different species of seals, sea lions and walruses which inhabit all the seas of the world. The walrus is the largest and most impressive of them all.

There are two kinds of walruses: *Odobenus rosmarus divergens* of the Pacific and *O. r. rosmarus* of the Atlantic, which together inhabit most of the arctic and subarctic salt waters. The Pacific walrus has fared better than the other, and its population is estimated at about 90,000 animals. About 23,000 (estimated in 1971) Atlantic walruses survive, mostly in Russian waters, and this species must be considered endangered unless its steady decline in numbers can be stopped.

An adult walrus is a large animal. Bulls

Walruses packed together on the beach, all of them bulls with massive tusks. The animal uses his tusks for self-defense, for levering his body onto the ice, and for digging mollusks.

reach ten to twelve feet in length (and a few larger individuals have been recorded) and one and a half tons in weight. Cows are smaller but still may reach a ton. Calves, which are most commonly born (in Alaska) during late April or early May when the animals are in spring migration, weigh from 85 to 140 pounds at birth. In the Bering and Chukchi seas, walruses migrate from Bristol Bay to the Point Barrow area in springtime and back again in the fall. Those John and I saw in Bristol Bay are bulls which annually and unaccountably remain behind for the summer.

The walrus cannot be considered a handsome animal, nor is it at home on land. Its brownish-gray (sometimes reddish-gray) hide is thick, heavily wrinkled and nearly devoid of hair. Males are inclined to grow warts or tubercules on the shoulders. Under the hide is a layer of blubber several inches thick. The most conspicuous features of a walrus are the facial bristles or moustache and the ivory tusks which grow to twenty-four inches or longer, and which are really elongated upper canine teeth. The tusks function in self-defense, in levering the huge bulk out onto the ice, and probably in digging clams and other mollusks from the bottom of the sea. A walrus also has powerful cheek teeth especially adapted for crushing and grinding clam shells.

The foreflippers of a walrus measure about a quarter of the body length, and there are five "toes" on each. The undersides are rough-surfaced to help provide some traction when traveling over the ice. The hind flippers are flexible enough to rotate forward, which is use-

I caught this walrus rolling on his back in apparent comfort. With the exception of some young bulls, walruses are not malicious or aggressive, but their size and great strength demand caution from anyone who approaches them.

ful for traveling over a solid surface as well as for swimming. The eyes of a walrus are small and piglike, and its eyesight is not too keen. The species is capable of trumpeting sounds similar to that of elephants.

Pacific walruses especially prefer shallow water areas close to ice or land, mostly because food is most abundant in such places. They have been credited with diving to 300 feet to dig clams. Even though the red blood cells can store enough oxygen to allow a walrus to stay underwater for up to twenty minutes, many mammalogists believe the 300 feet figure to be an exaggeration, with 100 to 150 feet closer to normal. When diving, a walrus's heart beats at only one-tenth of its regular rate but still supplies enough blood to the brain and other organs to function.

Walrus tusks have been used for unusual purposes. Let John J. Burns of the Alaska Department of Fish and Game describe one of them.

"I have watched a female walrus literally

demolish a heavy piece of ice to free her calf, which had fallen into a crevasse. The tusks were as effective as a pick-axe. The presence of twelve men, within thirty feet, did not distract her from her task. Our attempts to assist her in her efforts were met by furious charges, and a threatening noise made by rapidly opening and closing her mouth. This noise sounded much like a man banging a pipe with a hammer. We returned to our own tasks and in due time she freed her calf and swam off, carrying it on her back."

Cows will not abandon their calves, and vice versa. The cows make every effort to rescue their offspring, and often carry their dead calves away from Eskimo hunters. Walruses, especially young males, will push dead and badly wounded animals (often larger than themselves) off an ice floe, and out of the reach of the hunters. They frequently return to an ice floe as long as wounded animals continue to bellow, sometimes placing both men and their boats in jeopardy. This return is not a reprisal attack, but an attempt to lead the wounded animals to safety. A man imitating the trumpeting sounds of a walrus can frequently get them to return.

Walruses (with the exception of some young bulls) are usually not malicious or aggressive, but their inquisitiveness, size, and great strength demand caution of all those who approach them. Tusks are used a great deal in mutual display, the strongest animals, usually with the largest tusks, being dominant over the others. When animals on an ice floe are disturbed—and this is very often the usual state—they raise their heads high, prominently showing their tusks. Animals with smaller tusks usually move away, or become respectfully quiet. The only serious battles (and these are quite brutal) are between animals with the same body and tusk size.

Walrus hunting is conducted from all of the Eskimo villages near which the animals occur. However, the bulk of the annual harvests, usually around 1,700 in Alaska, are taken from such villages in or near the Bering Strait as Gambell, Savoonga, King Island and Little Diomede Island. Sadly, the hunting loss is very high and at least one animal is lost for each one retrieved, so the total annual kill in Alaska is approximately 3,400 animals. The harvesting of females is limited by regulation. Some walruses are also taken in Alaskan waters by Siberian Eskimos.

The most favorable period for hunting walrus is during the spring and summer when the animals are passing the villages on their way north. Hunting is good on St. Lawrence Island during May, and progressively later at the more northerly locations. Walruses reach the vicinity of Wainwright and Barrow during late July or early August.

Once the walrus was as important to Eskimos as the bison to Plains Indians and every bit of the heavily hunted animal was utilized. The dark red flesh and blubber were eaten, the skin was stretched to cover boats, the intestines dried for making rain gear, and the ivory carved into fish hooks, spear points or artwork for sale. But this value, this importance to Eskimos, is diminishing and that is fortunate for the walrus, monarch of the polar seas.

Muskox

IT WAS ALREADY midday when we cleared the cliffs of Cape Vancouver, on the Alaska coast west of the mouth of the Kuskokwim River. Pilot Fred Notti aimed his tiny float plane westward across Etolin Strait, the channel that separates Nunivak Island from the mainland. Nunivak, our destination, was a far-off dark shadow in the blue expanse of Bering Sea.

"This is luck!" Notti shouted above the drone of the engine. "I've never seen the ocean so calm here or the sky so clear."

For more than a week my son Bob and I had waited in Bethel, a remote Eskimo settlement one hundred miles inland on the Kuskokwim, for a break in the weather that would let us get to Nunivak. I had a major reason for wanting to go. That big, bleak island, seventy miles long and forty wide, is the home of the only muskox herd in this country. Along with us was Jerry Hout, a young wildlife biologist and assistant manager of two national wildlife refuges, Clarence Rhode and Nunivak, which maintain headquarters in Bethel. He is probably as familiar with the muskox on Nunivak as any other human.

At last the break came. After one very violent storm the overcast vanished, and by mid-morning Hout, Notti, Bob, and I were winging across the vast empty tundra of the Yukon-Kuskokwim delta. The shadow cast by our plane sent clouds of whistling swans, brant, geese, and sandhill cranes winging up from the ponds below us.

Etolin Strait, normally turbulent and angry, was millpond calm that morning, and the flight across it was pure pleasure. Less than thirty minutes from Cape Vancouver, we reached

Cape Manning at the northeast corner of the island. Then Notti headed the plane south. The bulk of the animals keep to the island's coastal areas, where wind sweeps away the heavy winter snows and affords pasturage. The animals' food is mainly grass, sedges, browse, reindeer moss, and lichens.

Flying at 300 feet, we spotted our first musk-ox at a place marked on our charts with the jaw-breaking name of Kanikyakstalikmiut. Between there and the southernmost tip of the island we counted seventy-five more musk-oxen, mostly in small herds. But not once was it possible for us to land and stalk them. We flew westward from Cape Mendenhall and found plenty of scattered herds and plenty of sheltered bays for landing, but we never found the two together. Then we came over the Binajoaksmiut River. Bedded beside it, a mile from salt water, was a band of five of the long-haired odditites that we were seeking. Then, a half-mile upstream, we spotted a lone bull and finally a second herd, numbering six.

Notti put the little aircraft into a steep bank, and we slipped down and touched the water at the mouth of the Binajoaksmiut, scattering flocks of eider ducks in all directions. Minutes later we were on shore, changing hip boots for hiking boots. Then we cut across country.

In ordinary going, a one-mile hike is a snap. But on the spongy tundra of Nunivak, it's something else again. We could have covered four miles on hard land in the time it took us to reach the first herd.

We spotted the herd from atop a high bluff. Treeless tundra, marked with patches of snow, stretched to the low hills on the horizon. Below us, clear as pale-blue crystal, the river was a series of roaring rapids with pools between, the pools crowded bank to bank with wallowing, splashing dog salmon. A tight formation of harlequin ducks winged upstream. That was an arctic scene I'll never forget.

But I didn't have much time to admire it. I unlashed a camera from my packboard and made a few shots of the bedded muskoxen 225 yards away. That was too far, even with a long telephoto lens. But if I couldn't get closer I'd at least have something to show for the trip.

Then a vagrant wind carried our scent to the animals. They jumped to their feet, splashed across the river, and lit out. A man couldn't possibly have kept up with them and we didn't try. Instead we headed up the Biak to stalk the second herd, but this try was even less successful than the first. The muskoxen broke and ran while we were still 300 yards away.

"I thought they were supposed to form a circle with their horns out, stand there, and let you walk up as close to them as you dare," Bob said to Jerry.

"Sometimes they do," he said. "That's the herd's ancient defense against wolves, but I guess they've learned that it doesn't do much good against a man. If they see or scent you, they're likely to do what these two bunches did. And once they run they go faster and farther than a caribou."

Taking photographs wasn't my only objective that day in August. I was anxious to see for myself the animals that have become the subject of a conservation controversy. The question is whether to hunt muskoxen or not.

The muskox, *Ovibos moschatus*, is a stocky, shaggy beast, a sort of polar buffalo with a sheep characteristic mixed in. The bulls reach a height of five feet at the shoulder and weigh as much as 850 pounds. Their horns, broad and massive at the base, turn down and then out and up to sharp tips.

Muskoxen are covered with the longest hair of any North American animal. Blackish-brown in color with a paler saddle over the back, the hair often trails on the ground. Underneath and mixed with that hair is a coat of extraordinary silken wool so dense that neither cold nor moisture can penetrate it. It is called qiviut. Despite his name, the muskox has no musk. Explorers have long reported and some writers still claim that there are musk glands in the skin or beneath the eyes and that the meat is sometimes musk-tainted.

Dr. John Tener, deputy director of the Canadian Wildlife Service, who lived among wild muskoxen off and on for ten years and is among the world's foremost authorities on them, says flatly that these animals are odorless. Dr. Calvin Lensink, manager of the Nunivak refuge, and others who have trapped them agree.

The natural range of the muskox today includes Greenland, the treeless plains of arctic Canada, and the big islands to the north. Official estimates are that Canada has some 10,000 muskoxen scattered over Ellesmere, Bathurst, Melville, Banks, and Victoria Islands and on the mainland between Great Bear Lake and the base of the Boothia Peninsula. Greenland has around 6,000 more. So the muskox is a somewhat rare but by no means endangered species. However, there is no open hunting season anywhere today.

Muskoxen vanished from Alaska in about 1865, when the last ones were killed. Their disappearance, most authorities agree, was a result of overhunting by Eskimos and whalers, but that may not be true.

In 1930 the U.S. Department of Interior took steps to reestablish the animals in Alaska. With Danish cooperation, seventeen bulls and seventeen cows, all yearlings, were captured in Greenland, sent by ship to Norway and then to New York, by rail to Seattle, by ship again to Seward, and then by rail once more to Fairbanks. The trip totaled almost 14,000 miles. The cost was $40,000, cheap at the time.

The herd was released in an enclosure at the University of Alaska, but the Fish and Wildlife Service soon decided that the muskox was a totally unpredictable animal—gentle one minute, aggressive the next—that wanted to be left alone and belonged in a more remote area than a campus. In 1935 and 1936 the thirty surviving animals were liberated on Nunivak Island, where there were no wolves, bears, or other natural enemies, and few humans. This stocking, it was hoped, would reestablish a vanished wildlife species and eventually provide a herd animal that would supply meat, milk, and wool for the Eskimos who live in the one village, Mekoryuk, on the north shore of the island.

But the muskoxen didn't take to being herded, and anyway the Mekoryuk people had more reindeer than they knew what to do with. The European reindeer, introduced in 1917, had overrun Nunivak. In 1961 some 2,000 were rounded up and slaughtered, and each year since then it has been necessary to kill about 1,000, but with no market for them. With that many reindeer, the Eskimos didn't care to fool with an animal as temperamental as a muskox.

So the muskoxen, left strictly to themselves,

Group of muskoxen huddle together on the bleak tundra of Nunivak Island. Beneath its long hair, the animal has a coat of silken wool so dense that neither cold nor moisture can penetrate it.

thrived. An annual count shows that the herd now (in 1971) numbers about 800–850 and that increase is at the root of the controversy.

Nunivak Island is a national wildlife refuge managed by the U.S. Bureau of Sport Fisheries and Wildlife. The bureau's biologists believe that the muskox herd is now too big for its range. The animals can survive only in limited areas along the coast, where there is wind strong enough to keep their winter food supply uncovered. Federal game men say that 700 is absolutely the top number the island can support and 400 to 500 is very high. Biologists of the Alaska Fish and Game Department concur. Apparently only a series of mild winters in the 1960s has staved off trouble. Given just one very severe winter or, worse still, a series of them and a large part of the herd or even all of the animals could be wiped out.

There is ample precedent for such a grim prediction. Wild animal populations restricted to a limited range by natural barriers have many times exhausted their food supply and nosedived as a result of wholesale starvation. I have already described the tragedy of the Arizona-Kaibab mule deer. The elk of Yellowstone National Park, where it has been necessary for park rangers to shoot as many as 4,000 in a winter, is another classic example. So are the moose of Isle Royale National Park in Lake Superior. On that island of 205 square miles, the moose built up to a population of from 1,000 to 3,000. Then winter food ran out, and the herd tumbled to about 150.

If the muskoxen on Nunivak are to avoid the same fate, some herd reduction must be carried out. There is no alternative. But to date permission has not been given by the Secretary of Interior to reduce the Nunivak herd either by regulated and controlled hunting or

Muskox bull I photographed on the Alaskan island of Nunivak, home of the only wild herd in this country. Thirty muskoxen were released on Nunivak in 1936 and today number about 800 animals, but they are in danger of overgrazing their range.

by a systematic slaughter. Opposition comes from misguided sentiment, from false information and all kinds of impractical proposals to domesticate the species. Many just do not consider muskoxen as big-game animals. Here is an uncommon case when shooting could help save rather than eliminate a species.

Some who oppose hunting point to the often described standard defense of the muskox in which the animals form a ring, with the calves inside, and stand in this defiant posture with lowered horns. The strategy works fairly well against wolves, but would invite slaughter by men with guns. There could be no sport in shooting a bull from such a circle.

The truth is that muskoxen seldom behave that way. The bands we stalked that day on Nunivak showed no inclination to stand and let us approach. Once they spook, they are impossible to overtake. The belief that muskoxen *always* form a defense ring seems to be based largely on the reports of Arctic explorers who shot them for food. What the explorers did not add was that they used their sled dogs in muskox hunting. Confronted by the dogs, the animals of course behaved as they would if wolves threatened them.

Any muskox's actions depend on circumstances and terrain. Cornered, they form a ring. A lone bull in a pocket from which he cannot escape will back his rump against a rock or bank and face his enemy. In open country muskoxen are likely to take to their heels. Sometimes they charge instead. Tener tells of one that chased him and a companion all the

way back to their canoe when they approached during rutting season.

The Boone and Crockett Club lists muskox heads in two categories, the Greenland race and the barren-ground or Canadian race, and now accepts muskox listings for record purposes only. The club does not consider the muskox a competition animal and does not accept muskox heads in its North American Big-Game Competitions. The same rule now holds for polar bears, and for cougars killed in any state or province that pays a bounty on them.

The real sport in muskox hunting would be not in shooting the animal but rather in getting into the Arctic and seeing one in its native range. If a hunter were to fly north, land his plane near a band, shoot a bull, and fly out with his trophy, all in a few hours, it wouldn't be much of a hunt. But if he stayed a week, enjoyed the country, and worked for the animal he wanted, then muskox hunting could be sport.

When Jerry Hout, Fred Notti, my son, Bob, and I left the Binajoaksmiut River that August day Notti headed the plane west. Between there and Ikooksmiut we counted 100 more muskoxen, but not one was near a landing place. About that time, I noticed that an overcast was building up behind us. Time was starting to run out on our chances for photography.

We were flying over steep sand dunes when Fred banked the plane and pointed down. "Single bull," he shouted. I glimpsed the animal in a little valley as we roared above it.

"I believe I can land right in the ocean," Notti announced. A few minutes later we were wading ashore on a sand beach. Luck had really smiled. A year might pass without another day calm enough to land a float plane on the open water of Bering Sea, and we had only to scale the dunes to get to the bull.

Fred stayed with the plane; Jerry, Bob, and I started inland. When we topped the last ridge the muskox stood only one hundred yards away, watching in our direction as if he had heard or winded us.

He gave me time to make a few pictures and then bolted away. But he made one mistake. His escape route dead-ended against the sea. We closed to within forty-five yards and took more pictures. Then the bull almost ran over us to get away. That was the last we saw of him, but he had given me what I went to Nunivak for.

Recently an expensive program of live capture and removal to try to solve the overpopulation problem on Nunivak was begun. But removing unwanted animals for stocking elsewhere has never yet proven to be a lasting solution to overcrowded range. Herds continue to grow, and sooner or later the surpluses must be killed off.

I happen to believe that the muskox deserves a place among the big-game animals of this continent, that he is a huntable trophy, and that it would be better to control the Nunivak population by shooting as many old bulls as necessary each year than to let the entire herd face the continuing threat of winter starvation. It is important to remember that hunters would take only the largest (and usually solitary) old bulls, impotent outcasts driven from the herd which nevertheless compete with younger animals for the very limited amount of available grass. In early 1971 there were about 200 surplus exiles on Nunivak, or about one-fourth of the herd. They are useless for stocking elsewhere; they play only a detrimental role in the health and survival of the Island's herd. It is cruel not to hunt them.

There is no dearth of domestic animals in the world: sheep, goats, cattle, yaks, and others. All have their uses, but none can equal their wonderful wild counterparts. Compare, for example, the sheep on a Montana ranch with the Dall or the bighorn, the plodding water buffalo of Asian rice paddies with his dangerous black cousin on the plains of Kenya, the tame reindeer of Lapland with our wild caribou.

Would anything be gained by adding the muskox to the long list of animals tamed to serve man, assuming that it could be done? Of course not. The muskox is a unique wild animal, a match for wolves and the fiercest blizzards of the polar plains. He should remain wild.

And he can be hunted, where and when his numbers warrant, under proper regulations and in the light of today's game-management techniques, without endangering his kind or their future. To date we're killing the muskoxen with our kindness.

Bison

As late as 1871 during a routine cavalry patrol of the Arkansas River valley, Colonel I. H. Dodge witnessed a sight that future Americans would never again see. For several days a herd of buffalos resembling an endless shaggy black carpet passed his pickets. Dodge calculated that the herd was fifty miles long, perhaps twenty-five miles wide, and contained four million animals.

About the same time on high ground between Oklahoma's Cimarron and Canadian rivers, an already famous American, Phil Sheridan, and two others not yet famous, George Custer and William F. Cody, reined in their horses. "How many buffalos have we passed today?" Sheridan inquired of his staff. The consensus was one quarter-million.

During the next fifteen years or so—through about 1885—the North American buffalo, *Bison bison,* was rendered virtually extinct.

In less than a generation an estimated sixty million bison which once roamed the western Great Plains were sacrificed to the advance and spread of civilization. The species once ranged from near the Mexican border far northward into Canada, and from Oregon to the eastern seaboard. In 1730 an early colonist wrote that Virginia "is a good place for Cattle and Hoggs. And fortunately there is a large creature of the Beef kind, but much larger, called Buffalo, which may be bred up tame and is good both for food and labour." There is no record that the species was ever bred tame enough for labour, but it was good to eat and for that reason, among others, it was completely eliminated east of the Mississippi by 1819. Seventy years later, just enough remained to stock a few zoos and small sanctuaries.

155

It has been claimed that the western buffalo herds during the early 1800s were the greatest herd animals the world has ever known. That is doubtful, considering the astronomical number of big-game animals which inhabited the virtually unbroken great plains region of Africa, stretching from Cape of Good Hope to the Red Sea. Even larger herds may have once existed across central Asia. Nonetheless, the American bison, little known to today's outdoorsmen, brought sportsmen to this country from around the world. Some of these hunts were great extravagances for the times.

The trend was perhaps started by the writer Washington Irving, who in 1832 made a trip into Arkansas and beyond with U.S. Indian Commissioners, with a Swiss, Count de Pourtales, and an Englishman, Charles J. Latrobe. The group traveled by steamer down the Ohio from Cincinnati to St. Louis, then the gateway to the Wild West. From there they continued overland to Fort Gibson and the Verdigris River, where they were met by a young Army officer who introduced himself as Sam Houston. (It is interesting to note how frequently, when researching material on the bison, famous names in American history turn up.)

Whether or not Irving and party pacified any restless Indians or marked any boundaries as they were supposed to do, they had a whale of a time hunting buffalos. Somewhere between present-day Oklahoma City and Norman, Irving dashed into a herd of several hundred animals and shot his first buffalo.

Irving later described the bison: "There is a mixture of the comic and the awful in these huge animals. They heave their great bulk forward with an up-and-down motion of the unwieldy head and shoulders. Their tails pop up like the queue of Pantaloon in pantomime, in the end whisking about in a fierce yet whimsi-cal style; and their eyes glare venomously with an expression of fright and fury." Irving had previously spent time in Europe, and his notes to friends there probably inspired other Europeans to come hunting in the United States.

Not much later Sir William Drummond Stewart, a Scottish baronet who had hunted widely in Africa, came to try his hand at buffalos. He was guided by a Kentuckian, Bill Sublette, and William Clark Kennerly, nephew of the leader of the Lewis and Clark exploration to the Pacific.

Buffalo herds still roam the plains of the West, protected in national parks and wildlife refuges, but their numbers are scant compared to earlier days. Bleached buffalo skull in Montana (below) stands as a silent monument to the slaughtered herds of yesteryear.

Stewart spared no expense in organizing his expedition. His commissary carts were loaded with fine smoked hams, sugar, flour, tinned fish from home, pickles, brandy and probably sour mash bourbon, which was becoming the popular frontier potable. There were eighty men in this group. Stewart rode afield in a white shooting jacket, jodhpurs and a Panama hat, none of which had been seen before in that raw, unsophisticated country. But since Sir William could ride and shoot with the best, he quickly quieted the snide comments about his elegant attire.

According to Kennerly: "We encountered buffalos in numbers which gladdened the heart of Sir William who had come 4,000 miles to shoot them. The horses seemed to enjoy dashing along beside the shaggy monsters until we could reach over and put the muzzles of our guns almost to the buffalo's shoulders. The prairie was strewn for miles with the bodies of dead bison." Kennerly admitted that the bag might have been excessive, but rationalized "What man could resist the temptation, when the whole earth it seemed, was a surging, tumbling, waving mass of these animals?" Sir William's party, records show, dined only on the tenderloins, humps and tongues of the buffalos, or on about eighty pounds of meat from each 1,500- to 1,800-pound animal killed.

The next noteworthy bison hunt was that of an Irish bachelor, Sir St. George Gore. The logistics of this venture were awesome. For transport he had 112 horses, eighteen oxen and an unstated number of mules and milk cows, plus twenty-one two-horse carts, four six-mule wagons and a number of ox wagons. For chasing game he used forty greyhounds and staghounds, and for shooting he ordered seventy-five muzzle-loading rifles, several of the new breech-loaders and many pistols.

Gore slept in a brass bed inside a green and white striped linen tent where at bedside was a library of books by Shakespeare and Scott. He had forty servants and hired additional guides and scouts, including Jim Bridger (another famous name), as he went along. The trip lasted three years and reached as far as the Rosebud and Tongue rivers. His bill was $500,-000. The bag, or toll, was over 2,000 buffalos, 1,600 deer or elk, 105 bears and assorted antelope, wolves, coyotes.

The Gore hunt was historic also as it precipitated the first known protest in America to slaughtering for sport. Resentful Sioux Indians, who depended on the game to live, made an official complaint to Washington. But elected officials were no more moved or concerned than they are today over contemporary conservation issues.

During the 1860s and 1870s, the Union Pacific railroad was carrying sportsmen on buffalo hunts which were widely advertised in the East. It was common for travelers to take pot shots at bison as they passed, even with no hope of retrieving the animal.

But the hunt which drew the most attention of all, and which rivaled the shikars of Indian maharajas on the opposite side of the globe, was one arranged for the twenty-two year old Grand Duke Alexis, son of Russia's Czar Alexander II, in 1872 during a state visit to America. At a White House dinner one evening, General Phil Sheridan, recent hero of the Civil War, offered to be the host.

The expedition became a series of hunts, beginning on the Platte River where a vast canvas camp was set up. Each carpeted tent contained a wood stove. Assembled on the spot to entertain the prince was the entire Second Cavalry troop with its fine band. Among the

To escape the annoyance of swarming insects, buffalo loosen the earth with their hoofs and roll around in the dirt. The dry dust filters through the animal's hair and chokes the insects. Called buffalo wallows, the same holes are used by buffalo year after year.

Colliding with a resounding crash, two bulls fight a tumultuous battle for the rights to a harem of cows—from ten to seventy. The bulls charge each other from a distance of about thirty feet, often taking the impact on their foreheads.

guides were Cody and Custer, who had a knack for being where the action was. Also on hand was a band of Sioux warriors and their families led by Chief Spotted Tail. To pacify and reward the Indians for staging a mock battle in war paint and eagle feathers for the prince, the army commissary requisitioned 1,000 pounds of tobacco. But the firewater was kept under guard.

Apparently the prince killed his first bison with Cody's rifle, Lucretia, after only wounding the beast with his pistol. The guest cut off the tail as a trophy and was toasted with champagne. That evening at a great buffalo barbecue, giant campfires warmed the cold night, and the prince flirted with Spotted Tail's giggling daughters.

The hunt, accompanied by the Cavalry, progressed westward to Denver, accounting for numerous bison along the way. Many dead buffalos later, it ended in Topeka, where the Kansas legislature recessed and held a big parade in honor of the blue-blooded hunter from overseas.

To be honest, Alexis and the other visiting sportsmen did not take a significant number of buffalos. But these hunts most likely set the pattern for the market hunting and senseless slaughter which soon followed as a way of eliminating the plains Indians from their natural environment. It became evident that the Sioux, Arikaras, Comanches, Cheyennes, Kiowas and others could not survive without this source of almost everything.

General Sheridan declared in 1869 that "Every buffalo dead is an Indian gone." This was the same unfortunate sentiment that the oil company executive expressed exactly a century later: "Who needs wildlife, anyway."

Without the bison, the Plains Indians indeed could not exist. They fashioned hides into all manner of garments, including moccasins, shirts, dresses and even bedrolls. They ate the nutritious meat fresh, smoked or dried, or pounded it with berries to make pemmican. Buffalos were converted into tents and saddles, into bone tools and sinew bowstrings, into everything from shields and quivers to glue (from the hooves) and sled runners. Maybe no single animal was ever more important to a race's survival.

The first European to describe the bison was one Antonio de Solis, who never saw a buffalo in the wild but did see what was no doubt the first of many buffalos to be consigned to zoos. This one, in the menagerie of the Aztec emperor Montezuma, was described aptly as follows: "A wonderful composition of divers Animals. It has crooked shoulders, with a bunch on its Back like a Camel, its Flanks dry, its Tail large, and its Neck covered with Hair like a Lion."

The Plains Indians obtained buffalos in a number of ways, at first by stalking on foot with only primitive spears and bows. The attrition must have been heavy because bison are not always as docile as they appear in parks, and when wounded can be very dangerous. On a number of occasions when taking pictures during the late summer rut, I have been chased by annoyed bulls, once up into a tree. When horses became available after the Spanish explorations of America, Indians could hunt bison on horseback and thereby tip the odds in their own favor. Still, a bison hunt required great courage and riding skill.

Among the most dramatic of all primitive hunts around the world were those in which bands of Indians drove or stampeded whole herds of bison toward the precipices of high steep cliffs, or "drops," figuring to force at least some of the animals over the edge to their doom. This called for great cooperation on the parts of the Indian stampeders because the effort could and often did backfire. The same drop areas were used year after year and there are a number of places in Montana where today the bone and skull remains of countless buffalos can be found in quantity at the bottom of cliffs.

The buffalo is doing fairly well today. About 15,000 wild ones live in a number of parks, national wildlife refuges and on many ranches. The largest herds live in Yellowstone, Custer State Park (South Dakota), and Wichita Mountains National Wildlife Refuge, Okla-homa. A herd has been established near Delta, Alaska, where hunting is allowed on a permit basis. The only other available hunting is on numerous ranches where it is done as a commercial venture.

The northern wood bison, *B. b. athabasca,* a slightly larger and darker animal than the plains buffalo, was hunted until an outbreak of anthrax in the 1960s put an end to it, at least temporarily. Most of the wood bison live in the Wood Buffalo National Park, Alberta, south of Great Slave Lake. There are about 15,000 animals here but most are really intergrades between wood and plains races, the latter having once been released there.

Many animals have played important roles in the history and development of North America, but none more important than the bison.

Gray Wolf

THE GRAY OR TIMBER WOLF, *Canis lupus,* is one of the world's wild dogs. His various geographic races go by a number of local names, including Alaska tundra wolf, Arctic wolf, Alaskan wolf, Labrador wolf, buffalo wolf, Texas gray wolf, and Mexican wolf, but they all belong to the same species.

In size and shape the wolf is somewhat like a German shepherd but has a longer coat, long legs, and bushy tail. Full-grown males average 120 pounds or less, with 180 pounds the absolute maximum for North America, in spite of tales describing larger ones. Females weigh one-fourth to one-third less.

Wolves are gregarious and tend to live and hunt in packs rather than as individuals. Packs, made up of one or more family groups, may vary in size from five to twenty animals. The gray wolf ranges in color from snow white to solid black, including all shades and combinations in between.

Females begin to breed when they are two or three years old, and there is some evidence that they mate for life. Litters of four to eleven pups are born from April through June in natural cavities or in dens dug by the parents. The pups, furred but blind at birth, grow rapidly and sometimes follow the older wolves afield when only a month old. Both parents feed the pups and care for them, and all close observers of wolf ways have marveled at the affection among members of the family.

Wolves are tireless travelers. Except when confined to the den with pups, they move in rough circles over a wide home territory and hunt along the way, often following the same routes time after time. It isn't unusual for packs to travel twenty miles in a day, and they have been known to cover more than one hundred miles in two days.

In order to live, wolves must kill other wildlife. They are carnivores, or meat eaters, as are lions, tigers, leopards, and even weasels and shrews. How they kill is either an exciting or a sickening spectacle, depending on the observer's viewpoint.

It is probably the gory killing manner of wolves that is responsible for human reaction against them. There's nothing pretty about seeing an animal eaten while still alive. African lions, however, capture a meal in an equally savage and cruel way; yet, we think of the big cat as noble and call him king of beasts. Wolves are often bountied, while today a license just to look for a lion costs as much as $500.

This is hardly logical.

At the end of World War II, when the preservation of rare or dwindling fauna was beginning to gain widespread support, a splendid book, *The Wolves of Mount McKinley* by Adolph Murie, an experienced and respected biologist, was published. Murie had lived with McKinley's wolves for years, and his work accurately described the important role of these important animals.

He pointed out that wolves had always lived in balance with the big-game animals—caribou, moose, Dall sheep, and grizzlies—of Mount McKinley National Park, even though they ate some of them and always would. Murie added that there were, of course, periodic or cyclic fluctuations in the populations of all these animals, wolves included.

Unfortunately, the book's publication coincided with a sudden drastic dip in sheep and caribou populations all over Alaska and Canada. The decline was caused by severe winters and probably other, unknown, factors. As a result, many hunters, guides, outdoor writers, and even some game authorities hit the panic button about wolf control.

In 1948 another book, *Wolf Predation in the North Country,* drew this conclusion: "This is it, brother. Extermination of the once-grand game herds of our North Country is as sure as death and taxes unless a strong restraining hand is interposed against the wolf. Failure to act now means the permanent loss of revenue, a meat famine for thousands of frontiersmen, the feeding and clothing of thousands of natives by the taxpayer."

It is no wonder that an all-out war on wolves followed. The sheep and caribou populations bounced back again in the next decade, as scientific observers had known they would, but the damage to the wolf's reputation was lasting. War on wolves is still being fought by many people, including legislators who make game laws and appropriate money for bounties.

When dealing with such a controversial subject as wolves, emotion usually wins out over scientific evidence. A prime case involves the Nelchina Basin, some 20,000 square miles of excellent big-game range in south-central Alaska.

Intensive control efforts by the U.S. Fish and Wildlife Service between 1948 and 1955 succeeded in removing more than 400 wolves from the basin. Only an estimated thirty-five wolves managed to survive the control program. In other words the wolf was almost extinct in that vast area. In 1955 the basin's caribou herd, which is one of Alaska's most important and which contains some of the best trophy heads, was estimated at 20,000.

The area was then closed to all wolf hunting as a test. Ten years later the basin's wolf population had increased again to 400 or 450, which might seem alarming. But in that same period the caribou herd had quadrupled to more than 80,000 animals!

During each of recent hunting seasons, hunters have harvested nearly 8,000 caribou, 1,750 moose, and about 150 sheep from this same Nelchina Basin, and the kill could be far greater if much of the region were not so difficult to reach.

Yet hunters often blame wolves when their luck is poor.

The only possible conclusion that can be drawn from the Nelchina study is that wolves exist in numbers compatible with the numbers of prey animals. Never really abundant anywhere, wolves are comparatively numerous only where such prey species as moose and caribou are very numerous.

Natural mortality factors, including disease, parasites, accidents, fights, and cannibalism, keep wolf populations in bounds. In turn the wolves help to keep the number of browse-eaters down to what the range can support; this is the same role other predators play in wilderness habitats all over the world.

Isle Royale National Park, 210 square miles of roadless wilderness in upper Lake Superior, is another case in point. Studies there by Dr. Durward Allen of Purdue University and Dr. David Mech of the University of Minnesota have thrown a great deal of light on the relationship between wolves and their big-game prey.

Isle Royale is uninhabited by humans except for a few tourists in summer. The island's isolated location makes it an ideal laboratory for such a study. By the mid-1930s the Isle Royale moose herd had grown to an estimated 1,000 to 3,000 animals. No wolves existed there, the moose ate themselves out of house and home, and a shocking die-off occurred.

By 1949, when the cyclic moose population was again on the upswing, wolves had invaded the park, probably crossing on the ice from Canada. Since then the wolf population has fluctuated from nineteen to twenty-five, made up of two or three resident packs and a few lone individuals. And the moose herd has held at a steady 600 or so, which is about the carrying capacity of the island's browse supply.

Besides Alaska and Isle Royale, only one other section of the United States has a substantial population of wild wolves. That area is the Superior National Forest in northern Minnesota.

The book *A Field Study of the Timber Wolf* by Milton H. Stenlund revealed that a population of about 240 wolves was helping to keep the number of whitetail deer, the chief prey species, within bounds on 4,100 square miles of the Superior Forest. Those figures prove out to a density of one wolf per seventeen square miles, meaning that the animal is a genuine rarity in Superior. And wolves are even less numerous over most of Alaska and Canada.

From 1943 through 1946, when big-game populations in western Canada and Alaska were very low, Ian McTaggart Cowan of the University of British Columbia, an authority on the subject, made a wolf-prey study in five national parks in Alberta and British Columbia. He concluded flatly that a depleted food supply, not wolf predation, was responsible for the low numbers of trophy game.

As nearly as can be determined by compiling the results of a number of recent wolf studies, an average wolf kills fifteen to forty large animals each year, the exact number depending greatly on the size of the prey.

At Isle Royale, Allen and Mech found that

Timber wolf on Alaska's American River tries to catch spawning sockeye salmon in shallow water (above) *while another looks on from the bank* (left).

a pack of fifteen wolves killed nine moose in twenty-eight days during 1959, fifteen moose in forty-five days during 1960, and twelve moose in thirty-seven days during 1961. These totals average out to a moose per wolf every forty-five days. Mech figured that an average wolf's requirement is ten to thirteen pounds of meat per day.

A surprising fact about wolves is that they are not totally efficient as hunters. Their unsuccessful attacks far outnumber their successful ones.

For example, Mech, reporting on three winters of aerial observation on Isle Royale, said that the island's big wolf pack detected 131

moose. Of these, the pack "tested" (chased or held at bay) seventy-seven. Of the seventy-seven moose, seven were wounded but escaped, and only six were killed—a surprisingly low hunting-success ratio.

I have been fortunate enough to encounter wolves on many occasions. This is rare luck because many people live out their lives in wolf country without ever seeing one.

Once on a hunting packtrip through British Columbia's Cassiar Mountains, John Moxley and I sat on a low ridge to eat a cold lunch. Idly we watched a number of caribou crossing a distant valley. Suddenly a single caribou cow came thundering toward us from behind. She probably didn't even see us in passing, nor did the three wolves that were in hot pursuit. We watched until the cow disappeared over the horizon. Long before that, the wolves fell far behind and finally gave up the chase.

Alaskan wolves seem to be more efficient killers than their Isle Royale counterparts, at least in winter, possibly because of favorable terrain and very deep snow which hinders the quarry. Or it may be that caribou, which make up a large portion of the kill of Alaskan wolves, are easier to take than Isle Royale's moose.

Bob Burkholder, a former Fish and Wildlife Service pilot who reported results of an extraordinary study in 1959, feels that Alaskan wolves are good hunters. By flying, and occasionally from the ground, Burkholder kept a pack of ten wolves in the Nelchina Basin under almost continuous surveillance for six weeks. There was good snow for tracking, and the wolves eventually became used to having an aircraft nearby or circling overhead.

Very seldom did this pack fail to kill after a target was singled out, and they did not have to chase many victims very far.

Mech, Burkholder, and most other observers agree that wolf attacks follow no set pattern. Rarely if ever do wolves hamstring their prey, as has often been reported. Instead they come tearing in, biting from all sides at whatever part of the animal they can reach, until it falls disabled. They will begin feeding, sometimes even playfully, while their victim is still alive. It isn't pleasant to watch, but nature is seldom merciful.

No matter how savage their attack, wolves are not wanton killers, as they have so often been pictured. Rarely do they kill more than they need.

Douglas Pimlott, then of the Ontario Department of Lands and Forests, spent the winter of 1958-59 following wolf packs in Algonquin Provincial Park with a helicopter. In five months he counted 219 deer that had been killed by wolves. Nearly all had been completely eaten.

"Only rarely did we find evidence of more than one deer being killed at a time by a pack," Pimlott reported. And he added, "We have grown into the habit of considering the killing of a moose or deer by wolves a bad thing. This is not true, either from the standpoint of sportsmen or from that of the moose and deer herds." Pimlott went on to call wolf bounties an utter waste.

There is still a great deal to be learned about the ways of the wolf. One summer, for example, I came across fascinating firsthand proof that wolves as well as brown bears are fishermen—or at least try to be. On the remote American River, just outside Katmai National Monument, I watched a large female wolf trying to catch spawning sockeyes in a shallow riffle. Other wolves looked on from the grassy banks.

Photographing the wolves on the American River wasn't easy. In fact, I found it impossible to get more than two of them in the camera's viewfinder at one time. I'd estimate that there were six to nine in the pack that loitered near, but out of sight of our camp which had been built to census the salmon run.

One wolf was far more trusting than the rest, once approaching within thirty feet. Most of them would come no closer than the opposite bank of the river, about 150 feet away. Most of my pictures had to be made with a 500 mm. telephoto lens.

I think that the wolves were drawn to this spot because the Fish and Wildlife Service team had built a weir across the river there in order to count the salmon. The fish were especially vulnerable just below the weir, and the place soon attracted several brown bears. I think that the wolves were lured to the partly eaten salmon strewn along the banks by the bears. When that source of food ran out, the wolves turned to fishing for themselves.

The truth about wolves is the hardest thing for most people to believe. Perhaps no other North American wild creature is so misunderstood, and few animals are feared and hated so much. From the very beginning of settlement on this continent, all hands have been turned to eliminating wolves wherever they were found.

It is doubtful whether wolves were ever a menace to humans. I have not been able to find, in any reliable source dealing with them, a single authenticated case of unprovoked wolf attack on man in the last fifty years. There are numerous tales of such attacks dating back to the 1800s, but it is hard to sort out truth from fiction.

There are many other stories, apparently true, telling how wolves came very close but either left or were driven off and did not actually attack. Wolves once had an unnerving habit of closing in around a man under the right circumstances, often getting within a few yards or even a few feet. And if these animals have killed few or no humans on this continent, they have scared many half to death.

These accounts, coupled with the many blood-chilling old stories from Europe (authorities believe that some of them may have been true), legends such as Little Red Riding Hood, and myths about werewolves, probably explain a good part of the reason wolves have long been considered to be wanton killers and outlaws we can better do without.

It must be admitted, too, that wolves kill their natural prey savagely. They at times robbed fresh graves in the early days of the American West, an action which contributed to their bad name.

Many outdoorsmen believe that the only good wolf is a dead one, and that is also the official attitude in most places. Wolves are unprotected almost everywhere they still survive, from Alaska and Canada (except in national parks) to Russia. They are poisoned, trapped, hunted by plane and snowmobiles.

In many places, there is still a bounty on their heads. Alaska at this writing still pays $50 per wolf. One bush pilot in southeastern Alaska told me that he can make a good living during the winter months by scattering poison baits along the shores of lakes in his area. He goes back later to collect the carcasses. His annual take is twenty-five to thirty-five wolves, worth about $4,000 in bounties and pelts.

To keep the record straight, in Alaska wolves are classified as both game animals and furbearers. But they are game animals on paper only.

In about seventy-five percent of the state, wolves receive absolutely no protection. In another ten percent (the Seward and Kenai regions), there are no wolves. In the remainder, there is a closed season on wolves and some restrictions on the use of aircraft in hunting them, but residents can still collect the $50 bounty on a dead wolf. Bounties on any wild animals are an outright waste. When they are paid on a vanishing species such as the wolf, their consequences are especially ugly.

Bounties have even tempted airborne hunters to invade such sanctuaries as Alaska's Mount McKinley National Park in quest of a fast and easy buck. The wolves there are par-

ticularly vulnerable since the country is largely tundra with little concealment, and it's easy to spot and kill the animals from planes.

It is hard to overcome deep-seated prejudice. But I submit that the wolf is an important and valuable member of the wildlife community and a splendid game animal. He deserves protection as much as does the grizzly, the polar bear, or the desert sheep. In fact, the wolf's need may be even more urgent today.

It's high time we made him a game animal wherever he survives. As Stanley Young says in his excellent book, *The Wolves of North America,* "Wolves are of surpassing interest as an outstanding group of predatory animals. There is no reason why they should not be accorded a permanent place in the fauna of this continent."

Does the wolf really qualify as a game ani-mal? My own answer is an unqualified and emphatic yes. He has all the qualities we demand in a big-game species. He is extremely shy, wary, and hard to hunt, and an autumn or winter wolf pelt is a beautiful trophy. The wolf is no more a wildlife villain than are any of the bears we regard so highly.

It's certainly true that for a man alone and on foot with only a gun, no large North American animal, except possibly the mountain lion or the jaguar, is harder to kill in fair chase. Fair chase, of course, rules out the use of aircraft or snowmobiles in actual hunting.

The need for regulations to give the wolf protection as a game animal is becoming more urgent because of the growing use of snowmobiles in some areas of the North. This problem is parallel to that of the improper use of aircraft in hunting big game. Wolf hunting done

172

Exciting symbol of our dwindling wilderness, the wolf should be protected by game laws to insure its survival for years to come.

as it should be, on even terms, is so great a challenge that only a handful of the animals are killed each year by hunters who are deliberately seeking them.

I like what Dr. Joe Linduska, acting director of U.S. Bureau of Sport Fisheries and Wildlife, has to say about wolves as game: "Of course they qualify. And they should be made game because birds and animals so classed are in far less danger of extinction than non-game species. The timber wolf is too important to become only a stuffed relic in museums."

Our wolves are important for still another reason. They are exciting symbols of a wilderness that is dwindling all too rapidly. The American outdoors wouldn't be the same if wolf tracks didn't cross new-fallen snows or if the wolf's eerie song didn't shatter the stillness of brittle arctic nights.

Africa

African Lion

AMONG THE MOST rewarding of all outdoors adventures left to man is the African safari, for shooting, for photography, or both. There is no experience that compares with it, and one important reason is the African lion, which is certain to be encountered.

The first encounter could come during darkness the first night under canvas, and the lion might not even be visible. But its penetrating roar reverberating on the night wind is guaranteed to thrill—and maybe chill—even a seasoned African traveler. And then, lions may be content to roar just beyond the perimeter of camp.

During a safari in June of 1965, our camp was beside the Semiu River in northern Tanzania, close enough to the Serengeti Plain that milling herds of wildbeest and zebras, of impalas and gazelles were almost always in sight

of the tent. My son Bob shared one tent with me, and professional hunter Neil Millar slept in another nearby. On moving into the area we had noticed the lion tracks on the bare ground all about, but no one gave it a second thought.

Late one afternoon we collected a zebra as camp meat for the crew and as a leopard bait. Because of the late hour and the long distance from camp, the animal was hurriedly skinned and loaded onto a lorry to be processed first thing the next morning. That night the skinners slept in the lorry, in fact, right beside the carcass of the zebra.

I am not certain of the time or who first discovered the prowlers, but suddenly in total darkness our camp was in complete turmoil. Crew members were running and shouting in Swahili, which I could not understand. I fumbled for a flashlight, stepped outside the tent, and in the beam of light saw seven lions dragging the zebra from the lorry. While I watched they dragged it away into the bush. The two men sleeping next to the zebra were left in complete shock, but Bob slept through all the commotion. I don't see how that was possible, but he did.

The rest of the night was quiet. It wasn't until daybreak that we heard roaring in the distance. The lions sounded well-fed and may have been gloating over what an easy meal they had obtained that night.

The African lion, *Panthera leo leo,* may not really deserve the popular title of "King of Beasts," but it is among the world's most magnificent and interesting residents. It is also much misunderstood and possibly overrated. As a result of recent scientific studies of the species, many new facts have emerged. For instance, simba is not the greatest hunter of the wildlife community and is not always raw courage and fighting fury. Under close observation, lions are not always good parents. At least in some parts of Africa they may live as scavengers which feed on the kills of hyenas, instead of vice versa. Still, it is an animal worthy of the attention of anyone who loves the outdoors. It symbolizes lovely wilderness Africa, the Bright Continent.

As recently as 1900, lions were abundant in suitable habitat all over the continent. They inhabited mountain regions to as high as 10,000 feet, as well as brittle deserts, dense bush and open plains from the edge of the Sahara southward to the Cape of Good Hope, and to the Atlantic from the Indian Ocean. The only places lions avoided were jungles and deep rain forests, places where prey animals were in small supply. In any areas where vast herds of plains game lived, as from the Red Sea southward through most of east and central Africa to Mozambique and the Transvaal, lions were abundant. Hunters on safari in the early 1900s could shoot all the lions their consciences permitted.

As late as the time of Christ the lion ranged the entire Mediterranean shore and into southern Europe. But today in Africa, the species occupies only about one-fiftieth of its original range, and that little bit is constantly dwindling. Everywhere simba's natural habitat is being plowed under or converted into pastures for livestock. Huntable populations, but just barely huntable, still exist in portions of Kenya, Tanzania, Uganda, Botswana, Ethiopia, Congo, Mozambique and Angola. Scattered animals live in Chad, Sudan, Somalia and Southwest Africa. But any real hope for the future anywhere lies in the protection afforded by large enough national parks and possibly in sound game management as it is practiced in North America. Management probably cannot survive Africa's exploding human population, however, and its demand to develop remaining undeveloped lands. Scientifically regulated hunting cannot eliminate the African lion, but progress will.

The lion and all its feline relatives are descended from the short-legged, long-bodied, small-brained Creodonta, a sub-order of extinct primitive mammals. Though there are missing links in its evolution, fragments of huge Pleistocene lions have been found in European caves and riverbeds. These large beasts came into conflict with prehistoric man and then vanished at the end of the Ice Age. Crude paintings of them are still visible on the walls of the Chambre des Félins of Lascaux in France.

Female lions and their cubs, part of a larger pride, take refuge from the midday sun. Composed of one or more families, the pride is organized for hunting and defending territory.

African lions are the most gregarious, the most diurnal and possibly the largest of all the world's great cats. Some Asian tigers may grow larger, but the two are very nearly equal in average size. They are also so similar in structure that with skins removed and placed side by side, only a skilled biologist on very close inspection can tell them apart. They have even been interbred in zoos.

Because of the lion's daytime habits, as well as its preference for more open country, the lion has always been the easiest of the big cats to see, and consequently to hunt. Keep in mind, however, that hunting pressure may have the greatest influence on whether any animal is diurnal or nocturnal. The more persistently lions are pursued in a given area, the more they tend to move and hunt only at night. On the other hand, when given protection, supposedly nocturnal leopards and tigers do at least some hunting in daylight. One point is certain: except in the parks and sanctuaries where they are unmolested and pay little attention to humans, lions are far more wary and furtive today than they were only a few decades ago. With the use of bait or baiting out-

Deadliest hunter of the pride is usually the female, seen at left stalking her prey in tall grass. Lordly male (right) arrives in time to benefit from the zebra kill, while the sated huntress crawls away to sleep off her dinner (below).

lawed almost everywhere, it is no longer easy to bag a trophy male lion, no matter if a whole safari is dedicated to it. Outside of national parks, heavily maned males are as wise as they are rare.

In traveling through the incomparable parks of east and south Africa, it is easy to get a wrong impression about lions, but it affords an ideal opportunity to learn about simba's social or family life. Because they are seldom very active during middays (which they may spend sound asleep in the shade and which is the time most travelers are afield), lions may appear to be lazy and indolent. That isn't true. A lion must devote a large part of life to hunting just to survive. It is simply that most hunting is done very early or late in the day, if not actually at night. Middays are used to recuperate.

The first thing a parks visitor learns is that lions live in prides, or groups composed of one or more families. The members are of all ages from tiny cubs to yearlings and adults of both sexes. As many as forty have been counted in one pride, and the largest I have seen contained twenty-seven. An average pride consists of eight to twelve animals. Occasionally two or more males will disassociate or are driven away from prides and thereafter travel together, rather than with a larger group.

Much remains to be learned about the organization of lion prides. Apparently a pride is territorial (as are individuals of other species), living, hunting and defending one specific area. However, the territories must be abandoned at least temporarily to follow game herds during their seasonal migrations in search of new green grass.

Interchange of members between prides seems almost inevitable, but qualified observers have noted that females in a pride will not readily accept a strange female and nor will pride males accept a strange male. There may be considerable conflict between them. Few prides ever contain more than two fully grown males, and three appears to be the maximum.

The pride system is the lion's best way to obtain enough food to survive. For comparison, a leopard lives in denser, darker environment where the stealth of one animal hunting alone is probably the most productive. In more open country where the prey is alert, fast afoot and has plenty of room to escape, hunting in teams is almost the only alternative. It is fairly well known that lionesses are more deadly hunters than males; at least they do the bulk of the killing. It is also true that certain lionesses become more skilled than others in a pride, and how well the group fares largely depends on them.

A full-grown, experienced lioness can be a sudden and fairly certain executioner. She hunts by sight and sound, rather than by smell. During dry seasons, one or more wait beside waterholes for game to drink. Then almost faster than the human eye can follow, a lioness is on the quarry, its neck is broken and its throat is severed. Larger animals such as zebras are harder to kill than gazelles, and some lions are bunglers, never becoming very efficient at killing even the small animals. Serious injury to any cat is always a possibility, especially from horned animals.

Prides may exhibit excellent teamwork in making kills, but I have watched some which were almost futile. The difference may be age of the animals and experience hunting together. Techniques differ greatly, but most often a pride will try to surround an animal or a herd of animals. That done, the lions either wait patiently in ambush, or try to close in, until the encircled quarry panics. Then, hopefully at least one animal will dart blindly too close to one or more crouching cats. The lion must wait to begin its final rush from very close range, because most plains animals can outrun lions when given the jump and over long distances. A lion seldom pursues an antelope very far.

When one lion of a pride makes a kill, all share in the dining but at times in order of seniority. Many have reported how the largest males, which may not even have bothered to join the hunt, eat first and preempt the choicest parts, while other pride members sit aside and wait. Though that may be true some of the time, most often all lions fall on the kill and share in a noisy, snarling, tearing meal until all their bellies are full or everything edible is gone. On one occasion in the Etosha Game Park, Southwest Africa, I watched a very large yellow female stand off an equally large male and smaller female while three nervous half-grown cubs fed on a springbok. I am not certain which lion killed the small antelope but believe it was the aggressive mother.

A large pride may consume a kill in one sitting. After feeding, lions usually drink large quantities of water. If any meat remains, it will normally be dragged into a thick, thorny corner where it is guarded from hyenas, jackals, vultures, or even leopards which might try to appropriate the prize. Often, packs of hyenas will drive away lions from their own kills.

The animals which most often fall prey to lions are the oldest, youngest, or weakest, simply because these are the easiest to catch and kill. When they are hungry or when little else is available, lions will tackle large animals, even adult giraffes and Cape buffalos, both of which are huge and powerful. In Manyara National Park, Tanzania, where they are very abundant, lions may subsist almost entirely on buffalos. One morning Neil Millar and I came upon the site of a buffalo kill.

The buff had been a full-grown male, judging from the heavy black horns and larger bones of the skeleton which were all that remained. But nearly an acre of ground and all the vegetation on it had been uprooted and leveled during the furious life-or-death struggle. Neil and I pondered whether one, several or a whole pride of lions had made the kill, but concluded that at least three or four cats were involved. Several days later we had some proof that we were correct.

It happens that the lions of Manyara are tree-dwellers (as they are also in other scattered places), and they spend daytimes sleeping in the wide-spreading acacia trees common in one part of the park, rather than on the ground. One explanation for this un-lionlike behavior is security from vengeful buffalos. Game scouts in the park normally have no trouble finding the cats in treetops for visitors to see and they located a pride early one morning for Neil and me, shortly after we had found the buffalo kill. Altogether there were eight lions in the pride, but only seven were "bedded" in trees. One of these appeared badly hurt from a puncture in the flank which was draining, and the eighth seemed so badly injured in the front shoulder that she could not even climb off the ground. The buff had taken a toll before it died.

Because it lives in a pride, a wounded lion has the chance to recuperate and survive its injuries because others will continue to kill. For such solitary animals as the leopard and the North American mountain lion, which I described earlier, death is almost certain after a serious injury. At times, injuries drive cats to become man- or cattle-killers because both are so much easier prey than wild animals.

Another incident John Moxley and I witnessed at Manyara in 1969 reveals still more of lion behavior. We had spent most of one morning photographing elephants and eventually came to the clearings near water's edge on the north side of Lake Manyara. Large herds of buffalos live here, and we found a herd of about sixty milling around beneath a large umbrella acacia tree which they had completely encircled. Taking a closer look, we spotted two lionesses trapped in the crown of the tree. Apparently they had been driven there by the angry buffs.

For a long time we watched the impasse to see what would happen next. One lioness appeared particularly nervous to get down and away. When finally given one small avenue of escape, she hit the ground running at full speed. The buffalos bluffed an all-out charge, but didn't press it, preferring to keep the other lioness treed. We followed the cat which escaped, and she led us to a pair of small cubs which had been hidden in a thick island of brush, probably while she went to attempt to kill. After purring and licking the cubs affectionately, the mother led them away where we could not follow in the jeep.

From two to four or five brindled or spotted cubs weighing a pound apiece are born about 105 days after a honeymoon away from the pride. When a female comes into estrus,

she is accompanied away from the pride by the dominant male, which might have to fight other males before doing so. If there is no clear-cut decision, which is sometimes the case, lionesses have been known to breed, usually noisily and often over a period of several days, with two or more males.

Some mothers, which may be attended by other females during and after birth, defend cubs with a fury and purpose difficult to describe. They have come out tearing and slashing at man, beast and even at a two-ton lorry which by accident was driven too close to where cubs were hidden. On the other hand, mothers have abandoned some or all of the cubs for little or no apparent reason.

Lions in Manyara National Park, Tanzania, spend the day sleeping in acacia trees, perhaps as safety from vengeful buffalos. One lion of the pride (right), badly wounded during an attack on a buffalo, remained on the ground.

Mortality is very high in lion cubs. Disease and parasites take a toll. And even a devoted mother must occasionally leave the little ones to go hunting. When this happens they are easy victims of leopards, hyenas and even their own father if he happens to be passing by. Males have been observed killing and eating cubs, and on one occasion a mother was seen to eat a cub which had been killed by a leopard during her absence. Cubs are weaned at about ten weeks and are independent at about one year, although they may remain with the mother until the next estrus within eighteen months or so.

A full-grown African lion is an extraordinarily handsome and athletic cat which (in a pinch) can swim, clear a twelve-foot fence, cover over twenty feet in one bound, and possibly reach fifty miles per hour in a short dash or charge. Males reach maximum size and development at five years, at which time the mane is the fullest, covering the head, chest and extending almost half way down the back. Mane colors range from salt-and-pepper gray to blond, brown, red and black. In some localities males do not grow manes, or at least very large ones. Elsewhere the dense thorny habitat may prohibit accumulating a large mane. The most magnificent manes I have ever seen were on old males in Tanzania's Ngorongoro Crater and in the Masai Mara Game Reserve of Kenya. Perhaps the majestic appearance of the

full-maned male is what first inspired the title King of Beasts.

It isn't any wonder that simba has always been considered among the most desirable big-game trophies. Stone Age men were the first lion hunters, but the earliest actual hunting records are those of the Egyptian pharaohs. Hieroglyphics now in the British Museum reveal that Amenhotep III, who lived from 1411 to 1375 B.C., killed 102 lions during the first ten years of his reign. That suggests the lion's former abundance.

Homer, of the *Iliad* and *Odyssey,* wrote of lion hunting in Greece, and according to the Bible, Samson was a lion hunter before his famous shave and haircut. In Roman times, lions were captured with snares and pitfalls and then shipped to the Colosseum, where lion-gladiator fights were popular with the spectators and Christians were popular fare for the lions.

Lions have been hunted by spearmen from horseback, with casualties accruing on both sides. Saint Louis of the Seventh Crusade amused himself with lions that way when he ran out of infidels to kill. Horseback hunting was also a common sport of the Tuareg tribesmen of the Niger region. If pursued too closely by an angry lion, a Tuareg rider would toss a pillow or garment overboard to the cat. While the lion stopped to maul the garment, the rider would swing about and use his spear.

Perhaps the last horseback hunter was Fritz Schindelar, who was also one of the first professional white hunters in East Africa. One day in 1913 while hunting with one Paul Rainey, an American motion-picture photographer, Schindelar rode a polo pony to try to flush a lion from a patch of cover. The cat had other ideas. It threw Schindelar from his mount instead, bit into his stomach, and three days later he was dead of the wounds.

Teddy Roosevelt was among the first of the well-known figures to make a safari, and some of his political opponents publicly stated that the African lions might do everyone a favor by keeping him in Africa. Hemingway and Ruark wrote of the drama and thrills of lion hunting. Today an estimated 2,000 American sportsmen are lured to hunt in Africa each year. Countless others go just for photography.

Virtually any kind of lion hunting can be exciting, but nothing can match a hunt on foot with primitive weapons only—spears, buffalo-hide shields and knives. Incongruous as it may seem, these hunts still take place in certain areas today, mostly because lions and livestock are not exactly compatible on the same range. When a cow is killed, the tribesmen still go after the killer, although this is becoming less and less of a problem as the lions evaporate into oblivion.

The tall, thin Masai of southern Kenya and northern Tanzania are the best-known lion hunters, and their exploits have often been described. But other tribes are also great lion hunters—the Nandi, Suk, Samburu and Karamojong, all of these also spearmen. Bushmen of South Africa, Wakamba of Kenya and the Midgans of Somalia use poison arrows, a hairy business since the lion might easily kill the hunter before the poison took effect.

After a Masai cow has been killed, all the young *moran* (warriors) of the tribe gather together. After frenzied dancing to build courage, they track the cat to its daytime resting place, which is usually in heavy brush. The brush is surrounded, and all effort is made to flush out the lion as the ring is tightened around it. When the cat does break out, invariably toward one of the *moran,* spears are

One of two frightened lionesses that were treed by a buffalo herd in Manyara National Park. This cat made a dash for it when she saw her chance, and eventually found her cubs.

A honeymoon couple steals away from the pride. The male sometimes has to fight for his right to lure a female into seclusion. In case of a draw, the lioness may breed with two or more males.

thrown and the attack is pursued with *simis*—knives—by all. What follows is a bloody melee which usually finishes off the lion and maybe a *moran* or two. Some fearful wounds are inflicted all around. And the rewards? The *moran* who tosses the first spear and the one who cuts off the lion's tail (while it's still alive) with his *simi* are thereafter regarded in the same light as the college football hero.

It is inevitable that some lions should become man-eaters, and the publicity given these few has not contributed to its survival. Every incident of a man-eater is invariably followed by the wholesale killing of other lions no more troublesome than the robins on the front lawn.

By far the best-known man-eaters are the Tsavo lions, a pair of maneless males of southern Kenya that once stopped construction of the Mombasa-Uganda Railway in 1898. In a nightly reign of terror, the two cats dragged away twenty-eight Indian coolies and dozens of native laborers from their barricaded quarters until all work had to be stopped. Finally one Colonel J. H. Patterson shot the lions and later wrote a book about it. The man-eaters' skins were shipped to Chicago, and today the mounted lions are on display there in the Field Museum.

During the next two years, other lions harassed workers on the same railroad. Near Voi a lion dragged a European engineer from his tent and ate him. Other workers kept vanishing until this lion was trapped and a one hundred pound reward paid to the trappers. As recently as 1955, lions were harassing station workers near Tsavo, and a campaign was organized to eliminate them.

Maybe lions simply develop a taste for railway crews. Thirty natives were killed on the Pungwe Flats during construction of the line from Beira, Mozambique, to Salisbury, Rhodesia. But rather than panic, as did the Tsavo Hindus, the Shangaans went out and eventually killed the man-eaters with spears. There was still more man-eater trouble during the building of the Eastern Line railway through the Transvaal.

Another famous man-eater, "Chiengi Charlie," terrorized the whole border country between Northern Rhodesia and the Congo in 1909. He was very light in color and would often appear in broad daylight to capture a woman here, a boy there, and then disappear for a day or two. Tremendous efforts to shoot the lion failed. A famous professional hunter was sent to bag the lion, but the lion dragged away his valet while the hunter was taking a bath. Eventually two other lions joined Chiengi Charlie to make it a threesome, and those of the local population who weren't already eaten looked for healthier latitudes. Finally a series of gun traps were set, and after killing two of the killers, that ended that.

Many man-eaters are old, mangy animals no longer able to catch and kill wildlife, as was Chiengi Charlie and the lion at Mgori, Tanzania, that in 1958 eliminated nearly a whole community. This one had had its teeth and lower jaw smashed by a shot from a poacher's muzzle-loader. It had therefore turned to catching porcupines and had fed on them until its feet and body were so full of quills that nothing was left—except people.

But just as many man-eaters are healthy and in the prime of life. The Tsavo cats are an example. One man-eater shot in Barotseland was a magnificent male in excellent condition. In fact, his pelt, which measured nearly ten feet, is among the largest of which there is record today.

Now and then a man-eater still puts in an appearance and is quickly dealt with. But mostly the African lion is a gentleman—a sort of hapless gentleman at that—content to live the way lions have always lived in some of the most beautiful wilderness left on the face of the earth. He is a very important balance in nature wherever vast herds of ungulates also live.

It would be a drearier, less exciting world without the lion and his characteristic roar. I have never shot a lion and have no desire to do so. Like royalty elsewhere around the world, the King of Beasts keeps steadily losing ground.

African Elephant

N O SPECIES OF wildlife behaves as much like humans as the African elephant. Every year as summer ends in the southern hemisphere, virtually all of the 7,700 resident tuskers in Kruger National Park, South Africa, go on an annual bender, much in the way people do every New Year's Eve. The reason is a fruit called marula.

The plum-sized marula grows abundantly in trees native to that rolling bush country. When the foliage begins to turn color, the fruit, which is best described as a cross between a mango and a lime, suddenly ripens and begins to fall. Monkeys and baboons love it but are invariably driven away by tribesmen and elephants who love it even better. The tribesmen brew a very volatile, intoxicating beer from the marula fruit and the tuskers merely eat it, but the results are the same.

After gorging a good load of fruit, the elephants go to water for a chaser, and the process of fermentation begins inside them. The pachyderm becomes, in effect, a distillery on four feet. Eventually the whole herd is drunk, but it affects individuals in different ways. Some only stand in a stupor and pay no attention to tourist-photographers who drive close to take pictures. But others, like some human drunks, grow vile-tempered and behave in an aggressive manner. Trumpeting, they chase cars and one another. Autos have been smashed and rangers killed by elephants under the influence.

Kruger Park naturalists have learned that (again like people) some tuskers kick the habit after one or two hangovers. But others keep eating the marula fruit as long as it is available.

Another parallel between elephant and

human behavior recently noted is how both overpopulate their habitat and thereby encourage their own destruction. In 1912, for example, only about twenty-five elephants survived in the area of present-day Kruger Park. When this became a park and all animals were given protection, the elephants multiplied rapidly and a careful census in 1958 revealed 7,701 animals, or an increase of 750 percent in less than a half-century. That is a density of nearly one per square mile, more than enough for them to threaten their own food supplies—even their own marula trees. Early in 1969 it was necessary to condemn 1,200 elephants to death for their own good, but unable to see a lesson in this, the human population in South Africa and elsewhere continues to grow at a frightening rate.

The African elephant, *Loxodonta africana,* which is the world's largest land mammal, is a marvel of natural architecture. Everything about the beast is on a grand scale. Its inch-thick skin may weigh a ton (or one-fifth of the animal's total weight), and, covering thirty-five to forty square yards stretched out, drape the animal like a pair of dark baggy pants. The skull of an adult may weigh between 600 and 700 pounds. A heart removed from a seven-ton tusker was found to weigh fifty-six pounds, lungs 300 pounds, liver 235 pounds and salivary glands eighteen pounds. These animals have very little fat.

African elephants are taller and heavier, and have darker skin, bigger ears and tusks, longer faces, less convex backs and carry their heads higher than their Asian counterparts. However, the size differences between the two are not as great as often claimed. Elephants of Asia seldom grow more than ten feet high at the shoulder. The tallest African bull on record (it was shot in Angola in 1955 and is now in the Smithsonian Institution) measured thirteen feet at the shoulder, but that is exceptional. Eleven feet is closer to average.

In another parallel to humans, elephants have adapted to many different kinds of habitats. They thrive best in open forests, but do well in jungles, savannas, swamps and marshes, in lowlands as well as high elevations as long as they are within reach of water. They grow to large average size in parts of Kenya's low, hot Northern Frontier and along the Nile in Uganda, and have been observed as high as 14,000 feet on Mt. Kilimanjaro. An elephant is nevertheless not as well adapted physically to as many different habitats as some other animals.

Well-cushioned feet spread when the animal's weight is on them but contract conveniently when the animal lifts its feet out of mud. The straight, pillar-like legs make it impossible for elephants to jump, run, trot or gallop. They can climb slowly up and down steep slopes and are fair swimmers. They move best on level or rolling ground over which they can travel great distances at good speed by means of a shuffling gait. When greatly alarmed or when charging, elephants can negotiate level ground as fast as fifteen to twenty mph, speed enough to catch a fleeing human.

The African and Asian elephants are the last survivors of 352 species of the order Proboscidea, which once roamed across all continents except Australia and Antarctica. Among these long-extinct ancestors were the woolly mammoth, the mastodon and a two-foot tall Eocene animal with only a short stub of a trunk. The elephant's closest living relatives today are the furry, rabbit-size hyraxes of Africa and the manatees and dugongs which are aquatic and have a much wider distribution. None of these surviving relatives has any sign of a trunk, the part of the elephant which is most distinctive.

Perhaps no other part of any animal serves so many purposes as an elephant's trunk. It delivers food and water to the mouth, showers and dusts the body, detects odors, identifies foreign objects by touch, trumpets with rage or squeals with pleasure, caresses a mate, chastises a calf, or plucks marula fruit from a tree. The trunk is really a muscular modification of the upper lip, measuring as long as six feet and weighing 300 pounds. It is powerful enough to uproot a tree, but sensitive enough to pluck succulent blades of grass from the forest floor.

But what has most intrigued man about the elephant has not been its strange appearance or its versatile trunk. Instead, humans have been attracted by the modified middle incisor teeth— or ivory tusks. If allowed to live out its natural lifetime, an African bull may grow a pair of tusks which weigh eighty to one hundred pounds apiece. The largest known single tusk weighed 237 pounds and came from a bull shot in 1899 in Kilimanjaro. The next heaviest tusk from an animal shot in Kenya weighs 226 pounds and measures slightly more than ten feet long. The opposite tusk weighs 214, the two totaling 440. Both are today in the British Museum of Natural History. The largest known tusk from a female weighed fifty-six pounds.

It is impossible to spend much time wandering in east Africa and photographing the region's wildlife without having elephant incidents. I have seen my share of them. One occurred in what is now Tarangire National Park in Tanzania, which at the time was open hunting country. Hunting Cape buffalos with my son Bob, then fifteen, I found fresh tracks of a herd of twenty or so leading away from a waterhole and toward a dense thicket. Since it was very early in the morning, we followed the tracks, figuring to overtake the animals before it became too late and too hot.

The trail led into brush so thick that we could barely see fifteen feet ahead. But we knew we were almost on top of the animals because we could hear and smell them. Occasionally we could glimpse a patch of black hide through the foliage. It was tense going.

Next thing we knew we were standing in the middle of an elephant stampede.

About a dozen tuskers charged past us on both sides, some trumpeting and some passing almost close enough to touch. There was no escape from the rush and nothing to do except stand still until it was over.

What provoked the stampede is difficult to say. Maybe the elephants were spooked or surprised by the buffs. But why? Maybe it was our scent that unsettled them. They could have run right over the top of us but did not. No matter what the reason, it drained away any interest in further following the buffalos that day.

Bob and I had another elephant experience during that same trip, this time in Uganda, and we were camping in an area not far from Murchison Falls. The tents had been pitched well after nightfall in a grove of acacia trees, and no one noticed in the dark that a bare, wide, well-worn trail wound through the tent sites we selected. After a late dinner, all hands fell into bed exhausted after a day-long drive from the Kenya highlands.

It proved to be a very short night. What woke me was not the sunrise, but the violent shaking of the tent. There was also a belly rumbling I should have recognized but which

Several families of elephants bathe and drink in a river flowing across the arid Kenya northern frontier. As long as they are near water, elephants can adapt to almost any terrain, although they thrive best in open forests.

at first I mistook for a nightmare. Then I saw the huge foot of an elephant planted squarely in the entrance to the tent. The tusker was tearing thorny branches from the tree just overhead.

Bob was sleeping soundly in the cot beside mine and I started to alert him. But any noise might startle the elephant—and where would it step next? So I just sat on the edge of the bed and waited, in a cold, cold sweat. Eventually the animal had its fill and moved on to strip the limbs from another tree. As he had when lions once invaded our camp, Bob slept through the whole incident and would not believe my account of it until he saw the huge footprints in the doorway.

Murchison Falls National Park is an especially good place to get acquainted with elephants. A number of very large ones were more or less permanent residents near Paraa Lodge and they can give tourists a few gray hairs as well as excellent photographs. One, called Lord Mayor, would regularly show up for the evening cocktail hour, and cocktails proved to be his own downfall when he discovered a barrel of pombe, a native banana brew, which he drank.

One day while I was fishing for Nile perch just below the falls at Murchison another tusker added gray to my own scalp. Immediately under the falls is a wild, turbulent maelstrom where the perch are concentrated. Just below that point the river is infested with some of the largest crocodiles known to man. To cast

Elephant's trunk is actually a muscular modification of the upper lip, powerful enough to uproot a tree, but so sensitive it can pluck a blade of grass from the ground. Here an elephant uses its multi-purpose trunk to dust its head of insects.

lures out into the fast water, it is necessary to climb out onto a steep, rocky peninsula which extends outward for about thirty yards from one bank. I had just landed a perch when I looked back, and there stood one of the largest bull elephants I had ever seen. Because of the roar of the falls, I did not hear the animal approach. Now it stood regarding me uncertainly, blocking my exit from the river.

If the elephant came much farther in my direction, my only exit was the river and I realized that odds for surviving both the current and the crocodiles were poor. But after tearing several tidbits from a bush with its trunk, the tusker continued on down the same trail which elephants have always used to make the circuit of Murchison Falls. I dressed my fish hurriedly and didn't do any more casting that day.

During Old Testament times elephants existed in almost every part of Africa. Today the northern limit is roughly the Twelfth Parallel, or a vague line running from northern Ethiopia and central Sudan through

Chad to Mali and Mauretania, where isolated herds may still survive. Perhaps 250,000 of the animals exist in lands around the Equator. The most live in the Congo and the least in South Africa, where virtually all are confined to Kruger National Park. In a few areas, notably Tsavo National Park, Kenya, and locally in Uganda, they are too abundant for their own good. It is regularly necessary to slaughter them.

Once the African elephant population was many times what it is today. Before settlement of the continent began, elephants roamed almost everywhere at will, except in the heart of the Sahara. Some natives pit-trapped or hunted the tuskers for food, but the hunting was more like tribal warfare with casualties on both sides. It wasn't really until the dawn of this century when firearms came to wilderness Africa and the great ivory market developed that elephants began to lose ground. Professional hunters killed unbelievable numbers, and Arab ivory merchants made fortunes from the harvest. At one time the trade in ivory and native slaves was one and the same. Captives were compelled to carry ivory to the coast where both were sold.

Early in the 1900s one famous elephant hunter, W. D. M. "Karamojo" Bell, alone shot several thousand bulls and wrote a bestselling book about his experiences titled *Wanderings of an Elephant Hunter*. It has been estimated that during the peak of market hunting—while numbers of mature bulls carrying heavy ivory was high—the kill was 45,000 animals annually for over ten years. Most of the ivory was fashioned into billiard balls and piano keys, both of which today are made of plastic which does not turn yellow with age.

Expanding civilization, especially the clearing of land for agriculture rather than hunting for sport or ivory, is the main enemy of the African elephant today. Even peaceful herds of from a dozen to several hundred animals migrating in search of food and water are not compatible with settlement and growing crops. The elephants, which cannot understand boundaries, fences, orchards or other obstacles in their path, have to eliminated. An individual adult tusker consumes at least 300 pounds of food each day. This may be of cultivated pumpkins, maize or bananas as well as wild swamp grasses and treetops. A whole herd can do a great deal of damage quickly. I have seen small villages completely trampled in mere passing.

Contrary to general belief, African elephants have been captured alive and trained, although not so willingly or as easily as Asian animals. As early as about 300 B.C. elephant catching stations were established by Ptolemy Philadelphus on the Red Sea coast, and the captives were to be used in war. The most famous elephants of antiquity were used by Hannibal, the Carthaginian, during his 218 B.C. crossing of the Alps and the invasion of Rome. These animals proved far more valuable as psychological weapons than useful in combat because Roman soldiers soon learned how to deal with them. The Hannibal elephants had been captured in Morocco and Algeria, where they were soon rendered extinct by the second century A.D. This was caused by the demand for ivory and animals for the bloody arena spectacles then popular over the civilized world.

Hunting elephants today can be an embarrassingly easy venture or genuinely grueling, depending on the time and place. In many parts of its range where the hunting pressure has long been heavy, a hunter might spend a

Among the most gregarious of large mammals, African elephants often travel in groups, the adults keeping the young out of trouble. Lone bull elephant (below) wears an unusually long pair of tusks by today's standards.

long time in the field before finding a suitable trophy. The large bulls with heavy ivory are no longer abundant or unsophisticated and they live in habitat hostile to humans. Nor is the hunting without an element of danger. A good many professional hunters consider the elephant the most dangerous of all African animals. Wild elephants are not at all like those which pose in national parks. It is necessary nowadays to have a very reliable outfitter to bag an elephant.

For me it is far more fascinating to hunt the species with a camera than with a gun, and I've had some background in both. Hunting with camera adds a new element to the sport, a greater consciousness of the beautiful environment in which the animals live. A photo of a live bull with Kilimanjaro or the Mountains of the Moon in the background is far more satisfying, more rewarding, than a huge dead carcass soon to be hacked to pieces by swarms of hungry natives who materialize out of nowhere for the meat. Photographing rather than hunting also provides a better opportunity to study the elephant and its habits.

African elephants are among the most gregarious of large mammals. Individuals in mixed herds seem to get along very well with one another. All seem to help in keeping young ones out of trouble, and there are many reports of animals helping stricken (wounded) elephants to escape. They are at least outwardly affectionate during courtship when there is considerable love play and squealing. Normal gestation lasts nineteen to twenty-two months, and when a young elephant is born in a secluded spot away from the herd, the mother is accompanied by one or more females who act as guards and companions. They become as devoted to the young one as the mother. The most furious charge I have ever seen an elephant make was by a fairly small female "aunt" of a newborn baby.

Young elephants—neonates—weigh about 200 pounds at birth, stand two and a half to three feet tall and are covered with fine hair which eventually rubs off. In a few minutes they are able to stand up and in a day or so can hike along with the herd. They suckle for about three years, and a year after that the mother usually conceives again.

African elephants display great intelligence and, many believe, the ability to reason. If so, they do it with a brain which at thirteen pounds (one-thousandth of their total weight) is very small for their body size. According to old beliefs, elephants never forget, but actually they appear to have no better memories than most other animals.

There is one final comparison worth making between man and the elephant: both have similar life spans. Both become sexually mature between twelve and sixteen years and have a normal longevity of about seventy summers. It will be interesting in the future to see if the elephant's longevity on earth compares with man's. Only time will tell.

Leopard

FROM THE SNOW-TIPPED Mountains of the Moon, astride the Equator, to the lush green valley of the Albert Nile, the small east African country of Uganda is rich in exquisite landscapes. It is also rich in big-game animals, some species found nowhere else, from the mountain gorilla to the Semliki Valley kob. To me no region is more fascinating than the Karamoja, which lies in the extreme northeast against the Kenya and Sudan borders.

The Karamoja has a strange and brooding beauty. It is arid, harsh, and mountainous, especially on the east side. During daytimes which are often windless and silent, the country bakes under a hot sun and seems to be empty of living things. But when late afternoon begins to blend into the yellow twilight, the landscape miraculously comes to life. The longer the purple shadows become, the more wildlife activity there is to see. That always is the best time to be afield.

One afternoon I had hiked a mile or so from camp to shoot a gazelle for camp meat. Along with me was Longollo, a Nderobo tracker and a splendid woodsman. The two of us climbed to the top of a rocky spine from which we had a long view of the dry country, all the way to 10,000 foot Debasien Mountain, and there sat down to survey it.

It is amazing how much wildlife I could see from my one spot. A herd of gazelles was visible, but it was far to the south and drifting even farther away. A bateleur eagle circled just overhead, and I suspect it may have been contemplating a dinner of the helmeted guinea fowl which cackled nervously nearby. A troop of baboons marched across country far below me toward a roosting place for the night. From shadows at the edge of a clearing nearby, a dik-dik studied me and then suddenly looked away. I turned in the same direction, toward a thorn bush which was twisted like all the others on the landscape.

There *was* something unusual about the bush. But it wasn't until I had stared at the spot for a long, long time that I was aware of watching a perfectly camouflaged leopard crouched under the bush.

Once spotted, its outline became very clear. But had the cat been there all the time? Or did it come to that place after our arrival? Was it trying to catch the dik-dik, or was that a coincidence? No matter, because the leopard must have sensed my recognition of it; at that instant it vanished, although I didn't see it go.

That was a typical leopard encounter. In a lifetime largely spent afield, I've never known an animal of similar size to match the leopard in stealth, in compatibility with its environment, and in the ability to be unseen. To my mind the African leopard is the most beautiful and most remarkable of all the world's cats. Next to the whitetail, it just might rank as the greatest game animal.

Many will not agree that the leopard is the most beautiful animal, and even fewer consider it such a great game species. But no matter how one regards it as a trophy, *Panthera pardus* is a marvelous beast equipped to survive—no, to prosper—in almost any situation. In the category of best "athlete," the animal most capable of doing the most things well, the African leopard has no serious competition.

Consider first its physiology. A full-grown male may reach 125 pounds and a female 100, which makes it the smallest of the genus *Panthera*. But the leopard moves at blinding speed and is so well coordinated that its rush appears as only a blur. Only the cheetah can run slightly faster for a short distance. Most veteran professional hunters probably consider the charge of a leopard to be the most fearsome and difficult of all to stop. The legendary John Hunter considered the leopard as the smartest, most cunning and dangerous animal in Africa. Hunter wrote: "I know of no beast I less wish to hunt in cover than the fast, savage, cunning leopard."

But the spotted cat is more than just fast. It can leap more than twenty feet horizontally and twelve to fifteen feet straight up into a tree without apparent effort. Leopards can swim when that becomes necessary and can climb anywhere any one hundred pound animal can go, and much faster. Leopards are as much at home in trees as on the ground. Flying is the only thing it cannot do, but there are African natives who even doubt that.

Chui, as the leopard is called in Swahili, has a remarkable natural radar. Long chin whiskers and bristle tufts on the forelegs are tactile organs which flash messages to the brain. The cat's vision must be secondary only to that of the vultures circling overhead which depend in part on sharing leopard kills to survive. The leopard's hearing approaches sonar in efficiency and helps explain why the animal is never surprised, and in fact seldom seen. Chui's scenting powers are keen enough, but probably not in the category of a good hound dog.

Baboons, the smaller antelopes, monkeys and bush pigs make up most of a leopard's diet simply because they are most readily available in the animal's world. But leopards are perfectly capable of killing animals twice their own size, and there are numerous records of their killing prey three times as large.

They kill by both biting and clawing. There

Standing poised and alert, a leopard watches from the shadows for a glimpse of its prey. The cat's spotted coat provides it with almost perfect camouflage in its mottled habitat.

are five sharp-pointed claws on each forefoot and four on each hind foot. Built-in mechanisms automatically retract the claws into a sheath of tough skin inside the soft, cushioned pads of the feet when walking. This keeps the claws from becoming blunted and worn as are those of a grizzly bear or dog which does not retract. When a leopard's legs are outstretched, whether to climb a tree or to attack, tendons automatically unsheath the claws. Retracting the claws also permits the cat to walk or run silently on any surface.

Leopards are very powerful, but probably not as powerful as has been supposed. After making a kill, the animal almost always drags

it (at times a very long distance) to a tree, where the carcass is lodged in a fork high enough to secure it from animals on the ground. Except to drink, the leopard may even stay in the same tree until the kill is entirely consumed, but just as often it will sleep elsewhere (probably nearby) and return at feeding times. Some kills prove too heavy to be dragged into trees.

On a photo safari in Serengeti National Park I saw a female of about eighty-five pounds which had killed a 150-pound topi. When we spotted her she was dragging it toward a large tree, the lowest fork of which was more than ten feet above the ground. The female was accompanied by a kitten about half-grown. But no matter how hard she tried, the cat could not get the topi into the tree fork, and finally the pair tore at the carcass on the ground. When they had finished feeding, they climbed into the treetop just above.

Before long the inevitable vultures appeared on the scene and a jackal also came. At intervals the leopard would suddenly drop to the ground, drive all freeloaders away, and then rejoin the kitten overhead. This continued throughout the afternoon until a pride of ten lions came along and ate the topi while the rightful owner watched sullenly from above. If the leopard had been a little stronger, the lions would not have enjoyed such an easy meal.

An excellent way to evaluate the leopard as a game species is to consider its status today. Once it lived in almost every part of Africa and Asia. Although that range is greatly reduced and chui has even been eliminated from most of Mediterranean Africa, its range has shrunk only a fraction as much as that of the lion, tiger or any of the other carnivores. In fact, the leopard is still far more abundant than many conservationists believe because it is far better able to cope with advancing civilization than the other great cats and the bruins. It is unfortunate that other great animals have not done so well.

In many parts of Africa leopards are fairly numerous but their presence still is virtually unknown. Credit this to their ability to be inconspicuous. Many have even adapted to living around the fringes of some African towns, as have whitetails in parts of North America, where less sophisticated wildlife was eliminated long ago. These "city leopards" are entirely nocturnal and can be immensely valuable to the villagers. They subsist on village dogs, baboons, hyraxes, monkeys, cane rats, bush pigs, mongooses and assorted other creatures which are a nuisance to garden crops.

It is nevertheless a temptation for villagers to set traps (although illegal most places), because the sale of one soft spotted pelt may be more than other income for an entire year. When trapped, most leopards show far greater intelligence than most other animals. Nearly all other cats go completely berserk in such a predicament, to their own disadvantage. But most leopards sit calmly while trying to pry the foot free, which they are often able to do.

The leopard's great beauty and the quality of its fur have been both an asset and a great danger, but hopefully the danger is diminishing as the United States and European countries now prohibit importation of the pelts for fur coats. (At the time of this writing, there is also a moratorium on hunting leopards in Kenya.) The spotted hide is a distinct advantage because it provides nearly perfect camouflage no matter whether the animal is crouched in dry grass or hiding in the leafy crown of a thorn tree. As long as the cat remains motionless, it is possible to look right at it and still not see it. Often all that betrays a leopard concealed in a tree crown is its tail carelessly left dangling.

African leopards live solitary lives, perhaps more solitary than their Asian cousins. The only times when two or more are likely to be found together is during mating and when kittens are with a mother. Leopards almost certainly do not mate for life, contrary to a popular romantic belief. The number of females with which a male will breed is limited only by the number of females within traveling distance, and vice versa. Even the actual mating is more noisy and acrobatic than prolonged

leisurely eat the small animal while sitting only a few feet from a front wheel. Then it evaporated into the night.

Even more fleeting was the moment on a clear, cold night when a cat would pass close to camp and utter it harsh, grunting cough. In the distance this very much resembles the grunt-ha, grunt-ha, grunta-ha of a forester hacking away on seasoned hardwood with a dull crosscut saw. The sound is enough to keep a man awake and alert for awhile thereafter. But leopards don't go around seeking trouble with people—they're much too smart for that.

One evening with the tracker Longollo, I sat at dusk in a lonely blind, watching a baboon bait which had been hung to attract a leopard for photographs. We were in the Karamoja region, and Longollo fell asleep with rifle across his lap shortly after sitting down. Not long after I thought I heard a leopard cough nearby. A guinea fowl flushed noisily from a ravine not far away, and then I knew a cat was near that spot. The leopard coughed again.

At that instant Longollo jumped up and leveled the rifle, but not in the direction of the cat. Instead he aimed directly at the nearest of three Karamojong tribesmen who had been approaching silently from behind us.

Completely naked except for paint daubed on their faces and for their spears and giraffe hide shields, the men faced us for a long moment and said nothing. Finally the trio broke and ran, their hardware ringing against the dry brush until they were out of sight. I sat down and in a cold sweat. Of course that spooked the leopard.

We were never able to learn the exact intentions of the tribesmen. Cattle raiding of neighboring tribes is a common pastime, and perhaps they just stumbled on us en route to a rustling mission. It's doubtful that they were stalking us, although it is a possibility. Longollo thought they were coming to steal the leopard bait, as putrid and decaying as it was. Later that theory appeared to be the best one when other baits mysteriously disappeared.

The hunter who decides to shoot a leopard, on bait or not, is wise to make his first shot a killing shot. An animal only wounded quickly escapes and when followed, as it must be, is almost certain to charge if any vitality at all remains. I have never been charged and have never seen it happen, but have interviewed many hunters who faced leopards in all-out attack. All agree it is the most chilling event in the African bush. Fortunately, a leopard's charge is not often as fatal as that of some larger animals, but unless stopped, the hunters can be badly mauled.

At least ninety-five percent of all leopards bagged in Africa today are shot over bait. Whole or part of a prey animal is hung in a tree where there is much fresh leopard sign, often along a waterway which the cat follows regularly during travels across its territory. Then the hunter builds a blind of natural materials overlooking the bait and not too far away, where he sits mornings and evenings waiting for a leopard to come along and find the bait. Very often the cat locates the bait, and if the hunter keeps his cool and is a good enough marksman, the hunt is over.

The one serious weakness in the leopard's character is that it cannot resist a free meal in a convenient place, and the meat need not be very fresh. In places where shooting over bait is not permitted, an African leopard is almost impossible to collect during a typical thirty-day safari in the best leopard country.

In fact, the greatest test of any hunter's skill today is to go afield with gun alone—no baits, no spotlights—and bag a leopard.

Cape Buffalo

MBOGO THE CAPE BUFFALO is a member of the so-called Big Five of Africa's dangerous game, the other four being the lion, leopard, elephant and black rhino. Today the buffalo is the easiest one to collect, and the only one which is completely legal to hunt everywhere. Shooting the Big Five was once the goal of every safari but is now a thing of the past. The buffalo is the only one a sportsman can be relatively sure of.

However, I have several times shot the Big Five on a single trip and once accomplished it in a single day in January, 1969. That was a safari with camera and telephoto lens rather than guns. The lion, rhino and elephant were fine large males, and they were shot early in the morning inside Ngorongoro Crater, Tanzania. What is most remarkable is that all were within sight at the same time. I cannot recall seeing, before or since, three of the Big Five at once anywhere. The leopard, which is the hardest for cameramen to shoot, was collected in late afternoon not far from the safari lodge at Seronera in Serengeti National Park. My buffalo was shot late in the morning on the cool 9,000-foot high rim of Ngorongoro; as a trophy it would probably rank the best of all. It was one of four bulls bedded in deep shade, and all had the massive curving horns characteristic of the species.

The first Europeans who explored far inland in east and south Africa were astounded by the number and variety of large animals they found. Among the most numerous were the Cape or southern buffalos which often appeared in herds of 1,000 to 2,000 or more. In a stampede these vast herds were similar to advancing tornadoes, both in sound and in the devastation left behind. An estimated ten million probably inhabited the continent before the European settlement began, and that figure may or may not include the smaller Nile and dwarf subspecies of western Africa.

Except for the lions, which at times made farming and ranching difficult along the settlement frontiers, the earliest settlers found the buffalos most impressive, but not because they were afraid of them. For years the idea persisted that the huge animals could be somehow domesticated, milked and trained to tow plows as Asian buffalos had been for many centuries before. But mbogo never was tamed, so the settlers shot them instead. The African buffalo today remains the completely incorrigible, magnificent animal it has always been.

There is no mistaking the African buffalo, the only animal on that continent with the distinctive features of an ox. It is powerfully built and heavily muscled, with a short, sinewy neck and stout, strong limbs. No matter how you view it, an adult bull is an awesome beast with a broad, naked muzzle, large ears, and thick black skin which often is badly scarred and may be sparsely covered with coarse hair. Both sexes have heavy horns, but both the boss (width) and spread are much greater in males, which may weigh a ton on the hoof. Altogether *Syncerus caffer* is sullen and formidable, if not downright evil-looking. Only rarely, however, does it become sullen or evil without good cause.

Buffalos cause a good many accidents, but they are seldom unprovoked. Wounded animals, or irritable old bulls which have been unduly harassed or surprised cause most incidents. No matter which, such animals are very dangerous. John Hunter considered only the lion and leopard as potentially more dangerous

Buffalos like to wallow in mud and allow it to cake on their bodies (right), *probably as insulation from the sun and relief from annoying ticks. A gregarious animal, the buffalo in open country forms large herds of bulls, cows and calves of all ages* (below).

and more to be feared, the lion only because it is a smaller target and so much faster afoot.

Several years ago Brian Herne, a good friend and professional hunter, had to interrupt a safari to deal with a bull buffalo which for no apparent reason had turned rogue. The animal had taken to ambushing villagers along a forest path between the huts and a river and had fatally gored one man after tossing him high overhead. A day later a government public health official came along to innoculate villagers, and the buffalo smashed his land rover and treed him and his driver.

Brian hurried to the spot and had no trouble finding the buffalo. In fact, it found him and was shot for its trouble. As Brian had suspected, it was a wounded buffalo behaving irrationally. It had been shot in the ribs and the behind, probably at close range by a poacher. That poacher, incidentally, was a resident of the same village under siege. Such cases are not unusual.

That buffalos have adapted to a wide range of environments is a mark of a great game animal. They thrive in dense forests as well as open plains, in heavy bush, savannas, the fringes of swamps, and in mountains to 13,000 feet. Everywhere the species is gregarious, living in herds, but the size of the herd varies a great deal with the environment. The denser the forest, it seems, the smaller the herd, with ten or twelve as the maximum. In more open country mixed herds of hundreds of bulls,

210

cows, and calves of all ages occur. There is usually one master bull in a herd, which is led by an old female.

Very old bulls, perhaps defeated in fierce intramural combat during the rut, or no longer virile, often separate from herds and live alone or in small bachelor bands. Wounded or injured animals have also been observed living together but away from large herds.

Despite their adaptability to different environments, buffalos are always found close to a source of water. During dry seasons when regular sources are exhausted, they will undertake long migrations to find it. The herd drinks twice a day, or twice nightly, and the vicinity of a waterhole is the best place either to find the animals or at least to locate the fresh spoor which leads to their hideaway. Mbogo likes to loll and wallow in water, too, and where unmolested may spend the best part of the day in it. Cape buffalos are often incorrectly called water buffalos, but the name is apt. Buffs apparently enjoy wallowing in mud and like to dry out allowing the mud to cake on their bodies. This may furnish some insulation from the midday heat and may be a means of eliminating great numbers of ticks which collect on the undersides of all buffalos, particularly around the genitals. Oxpeckers (often called tick birds) and drongos follow buffalo herds and feed on these insect pests, but are unable to eliminate all.

Buffalo habits vary where they are hunted and where they are not. Park and sanctuary animals have resembled herds of domestic cattle in behavior. They drink during daytime, are diurnal and nonchalant, and are usually visible. Most park animals soon become very tolerant of photographers and are the easiest of the common big-game species to shoot. Oc-casionally a solitary bull will rush a safari car, but only because it has been pushed too far by an unthinking driver.

In open hunting areas, buffalos behave much differently. They confine their visits to water to darkness, and before dawn retreat to the heaviest possible cover nearby to ruminate. There they spend daytimes in seclusion. Some herds in Tanzania, Sudan, Uganda and elsewhere are impossible to approach without great risk, so completely impenetrable is their daytime resting area. To look for a trophy bull in this kind of cover is the most tense, suspenseful hunting of all, because it means closing in at very close range to suddenly confront a terrible target.

Late winter or early spring is the calving time for cows, and single young are dropped by females. Gestation requires ten months. The calves are blond or reddish in color at birth and slowly grow darker with age. They are able to travel with the parent herds when a few weeks old, and during this wobbly, uncertain period they are most likely to fall prey to lions, hyenas and hunting dogs. Mothers, sometimes assisted by the entire herd, vigorously try to defend calves, but it is inevitable that a certain percentage is lost. African buffalos have been known to exceed thirty years of age, but average longevity is much shorter.

An extremely resilient and prolific beast, the buffalo is affected little by extremes of heat or cold, by tsetse flies or even by heavy hunting pressure. The more the species is hunted, the deeper it retreats into areas where hunting is difficult or next to impossible.

But disease from domestic livestock is another matter. During the 1890s in Kenya a disastrous outbreak of rinderpest among cattle spread to the wild buffalo and raced swiftly southward to the Cape of Good Hope, wiping out animals all along the way. The plague may have eliminated eight to nine million animals. At the time, it was estimated that only one of every 10,000 buffalos in east Africa survived, but the survivors developed a resistance to rinderpest and the herds grew rapidly. By 1912, buffalos seemed to have reoccupied most of their former natural range, and the population in 1970 was estimated at more than two million head continent-wide.

Hunting, particularly when limited to trophy bulls as it is, has no detrimental role in the future of buffalos. The old males are of no value to the herds and the species can stand a good bit of shooting. As with all other wild creatures, however, expanding civilization and the destruction of the wilderness will determine how long buffalos will survive.

The average horn spread of a large male buffalo is three to three-and-a-half feet. A four-foot spread is an extremely good one. There is on record a six-footer, a spread of horns wider than the average man is tall. When pressing a charge, during which the head is held high, the thick heavy horns of a bull either absorb or deflect shots from reaching the brain, the most vital area. Any Cape buffalo has extraordinary vitality and tenacity and may be the most difficult of all animals to anchor with a single shot. Charging elephants and rhinos can be turned away with shots that do not kill them, but buffs come relentlessly on until they reach you or are killed.

Opinions about mbogo's senses vary, but most agree that the eyesight is poor and the hearing only fair. The powers of scent are well developed, and animals on the fringe of any herd are always testing the air for messages or danger.

In addition to their own senses, buffalos depend on such other warning devices as the oxpeckers and cattle egrets which often accompany them. Both birds flush noisily in alarm when any danger—animal or human—appears. That usually sends the buffalos pounding in the opposite direction.

Except during mating season when there is considerable grunting, blowing and coarse bellowing, buffalos are silent animals, so they do not unduly attract attention to themselves. If the species has a weakness, it is its lack of speed, or at least acceleration, when trouble comes.

The stolid Cape buffalo has never excited the imagination of sportsmen around the world as has the lion, the tiger, the grizzly, or the elephant. Not many go on safari just to hunt or photograph this unhandsome ox. But for me the African bush would be empty without its black and ominous presence.

Rhinosceros

AT TIMES every outdoorsman becomes too careless for his own good and suddenly discovers he is in trouble. It can happen without warning when he climbs to a place on a mountain from which it is almost impossible to descend. Or precarious predicaments can result from overconfidence, or underestimating a wild animal. Both have happened to me, the latter during my first trip to Africa years ago.

At the time, I already had considerable experience hunting and photographing big game in North America, all of it without incident. Then came a thirty-day safari in (then) Tanganyika which was a great adventure, but where nothing of a perilous nature happened. At the conclusion of the safari, Keith Cormack and I drove to visit some of the game parks of Kenya with photography in mind.

In what is now Amboseli National Park we photographed several black rhinos, and a cameraman isn't likely to find any more docile, willing subjects than these. I was amazed at how undisturbed they were at the approach of our vehicle; even a female with a very small calf only stared dully at us. If the pictures lacked anything, it was motion or excitement rather than close-up detail, which I got.

Several days later we were in Tsavo Park, and driving along a lonely road we came upon another rhino. This one was lying down beside a mud hole in which it had been rolling. The mud was a brick red color and so was the rhinoceros. Any rhino is strange and prehistoric in appearance, but this dripping red one was pure nightmare, and I had to have pictures.

At the time I was using a 35mm camera with a 400mm follow-focus lens. The latter is long, heavy and cumbersome compared to newer gear, but with that equipment in hand I stepped from the car and walked closer and closer to the rhino, stopping to make exposures at intervals along the way. Like the Amboseli rhinos, this one seemed to pay little attention to me, only standing and walking away when I was thirty to forty yards distant. So I grew careless and hurried my pace to get a little closer, at the same time trying to focus the long lens.

Next thing I knew the rhino was pounding directly toward me!

It is lucky that he did not trample my photo equipment, which I dropped on the ground while climbing the nearest tree and driving a thorn into my hand in the process. The rhino ran right beneath the tree and kept on going.

What I will always remember about that encounter, however, is neither being treed nor the puncture in my palm. It is the astonishing agility and speed of that rhino. It still does not seem possible that an animal of such size and structure could swap ends and shift into high gear so suddenly. But many times since then I've seen rhinos repeat the performance—and each time was another valuable lesson.

The lesson, simply, is do not underestimate or take for granted *any* big-game animal. You might make the mistake only once.

Standing anywhere in the east or south African bush, the black rhinoceros, *Diceros bicornis,* looks every inch the prehistoric monster. A full-grown animal probably weighs a ton or more. It is five, maybe six feet high at the front shoulder and twice that long from nose to tip of tail. The skin, which is an inch thick, wrinkled, scarred and armor-like, is the same color as the earth on which it lives. That is usually some shade of gray and despite the name is seldom black. Two pointed horns, the

Black rhino, looking like an apparition from prehistoric times, squints at the world through little nearsighted eyes. Unexplained is the pugnacity of the black, the docility of the white rhino.

front one longer than the other, protrude out and up from an enormous piglike head. Viewed suddenly or for the first time, the rhino appears more an apparition than a flesh and blood animal.

No matter from which angle it's viewed, the rhino looks like a mistake. Its legs are too short for the long heavy body. At times its eyesight is so bad that it borders on blindness, and this may account for much of the animal's unpredictability and generally truculent behavior. The black rhino is often considered the only animal which will charge without provocation, although whether it is actually charging has often been questioned.

Professional hunter Brian Herne believes that a black rhino's nearsightedness is so acute that it permits a person who takes advantage of wind and travels quietly enough to approach too close before the rhino realizes it. The animal reacts by charging, or at least bluffing, mostly from fear or uncertainty. Herne may have something there. But how about that close cousin, the equally myopic white rhino, which is as docile as a barnyard milk cow?

No matter what the reason, black rhinos have a long history of taking on all comers, and that includes elephants, trucks, tractors and trains as well as hapless humans walking through rhino country. The Mombasa-to-Nairobi train has been derailed by a combative rhino, and each year in the national parks a number of passenger vehicles are overturned, sometimes with the passengers inside. There is a record of one animal battering itself so re-

Horn of the black rhino has unwarranted reputation among Orientals as an aphrodisiac and youth restorer. Illicit market in horns has caused poaching and a depletion of rhino herds.

peatedly against a farm tractor (which the driver deserted in panic) that it died from the injuries. Another fought a five-minute draw with a Chevy truck on the Mombasa highway.

In Kenya a game warden found a rhino hopelessly bogged down in a mudhole and unless rescued, doomed to die there. Using the winch on his land rover, the warden tossed a loop of rope over the rhino's horn and towed it out of its deathtrap. The rhino responded by smashing the land rover. Another rhino ended the life of Bwana Cotter, an Oklahoman who became famous as a professional hunter in east Africa. Still another killed four natives near Ole Debesse wells. So the record reads.

But it is not the rhino's bad temper which has reduced it to endangered species status. Rather, it is the usual combination of clearing the land for agriculture and the demand for its horn, which has no value at all (except to the rhino) but which nevertheless may sell for several hundred dollars a pound in parts of Asia.

It is now known that many Orientals consider ground rhino horn to be both an aphrodisiac and a restorer of lost youth. Although it is neither, it has created such a flourishing illicit market and has encouraged so much poaching that in the past, plains have been littered with decaying carcasses and bleached bones left behind after obtaining the horn.

The horn isn't actual horn. It is closely packed, hairlike fiber which grows out of the skin to almost the hardness of horn. An aver-

Cattle egrets often visit a black rhino and eat the grubs on its back—an arrangement that is most satisfying to both parties.

age-size front spike is about two feet, but it may grow to nearly four feet. Two very famous black rhinos of Amboseli Park, Gladys and Gertie (mother and daughter so named by park wardens), which have been photographed by thousands of tourists, both had front horns nearly four feet long.

Equally unusual is the black rhino's prehensile upper lip which is triangular in shape and very mobile. The lip is perfectly adapted for browsing on twigs and stripping the bark from the acacia and euphorbia trees that the animal relishes.

As members of the mammalian order Perissodactyla, the African rhino's only living relatives are the Asian rhinos, zebras, horses and tapirs, all of which also have odd numbers of toes on the foot—three for the rhinos. The black prefers dry bush country, particularly a thorn scrub habitat, but will live in open forests and has been found as high as 11,500 feet on the cloud-covered moorlands of Mt. Kenya. Whatever its environment, the species is crucially important to the other wildlife which share it. If rhinos exist to near-capacity of their range, they browse the scrub thorn heavily enough to permit other succulent plants and other animals to exist there. When the rhinos are eliminated, as has happened in too many and too vast areas, the thorn becomes so dense that few animals can live in it.

Once the black rhino's range included nearly all of sub-Saharan Africa, except the jungles and rain forests. But now there are only pitifully small pockets in Kenya, Tanzania, Uganda, Zambia and South Africa, the vast majority in national parks and sanctuaries.

Ironically, during the 1950s and 1960s there was worldwide concern for the white rhinos, which had been reduced to less than 400 head, all except a handful concentrated in Zululand, South Africa. What followed was a splendid conservation effort which has not only rescued the white from oblivion, but has also permitted restocking the animal to areas where it formerly existed. However, during all the concern for the white rhino, the black became equally imperiled.

A fairly recent black rhino slaughter took place between 1946 and 1959, when 50,000 acres of land in Kenya's Makueni District was cleared for agriculture by Wakamba tribesmen. The animals had to be removed, and John Hunter alone exterminated 1,088 black rhinos. But the farming was a failure, and the rhino killing served no useful purpose.

Anyone who has spent much time with or near black rhinos gets the strong impression that they are never happy. They are territorial, marking their areas with rubbed places on trees and piles of dung which grow huge from daily defecation in the exact same place. Rhinos eat tremendous amounts of browse, thorns and all, which are often passed through the body undigested and onto the dung piles.

"This," an African tracker once pointed out to me, "is what gives faru the ugly temper." Faru is Swahili for rhino.

An example of their extreme territorialism occurred when during a 1960-61 drought, 282 rhinos died of malnutrition in Kenya's Tsavo National Park. Almost all the casualties were sustained along the Athi and Tsavo rivers. These rhinos could have saved themselves by moving only a short distance over the Yatta plateau to the Tiva River where food was relatively abundant. But they preferred their established territories to the most bitter end.

If a rhino is ever happy, it is during its daily bath when there is enough water in the mud holes for that purpose. After feeding most of the night, the animal may wallow for an hour or two and snort (which suggests contentment) before emerging to bake in the sun. I once watched a black rhino emerge from its bath and trample down a few small trees, but not eat them, maybe just to show his happiness.

Even the black rhino's courtship and lovelife are all aggression. During mating, most wildlife parents are inseparable and at least do not appear angry at one another. But it is common for the female to attack her suitor, sometimes until he is so bruised and battered that he can barely stand on four feet. Bachelorhood seems much more attractive, and it is no wonder that the animals breed only every third year. About eighteen months after the nuptial battering, a single calf (rarely twins) is born in a lonely thorn thicket.

There is nothing cuddly about a black rhino calf, which is only slightly less homely than its mother. The female defends the little one at any cost, against any enemy, as long as the calf is still suckling, which may be as long as two years after birth. The baby always travels behind the mother rather than in front. Otherwise, a tracker assured me, the mother would charge it. Black rhinos do not reach maturity until five or six years, at which time they begin their own solitary and sullen lives.

It is much easier to describe the white rhinoceros, *Diceros simus*. Although the white is superficially similar in appearance, its behavior is exactly the opposite. For example, a white rhino calf almost always walks in front of the mother. And to provoke a charge from the white is virtually impossible.

221

There is no mistaking the white rhino for the black. The white reaches much larger size, up to seventy inches at the shoulder and from three and a half to five tons in weight, making it second (to the elephant) in size of all land mammals. The head is longer, heavier, and carried lower than the black rhino's, and it terminates in a broad square muzzle with no trace of protruding lip. The white rhino is rarely white. It is the same dark color of the mud in the nearest mudhole. The word "white" is an erroneous adaption of a Boer word meaning "wide," to describe the mouth. In fact, the name "wide-mouthed" rhino is still occasionally used for the species.

Whites are more social than their smaller and solitary relatives. They often move in family groups of four or five, and I once counted eleven in a herd. They are placid and even-tempered, traits which any wildlife cameraman will appreciate. During mating they become very aggressive, occasionally ferocious, among themselves and even the cows seem pugnacious.

The horns of white rhinos grow longer, thinner and straighter than the blacks' and may actually exceed five feet. The ears are large and fringed with stiff hair. The overall appearance is not one of grace and beauty.

Not long ago all of the surviving white rhinos (except for a dozen or so in Uganda) were in Hluhluwe and Umfolosi game reserves in Zululand. Soon after the animals were finally given complete protection from poaching, they multiplied beyond the carrying capacity of the two reserves. The government began a live-trapping program of surplus rhinos which resulted in stocking many areas (including Kruger National Park and several places in east Africa) where the species had earlier been eliminated.

Docile white rhino, the larger of the two, can be identified by its longer, thinner horn which may exceed five feet. Head is larger and heavier, and is carried lower than the black's.

Early in 1967 Karl Maslowski, a motion-picture producer, and I had an opportunity to photograph a white rhino capture at Umfolosi. Early in the morning we met the capture team, including the ranger in charge, a veterinarian, two Zulu game scouts mounted on horseback, and eight to ten other scouts. The animal for capture had already been selected and was a large cow of about four tons.

The actual shooting of the cow was to be done by the chief ranger with a Crosman CO2 gun, loaded with a heavy drug-filled dart. The maximum range with this was only twenty-five yards because of the bad trajectory; in other words, the ranger had to stalk within point-blank range.

The two horsemen wore crash helmets and heavily padded clothing all over. The horses also were protected with thick padding, and for good reason. Once the rhino was plunked with the dart, it would race away across country and far out of sight before the drug would take effect. The horsemen therefore had to follow right behind it, to pinpoint the exact location where it fell so that a large truck could be brought as near as possible for loading before the rhino revived. Without the padded protection, the riders couldn't possibly keep up with the rhino racing through thornbrush.

We found the cow lying down along with a large calf and a male in an island surrounded by open grassland. After carefully checking the wind, the ranger began his stalk on hands and knees, being careful to alarm none of the three. When only twenty yards away, he rose slowly

Enjoying a mud bath, their favorite diversion, two white rhinos display the sociability that distinguishes them from their relatives the blacks.

to one knee, aimed, and just as all the rhinos spotted him and suddenly stood up in surprise, the ranger fired. I heard the dart thump solidly into the flank of the cow.

Then all hell broke loose.

Rhinos were running in all directions, and I did not want to be in the path of any but did want pictures. I heard the horsemen shouting at their mounts. Suddenly everything was still again.

"Let's be ready to make tracks," the ranger said, "when a horseman returns."

We didn't have long to wait. The rider came back and reported that the cow was down in a fairly open area easy of access with the truck. A few minutes later we reached the spot and there, immobilized, the rhino looked even larger than it had in the field.

The next step was to back the truck as close as possible. The vet then injected a second drug to counteract the first and begin the rhino's revival. Gradually, the animal was able to stand up and while still in a stupor was half walked by the scout crew and half pulled by ropes and pullies into the padded bed of the truck. Not long afterward, it was well on its way to being released at Matapos National Park in Rhodesia.

Not all captures go as smoothly and without complications as that one. With so much practice the crews have become very efficient. But it is very hard, dangerous labor and there have been serious injuries. It is a wildlife conservation success story all too rare nowadays. Because of it, the world's population of wild white rhinos now stands above 4,000, and the animal appears secure. The ranger and game scouts of the Zululand reserves deserve an immense amount of credit for it.

Antelope

NO OTHER PART of the world matches Africa in the number, beauty and variety of large antelopes. Some species are very abundant and widely distributed over the continent. Other rare species live only in restricted habitats. At least one, the bluebuck of South Africa, is extinct and the survival of others is in doubt. The antelopes belong to several different families, but there is no point in listing them here.

The giant or Lord Derby's eland is the largest and most bovine in appearance of all the antelopes. Males may stand sixty-nine inches at the shoulder and weigh a ton. *Taurotragus derbianus* occurs in herds of as many as forty-five or fifty animals, but fifteen to eighteen is closer to average. With advancing age, bulls change from their fawn-to-chestnut color to gray or blue-gray, growing darker all the time. The flanks are marked with twelve to fourteen vertical white stripes. Matted dark hair on the forehead and a drooping dewlap which begins near the chin further distinguish the males. A bull's horns are massive and straight, with a tight spiral near the base.

In spite of its size and splendid appearance, the giant eland is shy and unaggressive. It is nocturnal and nowadays very rare, having been a victim of rinderpest and uncontrolled hunting over most of its natural range. It is common local practice to drive the herds into the open by setting brush fires. A race once fairly abundant from Senegal through Nigeria (*T. d. derbianus*) now exists only in scattered harassed bands. The central African race (*T. d. gigas*) of Chad, Sudan, and Congo has also lost substantial range and numbers but is not yet in such grave danger.

Slightly smaller than the Derby's is the common (or Cape, or Livingstone's) eland, *Taurotragus oryx*. Three races occupy suitable

Common eland range in large herds across eastern and southern Africa, in a variety of habitats. Despite its ponderous appearance, the eland is surprisingly agile—it can clear an eight-foot fence in a single bound.

ranges over a good portion of eastern and southern Africa. All are lighter in color than the giant eland, have only three or four body stripes, and a less prominent dewlap. The heavy horns are more parallel than V-shaped. Bulls at times reach 1,500 to 1,600 pounds, females somewhat less.

The common eland lives in fairly large herds of twenty-five or more, each containing one or two very large bulls. During migrations or periods of severe drought, several herds may band together, and the species is also often found in company with zebras, gemsbok, oryx and roan antelope. Older bulls may become solitary.

Eland occupy a variety of habitats from open plains, light forests and savannas to mountain grasslands, although they are browsers rather than grazers. They use their horns to break off and collect twigs or tree limbs; roots and tubers are dug up with their hooves. Daily water is a necessity. Like many other antelopes, eland are restless and move a great deal, especially during dry seasons.

The most surprising characteristic of the eland—again in spite of its ponderous appearance—is its great agility. As large and heavy as they are, eland can clear an eight-foot fence in one bound. When startled, they often jump over one another from a standing start, in the manner of impalas. Their agility never fails to amaze hunters.

In captivity, common eland soon become tame. The meat is delicious, marbled with fat, and the animals can be herded and milked.

Eland might far better serve the nutrition shortage in parts of Africa than do the herds of scrawny scrub cattle which infest and degrade the landscape.

Nowadays a good many hunters travel to Africa specifically in search of one or more of the magnificent antelopes. Perhaps the greater kudu, *Tragelaphus strepsiceros*, is the number one trophy. It is a most elegant animal about the size of a North American wapiti, with white-striped flanks, large ears, and a fringe of long hair from chin to chest on adult males. Most noteworthy are the massive spreading horns which grow upward in two to almost three spirals, to a possible length of nearly six feet (although average length is less).

There are three races of the greater kudu. The largest and darkest is *T. s. strepsiceros* of Angola, Zambia, South and Southwest Africa. One of the finest trophies I have ever seen

either on the hoof or in a museum was a kudu bull with absolutely massive horns at Etosha Game Park, Southwest Africa. The horns were so heavy that they seemed to impede the bull's travel. The park ecologist who daily roamed the area agreed that it was a most extraordinary animal.

The east African greater kudu, *T. s. bea,* ranges from Tanzania to Eritrea, the largest of this race being concentrated around Marsabit in Kenya's Northern Frontier. The western kudu, *T. s. cottoni,* is pale in color and is distributed from Chad to Ethiopia, where it was once abundant but is now very rare.

Altogether, though, the greater kudu is doing well, mostly due to furtive disposition and brushy habitat. The species is not easy to hunt, especially in mountainous areas which it often prefers and where it relies on stealth and excellent hearing rather than speed (greater kudus are actually slow and ungainly) to avoid

detection. Kudus live in small herds, usually family groups and as often as not without an adult male. Bulls tend to be solitary or to gather in bachelor herds, a common characteristic of antelopes. In the Etosha Game Park, which is the largest game reserve in the world, I saw one herd of eleven mature males, and the immensely large one mentioned before was in a group of five, all with huge horns.

One of the most exciting sounds of the African bush is the roar of bull kudus during the rut. It is not often heard except just before and after daybreak, when it can be helpful in locating the animals. The hoarse bark of an alarmed kudu is probably the loudest of any antelope, and it may be a hunter's only warning that he is near the game.

The lesser kudu, *Tragelaphus imberbis,* is more shy than the greater. It is also more graceful and faster. It reaches the size of a medium mule deer. Not as impressive at first glance and

229

Elegant greater kudu (left), with its characteristic massive spiral horns, is considered one of Africa's top trophies. Shy lesser kudu (right) is smaller, more difficult to hunt.

with spiral horns which rarely exceed thirty inches, the lesser is judged by most experienced hunters to be a more difficult trophy. My main impression is that it is always nervous.

Lesser kudus can survive without water for long periods. They therefore can live in arid country, where they spend daytimes bedded in the shade. The best times to see them are briefly at daybreak and dusk when males venture cautiously to the edges of thornbush cover to browse. Even where they are not hunted, lesser kudus try to keep humans at a safe distance. Near the riverside tent camp in Awash National Park, Ethiopia, was the greatest concentration of lesser kudus I have ever found. That included quite a number of splendid males. They were never difficult to see and should have been used to human activity, but it was never possible to approach close enough for good photographs. Maybe there was poaching in the area.

Except perhaps for the bongo, no antelope is more colorful than the bull nyala, *Tragelaphus angasi.* Adult males have dark gray, white-striped bodies, very long hair on the belly, reddish leggings, a snow-white mane the length of the back, and a white chevron on the face. Average weight is about 250 pounds. Its elegant overall appearance suggests to some observers more of an Arctic animal than a dweller of humid, lowland forests. Females are much smaller, chestnut in color and without the lyre-shaped, heavy, ivory-tipped horns of the bulls.

The range of the nyala is limited to Zululand and a portion of adjoining Mozambique, where it may be locally abundant. From my own experience, it is not as shy as most other antelopes. It is easy to see in the Zululand game reserves—Hluhluwe, Umfolosi, Ndumu and Mkusi. Virtually all of the world's hooved animals are good to eat, but of those I've tried, the nyala is most delicious.

The mountain nyala, *Tragelaphus buxtoni,* inhabits an even more restricted area than the lowland nyala. Splendid in appearance, the species was not discovered until early in this century. Today, just a handful of humans have ever seen them. No wonder, as mountain nyalas live only in the hagenia forests and heathlands of Ethiopia's Arussi and Bale mountain

231

massifs, above 9,500 feet and upward to about 12,000 feet. Today they are very rare, in fact endangered, because of the Ethiopian government's complete lack of concern for the future of its native wildlife. This is a tragedy similar to those taking place across northern Africa and so many parts of Asia.

Both the mountain nyala and its unique environment are international treasures which should be saved. But at this writing, that lofty, damp region is being invaded by graziers with flocks of goats, and large parts of the heathlands are being plowed under. The result is a terrible, unchecked erosion which can never be healed.

At least a dozen different races of bushbuck, *Tragelaphus scriptus,* inhabit much of the southern two-thirds of Africa. We normally think of some cats (such as the leopard) as the most nocturnal of big-game animals, but the bushbucks also do most of their living after dark. They sleep during daytimes in the seclusion of heavy cover, then move about and feed during darkness. Except when deliberately flushed from cover (which is done with dogs in South Africa), bushbucks are seldom observed except during first and last light of day.

The handsome bushbucks are the size of American whitetails or slightly smaller. The males (and a few females) have sharp, slightly spiraled horns which may average a foot long at maturity, and occasionally reach twenty inches. The many races differ mostly in size and coloration, ranging from tan to rich reddish to an almost glistening black in *T. s. meneliki,* a rare Ethiopian subspecies. Most have stripes or spots, very faint in some races. Everywhere they blend well into a variety of habitats from dense bush and riverine forests to nearly waterless thickets.

A bushbuck is neither swift nor agile, and especially young ones are favorite prey of leopards and pythons. Males are extremely tenacious, even aggressive, and can be dangerous if cornered or wounded. There are records of bushbucks killing leopards, and in one case both the bushbuck and the lioness which tried to kill it were found dead. The antelope had driven its dagger-like horns into the cat's throat before dying of its own wounds.

Long, curving horns that may exceed five feet in length are the mark of the famed sable antelope. Herds of ten to twenty sables roam the woodlands of southern Africa.

ankle joints and broadly splayed hooves permit easier travel over spongy ground than is possible for another antelope of equal bulk. Sitatunga can swim very well, and when surprised they can completely submerge in water with only the tip of the nose above the surface. An undisturbed sitatunga may spend a hot day either totally or partially submerged, now and then nibbling on aquatic vegetation. They are rather clumsy animals when traveling on dry land, an activity they try to avoid. Horns of males may exceed two feet.

Among the most coveted trophies on the Bright Continent—or in the world—is *Hippotragus niger,* the sable antelope. Standing about four feet at the shoulder and weighing 400 to 500 pounds, the glossy black bull sable is a handsome and challenging mammal to hunt anywhere in its southeastern Africa range. Many outdoorsmen consider the long (to more than five feet) curving horns as the most spectacular trophy anywhere.

A very specialized member of the bushbuck family inhabits many swampy areas of central Africa. The sitatunga, *Tragelaphus spekei,* which is confined to papyrus and reed swamps and occasionally to flooded forests, is a true marsh antelope. The species becomes exceptionally shy where it is hunted and as a result, hunting becomes most difficult.

Although the dark gray to chestnut coats of sitatungas do not blend with their green backgrounds, several unique escape mechanisms compensate for this contrast. Very flexible

Sables prefer the type of wooded areas which make them more difficult to hunt. They occur in herds of ten to twenty, and occasionally much larger groups, in which there is likely to be one fine bull. Otherwise, males remain solitary or join bachelor herds. Bulls are pugnacious, do a good bit of fighting among themselves, and are capable of defending against attack by single lions.

A subspecies called the giant sable, *H. n. variani,* is a rare antelope and larger edition of the common sable which lives only between

233

Dweller of dense forests or jungles, nocturnal in habits, the bongo is rarely seen by humans.

the Upper Cuanza and Luando rivers in Angola. Its numbers are estimated to be very low, and at this writing no hunting is permitted. But poaching and land-clearing (the worst enemy) go on. The giant sable may not.

A large antelope similar to the sable but rufous or tan in color and lacking the long curved horns is the roan, *Hippotragus equinus*. Four races are scattered over open or lightly wooded habitats in central, southern and subSaharan Africa. The animals prefer rough, broken, and often mountainous areas, and are seldom far from water. The irregular pattern of distribution is difficult to explain because roans seem to live only in certain small or isolated pockets, while they are absent from adjacent places where the cover is similar. Roans are disappearing from areas of former abundance, in some cases for no obvious reason.

The species lives in small herds of fifteen to twenty animals, each group led by a master bull. Other bulls gather in all-male groups in which there is constant jousting for dominance. The roan is a very aggressive antelope and so much fighting occurs even among male calves that the hides of nearly all are badly scarred.

I have never seen a bongo, *Taurotragus eurycerus*, which is surely among the most brightly colored and beautiful of all antelopes. The species is not actually rare, but its extreme shyness, its nocturnal habits and nearly impenetrable habitat make it an animal which nobody knows intimately.

There are two races of bongos: the western, *T. e. eurycerus,* from Sierra Leone to Katanga, and the eastern race, *T. e. isaaci,* of Kenya's Aberdares. Both dwell only in very dense forest or jungle. In Kenya they are confined to rain forest and bamboo-clad mountain slopes where hunting either with gun or camera has few rewards and is undiluted hard work. Bongos have excellent eyesight, good hearing, and are silent both vocally and when traveling through their dank environment. Full-grown animals may weigh 500 pounds. Some biologists suspect that bongos may exist in a few jungle areas where they have not yet been identified.

Both the fawn-colored beisa (*Oryx gazella beisa*) and fringe-eared (*O. g. callotis*) oryx are familiar to hunters in Africa because of their abundance and unmistakable striking appearance in the dry open bush and short grass savannas of east Africa. Beisa occur in herds of a dozen to twice that many cows and calves, and may be associated with zebra, Grant's or Soemmering's gazelles. Bulls tend to be solitary. The species has excellent vision and can live without water for a long time.

One morning in Ethiopia's Awash National Park I came upon two bulls in serious combat. Both had lowered their heads to between the forelegs, aiming their long sharp horns forward and low, parallel to the ground. In a cloud of dust, each was thrusting forward, probing for openings to impale the other. Lions have been killed by oryx defending in this manner and after that demonstration, which ended when the bulls spotted our jeep, it is much easier to understand. The skin on an oryx's neck may be one and a half inches thick, useful as pro-

tection or padding for the constant conflict with other males.

A close relative of the east African oryx is the gemsbok, *Oryx gazella gazella,* which is similar in structure (powerful shoulders, lower in the rump, long rapier horns which may measure four feet) and differs mostly in the coarse black hair on rump, tail and upper hind legs. Its range is confined to Southwest Africa, the Kalahari Desert and Botswana, where in places it remains extremely abundant. On the dry plains and sub-desert of Etosha Game Park I have seen many herds of forty to fifty animals and one group of more than a hundred. The species is nomadic, traveling far for water or food, but can go without water for long periods. Gemsbok are grazers but may also eat wild fruits and melons. At times they depend on the latter for all their water needs. Either the oryx or gemsbok is responsible for the unicorn legend. Viewed in profile, this handsome larger antelope appears to have only one horn. Nor is it unusual to encounter gemsbok with one horn broken off, probably by fighting.

The scimitar-horned oryx, *Oryx tao,* is a large white antelope, ruddy brown on the chest and neck, with backward curving rather than straight horns. At a distance it is ghostlike in appearance, particularly through desert dust and heat waves. Once the species ranged in vast herds all across northern Africa, often numbering into the thousands and mixed with equal numbers of dama gazelles. Ancient Egyptians domesticated them, but the only specimens (if any) remaining in Egypt are now in Cairo's dingy zoo. The scimitar is extinct over much of its original range, and less than 10,000 total remain, about half of those in northern Chad.

Herd of oryx, carrying their long, sharp horns like lances, trots across the dry bushland of Awash National Park, Ethiopia.

Scimitar-horned oryx (left), once abundant in northern Africa, is now extinct over most of its original range.

Addax (right) once inhabited much of southern Africa, is now threatened by overhunting.

Nomadic gemsbok (below), possibly the inspiration for the mythical unicorn, roams the arid ranges of Southwest Africa.

The addax, *Addax nasomaculatus,* is another large antelope gravely threatened. It once roamed much of Saharan Africa, often far from any source of water. It used to migrate widely, as far north as southern Algeria and Tunisia. It is a handsome animal which weighs more than 200 pounds when full grown, with spiraling antlers similar to the kudu. The hooves are enlarged for better walking on a soft or sandy surface.

Addax survived fairly well even when heavily hunted by desert nomads on horseback. Military vehicles and long-range military rifles, however, were another matter. Not one reserve anywhere has been established for the animal's protection. And no North African government appears concerned.

A combination of factors has been responsible for the decline. The encroaching Sahara Desert, a result of centuries of overgrazing by domestic livestock, is one. Mass killings by military personnel in vehicles and with automatic weapons have been more recent and more dramatic. Oil explorers and surveyors have also taken their share, until today there is need to stop all shooting everywhere. And a national park is needed in Chad to save the addax and slender-horned gazelle as well as the scimitar.

The Arabian oryx, *Oryx leucoryx,* smallest (three feet at the shoulder) and rarest of the three species, is also endangered, thanks again to encroaching desert and undisciplined soldiers and oil people, all using cars to surround and herd the animals to mass slaughter. Arabia's former King Saud once shot a hundred or so in a day for amusement. Now only a few hundred survive wild in Oman, and there are small captive herds in Arabia, Qatar, Kuwait and Phoenix, Arizona, zoo.

A BEWILDERING number of medium to small antelopes exist or once existed in every part of Africa. The abundance covers the number of species and subspecies as well as the total number of animals. A list of the world's greatest remaining wildlife spectacles must include the massed wildebeest, hartebeest and gazelles in such national parks as Tanzania's Serengeti and Kenya's Masai Mara. It is not unusual to stand atop a rocky outcrop on the Serengeti Plains and see below herds of thousands of antelope mixed with zebra in every direction. Smaller concentrations even exist in regions which are not included in national parks or reserves.

The numerous species of antelopes have a number of things in common. First, they are herd animals. Most prefer open to timbered habitat and therefore are agile and fast. They have to be. The males and occasionally the females of the species grow horns which are not shed and which grow with age.

The defassa waterbuck, *Kobus defassa*, and common waterbuck, *Kobus ellipsiprymnus*, are common antelopes which are slightly atypical. The two differ mostly in range and the color pattern of the rump, the common waterbuck having a conspicuous white ring on its behind resembling a target with bullseye. The two species interbreed where their ranges overlap, and the result can confuse someone trying to identify them.

The main characteristics of waterbucks are the long, coarse, dark hair of both sexes and the heavy, ringed, forward-curving horns of males which are extremely handsome. The coat is oily, which may explain the animal's strange musky odor and the flavor of the meat which many consider unpalatable. The nearness of waterbucks can be detected by odor alone, and experienced native trackers can follow the animals for long distances by the lingering scent. Small herds of four or five to twenty, each with a master bull, are customary, but it isn't unusual to see herds without males. Where they are not hunted in parks, waterbucks soon become very tame. On more than one occasion I have awakened in the morning to find a cow staring directly into my open window.

Both defassas (of which there are four races) and commons require well-watered areas. The range of the defassas covers most of central and eastern Africa, except jungles, dense forest and arid regions. The common lives to the southeast of this, from Tanzania to Zululand, Zambia and Rhodesia.

A close relative of the waterbuck, but dissimilar in appearance is the kob, *Kobus kob*, of central Africa. Buffon's kob (*K. k. kob*) inhabits a range from Gambia to Chad and the Central African Republic. The white-eared race is restricted to the very narrow border area between Sudan and Ethiopia. Most abundant is the Uganda kob (*K. k. thomasi*) which is so common in Murchison Falls National Park, nearby Semliki Valley, and the surrounding Nile bottomlands.

The Uganda kob is as entertaining as it is attractive. Where the population is high, males establish territories on mounds or low ridges which they defend vigorously from all other males. That means a good bit of defending, because these territories may be no more than one hundred feet in diameter and a dozen or more well-trampled territories are often crowded side by side. Activity is brisk and fighting almost continual when a female in

Oily coat of the waterbuck gives off a strong odor, enabling trackers to follow the animal for miles. Males wear heavily ringed horns, which they use in mating battles (below).

Uganda kob, most abundant of the kobs, travels in large herds. The males establish territories on small mounds or ridges, which they defend vigorously—especially when a female appears.

estrus appears in the vicinity for mating. Hair and dust fly in a noisy clatter of horns. Otherwise, the kob live in fairly large, loose herds, sometimes to one hundred or more. Early explorers in Uganda report seeing them in herds of thousands.

My several trips to Africa have been successful and fulfilling experiences, with one minor exception. That was an expedition with old hunting friends and an inept outfitter from Addis Ababa into the Gambela-Baru rivers region of western Ethiopia, after white-eared kob and Nile lechwe. We saw neither antelope because of frequent mechanical breakdowns en route to kob country, rivers too deep to ford, and finally just bogging down in country

where the grass was six to ten feet tall. The white-eared kob has seemed especially elusive since, and it certainly is.

In size and silhouette it resembles exactly the Uganda kob. Weights of both average 150-175 pounds. But mature males become a very dark brown, almost black, with white throats, bellies, spectacles (eye rings) and ears. White-eared kobs are highly aquatic, feed on aquatic vegetation and might spend long periods in the water.

The puku, *Kobus vardoni*, would be practically indistinguishable from the Uganda kob (which has thin black edging on the forelegs) if both shared the same range. But on close inspection, the males have shorter horns which are heavier at the base. The puku's range includes southern Congo, southern Tanzania, Zambia and Rhodesia, where it prefers the open flats bordering rivers and marshlands. Its habits are similar to the kob's, but smaller herds are the rule.

Three races of the common lechwe are distributed in the swamps and wetlands of southern Africa. The red lechwe (*Kobus leche leche*) of Botswana and western Zambia is bright chestnut in color. The black (*K. l. smithemani*) of southeastern Congo and adjoining Zambia has a black or dark brown tinge on back, neck and flanks. A third lechwe (*K. l. kafuensis*) is confined to Zambia's Kafue Flats and is distinguishable from the others by a blackish shoulder patch and normally by longer, thinner horns of the males.

Of all antelopes, only sitatungas are more aquatic than lechwes, which can swim well and travel much better across swamps and marshes than over hard ground. They congregate in large herds and are at the mercy of fluctuating water levels; during drought too many are confined into too small areas and the toll by many predators becomes severe. In recent years there has been concern over the disappearance of lechwes from much of their former range, even from the Bangweulu swamps and Kafue Flats where the population was highest.

Kobus megaceros, the Nile or Mrs. Gray's lechwe, is separated by almost 2,000 miles from the common lechwes. But this graceful, long-haired antelope is also highly aquatic, living only in dense swamplands along the White Nile, Bahr el Ghazal, and some tributaries in fairly large herds. Females are chestnut in color. Males grow darker with age to a chocolate brown color at maturity, when they might conceivably be confused with white-eared kobs. But a saddle-shaped white patch on the nape of the neck is certain identification. The inaccessibility of the species plus its beautiful, ringed, lyrate horns make the Nile lechwe an especially desirable trophy on the wall or on color film.

Early one morning in Nairobi National Park, I had set up a tripod and mounted a camera and telephoto lens to photograph the birds around a small waterhole. During the next fifteen or twenty minutes I kept busy photographing and changing film and film magazines, in other words, making considerable disturbance. It wasn't until I picked up the tripod to depart that I noticed dark liquid eyes staring at me from tall grass about eight feet away. Next I noticed the short, forward-curving horns and so identified the animal which had been watching me all the while as a bohor reedbuck, *Redunca redunca.*

It's difficult to explain why the young male antelope chose to sit in place rather than flush with a possible enemy so near. Maybe by remaining motionless he felt perfectly concealed, and in fact was unnoticed for a long time. More likely, that is just the nature, the instinct, of the species.

It is nearly impossible to tell apart the several races of the bohor. One (*R. r. redunca*) ranges from Senegal to Ghana. Another (*R. r. nigeriensis*) lives in a strip from Nigeria to the Congo. The Abyssinian bohor (*R. r. bohor*) is peculiar to Ethiopia, and there is also a Sudan race (*R. r. cottoni*) with very widespread horns. By far the most common is the eastern bohor (*R. r. wardi*) of Kenya, Uganda, and Tanzania. These live singly, in pairs, or very small family groups wherever grass and wetland-edge vegetation is tall or lush enough to conceal them. Perhaps they are much more numerous than generally believed, because of

Exhibiting the characteristic trait of the species, a southern reedbuck stands motionless in the face of possible danger (in this instance, only a photographer). Even the swarm of insects does not disturb its statuesque pose.

their furtive (and possibly nocturnal) habits. When a bohor is flushed, it runs with a unique rocking-horse motion, usually toward the closest dense cover.

The southern reedbuck, *Redunca arundinum,* is larger than the bohor. Its range begins in Tanzania and extends southward along the South African Indian Ocean coast. It is quite abundant in coastal Zululand, preferring treeless, grassy country along rivers, and near water no matter where it lives. The southern species has the same habit of sitting or standing motionless, rather than flushing, in the face of potential danger.

Smallest and most gregarious of the reedbuck species is the mountain variety, *Redunca fulvorufula.* Bohors and southerns are comparable to whitetail deer in size, but mountain reedbuck seldom exceed sixty or sixty-five pounds. In herds of as many as ten head, they live in widely separated ranges. Chanler's mountain reedbuck (*R. f. chanleri*) is found in the broken, rocky highlands from Ethiopia to Kenya. The southern mountain race (*R. f. fulvorufula*) is scattered across a similar habitat south of the Limpopo River. A third even smaller mountain reedbuck has been found isolated in the Adamawa Mountains of Cameroons.

Because the two at times share the same habitat in hilly southern South Africa, the mountain reedbuck might be confused with the vaal rhebok, which though actually slightly smaller is similar in size, behavior and habitat preference. Rhebok tend to be more

grayish in color, to live in larger groups (at times to twenty or twenty-five head in a herd) and to prefer higher, more open country.

Vaal rhebok, *Pelea Capreolus,* are slender of build with thick, woolly hair and meat that is not considered edible. Males have short, straight, vertical, and parallel horns. They are pugnacious among themselves, but almost certainly do not attack domestic sheep, goats and mountain reedbucks as they have been accused of doing.

If there is a category of African antelopes which might not be considered handsome, it is the family Alcelaphinae which includes the hartebeests and the wildebeests. These are of medium size and possess some peculiar features. All may appear clumsy and stupid, but this is deceptive. The most noticeable features are the long narrow faces and withers, which are much higher off the ground than the rumps. All are gregarious, live in large herds with high reproductive potential, and appear remotely horse-like. All species considered together, the family inhabits a major portion of the continent.

The common hartebeest, or kongoni, *Alcelaphus buselaphus,* is an antelope averaging 300 pounds and including several races or subspecies about which mammalogists have never agreed. All are uniform fawn to rich brown in color, with horns which curve out, up and back, or vice versa. The strange shape of horns on top of the elongated face is slightly ludicrous at close range, although the whole animal is very tenacious and can generate good speed when that is necessary to outrun a pride of lions.

Coke's hartebeest (*A. b. cokii*) of Kenya and Tanzania, and Jackson's hartebeest (*A. b. jacksoni*) of Uganda and Kenya are the two sub-

to consider. The red hartebeest, *Alcolaphus caama,* is a richly colored antelope of south Africa from the Cape of Good Hope to Southwest Africa, Botswana, Transvaal, and the Orange Free State. By 1875 this species was nearly extinct but since has become abundant both in parks and on some private lands. A large red hartebeest bull, probably stimulated by the rut, was one of the few animals ever to have charged me with apparently no provocation. The place was Giant's Castle, Natal, and the result was a footrace toward a jeep which, although carrying cameras, I barely won.

Lichtenstein's hartebeest, *Alcelaphus lichtensteini,* which inhabits mopane woodlands from Tanzania to Mozambique, is considered by many to be the most stupid looking of its clan. Males of the species can also be among the most fascinating. They are highly territorial, selecting mounds (in the territory center) on which to rub the sides of their heads, to urinate, and prance in a comic manner when another animal approaches. Once near Mikumi, Tanzania, I saw a Lichtenstein's bull firmly stand its ground on a mound while a herd of a dozen elephants passed close on both sides of it. The animal only snorted loudly and this the tuskers ignored.

The topi, *Damaliscus korrigum topi,* is one of the most abundant and familiar antelopes of east and central Africa. Topis are highly gregarious, gathering in vast herds. Their close relationship to the common hartebeests is evident in their awkward and angular

species best known to hunters and cameramen in eastern Africa. In central Africa there are lelwel and Roosevelt hartebeests, and maybe others according to some authorities. The hartebeest of western Africa is *A. b. major;* the rare and vanishing Swayne's (*A. b. swaynei*) lives in Ethiopia and Somalia. And the typical race (*A. b. busephalus*) once widespread in northwest Africa has long been extinct.

There are yet more species of hartebeest

Related to the hartebeest, the topi is seen in large herds in east and central Africa; it is one of the most abundant antelope in the region.

appearance. But topis are richer, metallic copper-red in color, and the ridged lyrate horns are more attractive. During the rut, males settle on individual stamping grounds which they spend a good bit of energy defending. Once in Kenya, Frank Sayers and I came upon a pair of bulls so busy fighting that neither saw the lion crouching closer and closer in tall grass less than one hundred feet away. Our own approach in a jeep flushed the lion and probably saved the life of one bull.

Another kind of topi called korrigum, *D. k. korrigum,* is larger, has a reddish-orange coat and lives from Senegal to western Sudan. The tiang, *D. k. tiang,* of Sudan and southwest Ethiopia is smaller, rufous brown with purplish tinge, and much shorter horns. All of the topis prefer open savannas or parklike woodlands, where they are not difficult to hunt.

Damaliscus lunatus, the tsessebe (or sassaby), is a 300-pound antelope resembling the topi which is less gregarious. Small herds of eight head or so are most common. It's a resident of flats and swampy flood plains in Botswana, eastern Mozambique and Zululand. Strictly a grazer, the tsessebe may be the fastest of all African antelopes, particularly over long distances.

Two darker antelopes superficially resembling the topi and tsessebe are the bontebok (*Damasliscus pygargus*) and the blesbok (*Damaliscus albifrons*), look-alikes of South Africa. The coat of the bontebok has a glistening metallic sheen which changes from purplish to reddish-brown in different lights. It is pure white on the lower legs, face and rump. The blesbok is smaller and paler in color.

Both the bontebok and blesbok once hovered on the edge of oblivion. The former was numerous more than a century ago within the restricted range of southwest Cape Province.

Their coats glistening in the sun, two bonteboks cast a curious glance at an intruder on the plain near Cape of Good Hope.

But hunting and agriculture reduced the number to less than one hundred animals until a few landowners became alarmed and a national park just for the species was created. Today, the population exceeds 1,500 and under protection is increasing on private lands.

The blesbok's range was less limited and historically the species itself was more abundant. Still, it was once seriously reduced and only during recent decades has the animal become plentiful enough to be hunted again in Transvaal, Orange Free State and western Natal.

Conservationists everywhere are seriously concerned about *Damaliscus hunteri,* Hunter's hartebeest, the most graceful and lightly built antelope of the topi-hartebeest variety. A species of open grassy plains and dry thornbush country, its range today is nevertheless restricted to a narrow strip of semi-desert thorn scrub in the Garissa District, Kenya, or from the Tana River north to the Juba River in Somalia. Less than 1,000 survive in Kenya, and possibly all have disappeared in Somalia.

At this writing, the survivors have been threatened by a scheme to resettle 75,000 African families on lands just south of the Tana. But a spillover to the north certainly would occur, plus poaching, putting more pressure on these shy antelopes. An attempt has been made via plane, naval vessel and helicopter to trap, transfer and try to establish Hunter's hartebeest in Tsano National Park. So far it has been unsuccessful.

Blue wildebeest are a familiar part of the land-scape in Kenya and Tanzania. These antelope are an important prey of lions and hyenas.

The brindled gnu, or blue wildebeest, *Connochaetes taurinus,* is one of Africa's unmistakable, most easily seen antelopes. The ox-like animal with massive shoulders, sloping back and flattened bristly muzzle occurs in huge numbers on Kenya's and Tanzania's plains, particularly in the plains national parks. Herds of many hundreds usually associated with zebras, Grant's and Thomson's gazelles are commonplace. The southern race (*C. t. taurinus*) has a black beard; the northern subspecies which ranges from central Tanzania northward has a light gray beard.

Wildebeests are migratory, traveling in scattered formations to search for food and water. Often herd numbers are so large that they rapidly graze down all the grasses in an area and must continue on. They move day and night, sometimes more than thirty miles in a day when water supplies are short. During the rut, a few dominant males keep the cows herded in tighter groups, each driving away other bulls from their own section of the herd.

In some regions, wildebeest supply more than half the diet of local lions and perhaps even more than that of spotted hyenas, hunting dogs and cheetahs. All of these predators take a heavy toll of newly born calves, sometimes capturing them as soon as they are dropped by the females.

The white-tailed gnu or black wildebeest, *Connochaetes gnou,* is a large and somewhat grotesque antelope peculiar to South Africa. Except for a long white tail, it is dirty blackish in color, weighs about 300 pounds full grown, and has outward then upward curving horns. The species is another which was once numerous, having associated in vast aggregations with quaggas (extinct) and ostriches over South Africa's central plateau. But they were

aggressive and unwary, easy marks for Boer farmers who systematically tried to eliminate them and almost succeeded. In 1948 less than 1,000 remained and the number later dropped lower. Today the animal receives protection on many ranches and a number of wildlife reserves so that although in small supply, it is no longer endangered.

Africa contains many antelopes which are remarkable examples of adaptation to specific habitats. Of these, the gerenuk, *Litocranius walleri,* is most outstanding. The species is also known as giraffe gazelle because of its very long, thin legs and elongated neck, which make it possible to stretch out and browse high on tender tips of prickly bushes and trees in very dry or desert country. The animals are adept at standing on hind legs to stretch even farther, using their forelegs to bend and break off lower limbs.

The brown-eyed gerenuk, which is solitary or a member of a very small group, is bambi-like in appearance. It drinks very little and may require no water at all. When running, the long neck is stretched straight forward in line with the body for easier passage through dense thornbush.

An animal which somewhat resembles the gerenuk is *Ammodorcas clarkei,* the dibatag, which some authorities consider to be a reedbuck. It is long-necked but not so long as the gerenuk, and its smaller horns curve forward rather than backward. This is a fairly rare animal of eastern Ethiopia and Somalia, where overgrazing by domestic stock is turning the dibatag's habitat into barren, lifeless desert.

The impala, *Aepyceros melampus,* is among the most adaptable of antelopes, thriving in a variety of environments. Hunters on safari figure to encounter it almost anywhere, except very far from a steady source of water. Impala bulls collect harems of fifteen to twenty females with which they consort. Groups of bachelors also travel together and fight noisily among themselves during the rutting season, perhaps to no avail.

Few animals anywhere are as graceful and sure-footed as impalas, which can make prodigious leaps of thirty feet almost from a standing start. The sight of a startled herd of impalas in flight, many jumping over others at the same time, is poetry in motion and one of Africa's most beautiful sights.

Impalas are similar to whitetails in size and are rufous-fawn in color with paler flanks. The southern impala (*A. m. melampus*) ranges

Blue wildebeest often mingle with zebras and gazelles in herds so large that they quickly overgraze a range and must move every day.

Long-necked gerenuk, also known as the giraffe gazelle, is well equipped to browse on high, tender tips of trees in its arid habitat.

Among the most graceful animals in Africa is the impala (right and below), capable of leaping thirty feet from a standing position and jumping over one another when a herd takes flight.

from southern Tanzania, Congo and Zambia to South Africa. The east African race (*A. m. rendilis*) has the largest horns. An Angolan impala (*A. m. petersi*) has a dark mask on the face and a bushy tail.

The family Antilopinae is composed of medium to small, graceful gazelles, all capable of great speed and dwellers in open country, occasionally the driest of all open country. Their water requirements are ordinarily negligible, and though the group ranges from Africa across Arabia, to central Asia and India, Africa is really the gazelle continent.

Northernmost is the dama gazelle, *Gazella dama,* of the Sahara and sub-Sahara. It is an exquisite reddish animal with white face, belly and rump. It is also very rare nowadays. Damas often occur in mixed flocks of pale sand-colored, much smaller dorcas gazelles, *Gazella dorcas*.

Soemmering's gazelle, *Gazella soemmeringi,* is fairly large, pale fawn in color. It can somehow survive in the driest, bleakest habitat, but even this resourceful antelope is being forced from its natural range in Ethiopia and Somalia by the senseless overgrazing of domestic livestock and camels. During January 1969 I hunted for Soemmering's in formerly good country of eastern Ethiopia. But vast expanses of country there had been reduced to bare flats covered only by a layer of powdery dust. Camel caravans en route to water wells (at which gazelles could not drink) were detectable from miles away by the plumes of yellow dust. It was a terrifying example of how overgrazing can destroy a grassland, possibly forever.

Gazella granti, Grant's gazelle, is soon familiar to every east African visitor. It is handsome, abundant, and in the parks not very shy or difficult to approach at close range. Several

256

Handsome little antelope of east Africa is the Grant's gazelle, abundant in the parks and easy to approach.

257

Above, rare dama gazelles of the northern deserts. Right, Thomson's gazelle of the Kenya plains.

races differing in shape or curvature of the horns exist. *G. g. granti* belongs to the Serengeti region. Robert's gazelle, *G. g. robertsi,* has the most widely diverging horns. Bright's gazelle, *G. g. brighti,* roams Uganda's Karamoja and Kenya's northern Turkana. *G. g. lacuum* is from Ethiopia, *G. g. petersi* from the Kenya coastal districts, and *G. g. raineyi* belongs in Somalia. Living habits of all are at least very similar, every one being gregarious.

The Dorcas gazelle already mentioned is marvelously adapted both in color and physique to survive in North Africa's desert and eastward into Israel, Syria and Arabia. But because of shooting (*not* sports hunting) pressure, it is not doing well anywhere. If it survives at all in Asia, small bands may still roam Israel's Sinai, or there may be isolated groups in the rockiest, least accessible portions of Arabia's desert. A subspecies, *Gazella dorcas isabella,* the Isabelline gazelle, is restricted to Ethiopia and Sudan.

Pelzeln's gazelle, *Gazella pelzelni,* of Somalia's Gulf of Aden coast is now very scarce. Rarer still is the rhim or slender-horned gazelle, *Gazella leptoceros,* including the Arabian race, *G. l. marica.* These are very light in color, almost white, and possess splayed hooves for convenient travel over sand. That has not spared the species from over-shooting. They are now gravely endangered.

The red-fronted gazelle, *Gazella rufifrons,* is another sub-Saharan species with a future in doubt. So is Speke's, *Gazella spekei,* of interior Somalia. The status of the handsome Thomson's gazelle, *Gazella thomsoni,* fortunately is far brighter. The tiny Tommy still exists in good numbers throughout most of Kenya's plains country and is a common animal in the parks. Tommies often mix with Grant's, zebras and other plains species.

The most abundant antelope in southern Africa is the springbok, *Antidorcas marsupialis,* the only gazelle found south of the Zambesi River. It is highly gregarious, literally swarming in huge herds. At Etosha Game Park I have seen springbok extending from nearby almost to the horizon. The species is small, weighing no more than seventy pounds, and nearly silent. When frightened, surprised, and maybe at times for their own amusement, springbok bound into the air as high as ten feet, repeating this bouncing (called "pronking") several times. At the same time, they arch their backs and expose a fan of pure white hairs on the rump. The spectacle of several springbok in a herd pronking at one time is unique and exciting.

Before settlement of South Africa, springbok existed in such numbers that during mi-

grations in search of food or water the density of the packs caused some to be trampled to death. At intervals of several years there were enormous losses due to drowning, malnutrition, disease, or from drinking saltwater when reaching the seashore. This was a natural control for overpopulation and could best be compared to the Arctic lemming's migration to the sea. Today, the surplus of springbok numbers is taken by hunters because the meat is extremely good.

A few other African mammals might be considered in this chapter, although it is difficult to look upon them as big game. There are the numerous and varied species of duikers, for example. Add also the oribi, klipspringer, steinbok, and the grysboks. With or without them, the list of the continent's antelopes is long and impressive.

Tiny springbok, only gazelle found south of the Zambesi River, forms large herds; when frightened, it bounds high in the air (below).

Other African Big Game

Besides the Big Five of dangerous game and the antelopes, Africa is the home of several other contrasting species of big game. Heading the list are the wild sheep and the ibex of the family Caprinae.

The Red Sea hills of Eritrea and Sudan from near sea level to 6,000 feet are the home of Nubian ibex, *Capra ibex nubiana*. A few also survive in the Sinai Peninsula and possibly in Arabia. This is a wild goat with horns carried by both sexes, which are much longer and heavier on the males. Horns of billies may exceed three feet. Nubian ibex live on the steep cliffs and mountain slopes in dry, blazing hot desert country which can be an ordeal to hunt. The species lives in small herds, with the males being solitary most of the time. They move about and feed when the sun is low, but spend daytimes in the shade of caves or crevices.

By contrast, the walia ibex, *Capra ibex walie,* lives in a damp cool environment on top of Ethiopia. The rare species is confined to thin ledges, crags and sheer cliff faces 8,000 to 11,000 feet high on the northwestern escarpment of the Semien Mountains, one of the most spectacular mountain massifs on earth. At one point vertical precipices from 2,000 feet to nearly a mile high stretch unbroken for twenty-five miles. The few outsiders who have seen both consider it more awesome than the Grand Canyon. Yet the formidable landscape has not been protection enough for the walia ibex, because of intense grazing and farming of the plateau on top.

Today the walia ibex is among the rarest of all mammals. An estimated 150 survive in an area which desperately needs national park status. The Nubian ibex are not doing much better, and their population in Eritrea is estimated at 300. In this case uncontrolled shooting, most of it by "liberation guerillas" is responsible.

The status of the barbary sheep or aoudad, *Ammotragus lervia,* is more secure than that of the ibex for two important reasons. Their natural range in the hot and rocky mountains of the Sahara is extremely remote and away from beaten paths. And it is impassable even to four-wheel drive vehicles, a factor which has excluded the military vehicles which have decimated other Saharan game.

Barbary sheep are excellent climbers and jumpers, at home in the most terrible terrain. They are most active at night, sifting down into valleys to graze and browse, and then retreating at daybreak toward higher ground. There in desert shadows aoudads are virtually impossible to see because their coats blend so perfectly into their backgrounds. In addition to the natural camouflage, this sheep's hearing and eyesight are keen.

Aoudads are sandy brown in color and the soft hair is long; on the chest, it is apron-like. Weights of 200 to 250 pounds are attained by males which grow massive enough horns to be valuable trophies. It is ironic, however, that trophy hunting for barbary sheep in the future may be best in New Mexico and on many Texas ranches where the species has been established.

One or just possibly two deer exist in Africa. Barbary deer, *Cervus elaphus barbarus,* once ranged from Morocco to Tunisia. A few survived World War II in Algeria, but none have been observed anywhere since the late 1960s. The subspecies is probably extinct. Fallow deer, *Dama dama,* have been

High in the hot and rocky mountains of the Sahara, the barbary sheep have managed to escape the fate of other African game. Not even a four-wheel-drive vehicle can penetrate their remote habitat.

introduced onto some ranches in Transvaal, South Africa, where some hunting is done.

One of the continent's most unusual and least elegant animals is the warthog, *Phacochoerus aethiopicus,* a wild pig with enormous flattened head covered with tubercles or warts. The species is unmistakable, sure to be seen by anyone on safari because it exists over most of central and eastern Africa. Adults weigh more than 100 pounds and males have been weighed at nearly 300.

Warthogs are grazers of fairly open country. They sleep, take refuge and raise young in aardvark and ardwolf burrows, which they enter backwards. Some of their habits are comical. When grass is very short, warthogs drop down on foreknees to feed. They travel in family groups, or sounders, and when alarmed all run off with tails erected as stiffly as antennae. Apparently a warthog's sight is poor because when the wind is right, it is possible to approach very close. But their senses of smell and hearing are good. Warthogs are very prolific, as they have to be, because the species is an important prey of all the major predators.

An abundant resident of high or mountain forests and dense bush is the bushpig, *Potamochoerus porcus.* It is smaller than the warthog and resembles domestic swine. Bushpigs gather in larger sounders of from twenty animals (the usual number) to fifty head. They are omnivorous, eating everything from insects, reptiles and carrion to succulent grasses, roots and

Warthogs are found in open country over most of central and eastern Africa. These two have dropped to their knees to feed in short grass—a characteristic habit of the species.

farm crops. Bushpigs can be very destructive to truck gardens because they multiply rapidly where leopards and other natural predators have been eliminated. This is an important prey species, but as a group it is formidable and capable of driving a leopard away.

The giant forest hog, *Hylochoerus mein-ertzhageni,* is a huge, powerfully built pig which weighs up to 500 pounds. Because it is restricted to the most dense forests of central and eastern Africa, it is seldom seen and little is known about its habits. An occasional hog is observed at Treetops, Kenya, but almost nowhere else. It is most likely a nocturnal spe-

cies which leaves less sign than other pigs because it seldom roots for food. However, it follows regular pathways through the dense forests, leaving tunnels which are telltale evidence of its existence there.

Sus scrofa, the Old World wild boar, once probably roamed across northern Africa but today its survival is doubtful. The Egyptian boar, *S. s. sennaarensis,* only exists today as a mixture with feral hogs in Sudan.

Zebras may or may not be considered as big-game animals, but they are hunted and their striking presence is so important on the

266

African scene that they should at least be listed here. Except for the wild ass, all are distinctively striped. They are highly sociable, prolific, citizens of open plains or bush, rather than forest.

Both the Nubian and Somali races of the wild ass, *Equus asinus,* are rare and rapidly disappearing. Grevy's zebra, *Equus grevyi,* of northern Kenya and southern Ethiopia is the most exquisitely patterned, with thin stripes on a white body. Burchell's zebra, *Equus burchelli,* has broader black stripes and the greatest range of all from Kenya to Mozambique. A subspecies, Chapman's (*E. b. antiquorum*), is buff-colored on the back and neck and has buff shadow stripes between the black bars on the rump. Two races of the mountain zebra, *Equus zebra,* live in isolated areas of high country in South and Southwest Africa.

The cheetah, *Acinonyx jubatus,* fits the big-game category, but for no reason should it be hunted except with camera. It is an unusual sway-backed cat with many canine features. More than any other animal it resembles the leopard (with which it has been confused), but the long, thin legs and smaller head should make it unmistakable even at a distance.

The cheetah is one of eastern and southern Africa's rarest jewels. It is more graceful than a greyhound, and swifter than the human eye can follow. Few birds can fly as fast as a cheetah can run for two hundred yards or so, which makes it the fastest animal on earth.

Whereas a leopard's spots are really rosettes, a cheetah's spots are solid black. The two animals are about the same length from nose to tip of tail, but the cheetah is taller at the front shoulder. Even when full-grown, a cheetah seldom weighs more than 120 pounds. It is not nearly as sinister looking as the leopard because the yellow-brown eyes are almost mild in appearance. Pronounced black "tear" lines extend from the front of the eyes to the muzzle. There is a short, wiry mane behind the shoulder which is most pronounced on old males. The tail is ringed and has a white tip. Neither the jaws nor the bridgework are as powerful as the leopard's.

Although cheetahs are far less common than leopards, they can be more easily seen and photographed because they are diurnal in habits. Of all the world's large cats, only the lion is more frequently observed.

A cheetah's success in hunting depends on a combination of surprise and bewildering speed, because it lives in open plains country where ambush is difficult. Cheetahs are never found in dense bush or jungle. First, the animal tries to stalk as close as possible to its target, using tall grass or some such natural feature as a gully or depression for concealment. Then it races for the victim, trips it up, seizes it by the throat, and strangles it to death.

The cheetah is not always successful, however, and the odds may be fairly low. Many of the small antelopes which the cheetah preys upon are also very fast. Unless they can be caught within two hundred or three hundred yards, they normally outdistance the cat, which has less endurance. Some of the very small antelopes, including dik-diks and steinbok, can elude a cheetah by dodging about as they flee.

I have never seen cheetahs in action as much as I would like, but once I held a ringside seat for an exciting and finally futile chase. The cat appeared to be a young one, and after stalking to within about forty yards of a band of Grant's gazelles, it began its deadly rush toward the nearest. In less than one hundred

More graceful than a greyhound, swifter than the human eye can follow, the cheetah is one of Africa's rarest jewels. Living on the open plains, the cat must stalk its prey where ambush is difficult and rely mainly on surprise and its bewildering speed.

yards, he caught a gazelle, and the two rolled over and over together in the grass. That should have been the end, but suddenly the gazelle broke away and ran, and the cheetah gave up, apparently too winded to follow.

Alongside its lack of stamina, another great handicap is the lack of retractable claws. The cheetah's are blunt and canine and so can be only partially withdrawn. If it weren't for the marks left by the cheetah's claws, it would be impossible to tell its pawprint from a leopard's. Both are the same size and shape.

Cheetahs have never been in conflict with man. There are no records of man-eaters, and they do not molest livestock. When wounded or cornered they are not known to retaliate, or do much more than snarl. The species is rather easily tamed; when captured young, they become fascinating, affectionate, and reliable pets. However, in captivity they seem to lack the intelligence of dogs or even of such wild pets as raccoons and other wild cats.

Unfortunately, cheetahs in the wild are a vanishing breed. (The cheetahs of Asia are already extinct.) They have never been seriously hunted in Africa, as have other cats, and have been protected for a long time almost everywhere. Still, the number declines and nobody can say exactly why. Fully grown cheetahs have no natural enemies except packs of hunting dogs which have sometimes run them to exhaustion. But young cheetahs are vulnerable to any predators which happen to come along.

Two to four cubs, or kittens, are born at any time of year. At first, they are plain smoky-gray balls of long, woolly fur. They utter a strange, birdlike chirp which sounds unnatural coming as it does from a cat. Eventually the chirp becomes a mew and purr. The gray color gradually blends into pale yellow as spots begin to appear, first on the legs and later on the body.

Although it seems completely contrary to their nature, there have been incidents of cannibalism among cheetahs. Records exist of males killing and eating kittens, and there is an instance of one cheetah eating another which had been caught in a poacher's trap.

No cheetah is very well equipped for climbing, but it is not unusual to see one perched in a low tree. Once I saw how they get up there. It was early morning in the Karamoja, and while glassing the landscape for a band of roan antelope which should have been in the vicinity, I spotted a cat walking at the base of a huge rockpile. There were several umbrella-shaped trees nearby. Because at that distance its spots blended into its body, I decided it was a lioness. But I was surprised when the "lioness" made a mighty leap upward onto a branch directly over her head. It wasn't until I moved much closer that the cat in the tree became a cheetah. Unfortunately I didn't get close enough for a picture before the cat dropped down and vanished into the bush.

How fast can a cheetah really run? Some Africans swear it is so fast that the animal's feet never touch the ground. Estimates of its speed have been as much as one hundred miles an hour. An experiment halfway around the world from the cheetah's natural range, however, found the truth.

The laboratory was a Florida dog-racing track in the United States. The cheetah used

Serval is a small east African cat that is nocturnal in its habits but may be encountered during the day. Weighing about forty pounds, the serval has a handsome, spotted coat and over-large ears.

Although hardly entitled to be called a game animal, the hippo has multiplied in certain areas to the extent that it has had to be hunted for its own good. Both in the water and on land, the hippo is dangerous.

in the experiment had been born and raised in captivity but had been kept in good physical condition by regular workouts. During a half-mile sprint, the cat briefly exceeded seventy miles per hour, which was faster than any greyhound or any other animal could ever do.

Two other African cats, the caracal or African lynx, *Felis caracal*, and the serval, *Felis serval,* may be of some interest and importance to hunters. The caracal has long, distinctive ear tufts, and the serval is handsomely spotted. Top weight for both is about forty or forty-five pounds and although the two species are nocturnal it is not unusual to encounter them in eastern Africa.

Not exactly a big-game species is the hippopotamus, *Hippopotamus amphibius,* a huge, fat, aquatic animal which has recently had to be hunted for its own good. In many of the national parks, hippos have multiplied to the extent that they have damaged and even destroyed their own habitat.

Hippos once lived in all permanent water areas of central and eastern Africa as far southward as St. Lucia, Zululand. Today the range is limited to places where human population is small, where there is little agriculture (with which hippos are not at all compatible, since they relish everything from pumpkins and maize to radishes and castor beans), and inside the boundaries of national parks. The best places to see hippos today are at Mzima Springs, Tsavo National Park, in the Nile below Murchison Falls, and Queen Elizabeth Park.

Hippos average a ton in weight and may reach two and a half tons. They are gregarious, living in herds of from twenty to thirty or more, and sedentary, staying in a particular place to which they have become attached. Hippos in Africa may account for more human deaths and injuries than all the so-called dangerous five put together: the hippopotamus ranges far on land at night to graze, and encountered at this time, it may become very aggressive. When tormented by poachers, hippos can overturn small boats and attack the occupants in the water. Hippo-poaching, in fact, is a high-risk occupation. Young hippos are likely prey for lions and especially crocodiles.

Asia

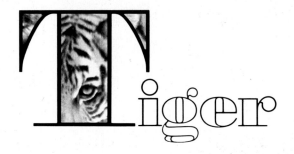Tiger

THE SOFT Indian twilight had faded into dusk when a sixth sense warned me that I was no longer alone. Not a twig cracked. No birds or monkeys sounded an alarm as they often do. No living thing moved, and from my confined quarters in the crown of a tree I only dimly saw the carcass of a buffalo on the ground below. But all at once I forgot my complaining muscles and the insects whining about my ears: I felt the first symptoms of buck fever.

Time passed so slowly then that I decided my sixth sense was all wrong. The buck fever all but disappeared. It wasn't until I capped a telephoto lens, preparatory to leaving the blind, that I saw the tiger. It appeared beside the kill below as suddenly and as silently as a figure projected onto a screen in a darkroom. A moment later it was tearing flesh from the buffalo's flank.

The loud noise I heard was not the tiger, but my own heart pounding.

Only seconds after it began to feed, the big yellow cat turned to look directly at me, hesitated, and then evaporated into the dark jungle. That's all there was to it. All daylight was gone before I felt calm enough to climb down from the tree, a few years older.

Brief as the encounter was, it remains unforgettable. That was my first glimpse of one of the most splendid animals on earth. The tiger is a species which fewer and fewer sportsmen will ever see in the wild as I did, not even in a national park or game refuge. And sadly, that is the same fate of most big game on the Asian continent, as we will see.

As recently as a quarter-century ago, a sportsman could travel to India and without spending too much time or suffering any

Shading itself beneath a shattered tree trunk, a tiger rests between hunting forays. This species originated in northern Asia. As its adaptation to the tropical climate of Southeast Asia and India is not yet complete, the cat hunts nocturnally, spending the day trying to stay cool.

hardship, enjoy a shikar for tigers with other game thrown in. Chances were good that if he could shoot straight, he would return home with at least one handsome striped rug. But those days are gone forever, because tiger hunting belongs to a happier past.

One by one the various states of India, which along with Nepal is the last stronghold of the species, enacted legislation to prohibit killing the big cats. In most cases there were none or very few tigers left to kill. In some states, the legislation resulted from a belated twinge of conscience for allowing such a magnificent animal to reach the brink of extinction.

In the history of man, few animals have so greatly excited human imagination. Some native peoples regard the tiger with awe and terror, as a punishing God to be appeased. The species is big, powerful, exquisitely beautiful, and potentially dangerous. Once it was also very abundant. There have been many man-eating tigers, and stories about them are well known around the world. At one time no one could really claim to be a big-game hunter until he had traveled to India for tigers, hopefully to account for one of the man-eaters.

Here was one kind of wildlife which any schoolboy could readily identify in the zoo, in a circus, or a textbook. Remember Little Black Sambo and the tigers? And in recent years the mystique of the big striped cats has been used extensively in advertising.

Yet few animals are so little known and understood, even this late, in the last phase of their existence.

The tiger, *Panthera tigris,* is a native of Asia and no other continent. The genus *Panthera* includes lions, jaguars and leopards, all large cats characterized by a larynx which is attached to the skull by long hyoid ligaments. This adaptation for swallowing large masses of unchewed food enables a tiger to down a chunk of raw meat weighing three pounds or more.

Although we normally consider the tiger as purely Indian, seven separate races or sub-species once ranged completely across Asia from southeastern Iran through Afghanistan, Nepal, most of India, Burma, Malaysia and Indochina to Indonesia. Northward it extended into Korea, across China, and into Manchuria and portions of Siberia. Of all the world's great cats, only the leopard had a greater original range, being a resident of most of Africa as well as Asia.

The tiger is very adaptable. Within its range, it occupies a variety of habitats from rain forest to humid mangrove swamps and from cold coniferous woodlands to arid semi-desert scrub. Tigers have been tracked in Himalayan snows as high as 10,000 feet and on tropical saltwater beaches of the Malabar Coast. But the species is most at home in deep forest shadows. Its behavior varies slightly in these different environments, but no matter where it lives, the constant search for food consumes nearly all of the tiger's life.

It would appear that a tiger's life is easy, what with its splendid physique and arsenal of weapons. Its senses are acute, especially its short-range vision and hearing. A tiger can easily clear a seven-foot fence, cover twenty feet in a single bound, climb a tree, or swim. It has great speed (although only for short sprints) and possesses formidable claws and teeth. Only the sense of smell is poorly developed, and this is used more to find a mate than

Eyes fixed and ears up, two tigers (left and below) prowl through underbrush. It is these two highly developed senses —vision and hearing—that tigers rely on in hunting; their sense of smell is quite poor.

a meal. It probably is not as intelligent or re-sourceful as the leopard.

A tiger needs near-perfect cover conditions to make a low, crouched, fluid stalk. Most stalks must be made on other animals whose senses are equally acute and which are even faster afoot for long distances. That means the tiger must approach very near before making its move on a nervous target. According to old-time hunter Jim Corbett, author of the classic adventure *Man-Eaters of Kumaon,* a tiger might make a dozen unsuccessful attempts be-fore finally catching a meal. Other qualified observers believe the success ratio is even lower.

Actually there have been very, very few close observers of the tiger except over the barrel of a rifle, and this is no way to learn much about a creature which is very shy and retiring. Unlike more gregarious, open coun-try lions, tigers normally travel and hunt alone, tending to stay in dense cover. They try to avoid man as much as possible, so much so that natives who have lived their entire lives in tiger country never see one. Even tigers pro-tected in parks do not grow to trust man as do the lions in East African game reserves. The same striped coat which is so conspicuous and eye catching in a cage or compound blends very well into the animal's lush background. It is very easy to look directly at a tiger with-out seeing it.

Probably the best qualified living observer of the Indian tiger is a young biologist, George Schaller of Johns Hopkins University and au-thor of the bestselling *Year of the Gorilla.* Schaller spent a good deal of time in Kanha National Park of Madhya Pradesh state, cen-tral India, practically living with the tigers which find sanctuary there.

Too few sportsmen and tourists ever see Kanha. Most international travelers visit the Taj Mahal, the burning ghats of Benares, and similar examples of India's extravagant past, but there is no more lovely place on the entire subcontinent than Kanha, with its open mai-dans, sal trees and cool rest houses. Here is one of those rare retreats in India, only ninety-seven square miles in size, not yet devastated by humans, and where the wildlife still exists as it did centuries ago. It is also one of the few places left on earth where a person can see a tiger in the wild, and even at Kanha that is an uncertain proposition. (No doubt the best place to see and photograph tigers in the wild is Tigertops near Meghauli, Nepal.)

Schaller learned much about tigers that here-tofore has been either unknown or misunder-stood. For example, they are not the cunning wanton killers, either of other animals or of humans, depicted in some literature and folk-lore. When a tiger makes a kill, it is only for food and its entire life focuses on the dead car-cass. The cat (often its friends and family as well) lives and sleeps near the kill until every last rotting scrap of it, including viscera and hooves, is eaten. Sometimes the tiger will drag the carcass into a ravine or depression and cover it with earth or debris for concealment. But covered or not, the cat must always remain nearby to drive away such scavengers as the jackals, hyenas, crows and vultures which soon appear.

How long a tiger lingers by the kill depends on its size and not upon the degree of spoilage under the hot Indian sun. An adult chital (the spotted or axis deer) which may weigh more than one hundred pounds might last one cat three days. A larger sambar or a swamp deer lasts twice that long. Or the tiger may actually spend weeks in the vicinity of such a larger kill as a gaur or buffalo, although adult bulls of these wild oxen may be more than a tiger can handle.

In areas where hunting pressure has long been heavy, tigers behave differently. There they have learned to feed on the prey only immediately after it has been killed; then they abandon it. There is good reason for this behavior, because one very effective hunting method involves locating a tiger kill by watching for vultures circling overhead and then building a machan or tree blind nearby, overlooking the kill. There the hunter waits for a shot at the tiger the next time it returns to refuel. Apparently tigers in certain localities have learned to avoid this trap.

In carefully checking the remains of 200 deer killed by Kanha tigers, Schaller found that many were young or old, while proportionately few were in the prime of life. The main exceptions were hinds carrying fawns and therefore less able to escape. As elsewhere, the big predators eliminated the least fit, easiest-to-catch prey.

As soon as a carcass has been devoured, the tiger must begin hunting again. This usually occurs between twilight and daybreak. However, a tiger will not pass up the opportunity to make a kill in daylight and in sanctuaries does considerable hunting before nightfall. It appears that most hunting is done in the same familiar area or territory by roughly following the same circuit, which may cover between fifteen to twenty miles between dusk and dawn. Exactly how far depends on the abundance of the prey: the less abundant, the greater the distance. Anything is fair game, alive or dead, including everything from jungle fowl and peafowl to wild boar, monkeys, and any of the native deer or antelopes. Young elephants have been fair prey. Neither will tigers pass up frogs, bird eggs and probably some reptiles.

Almost everywhere in India nowadays, a tiger depends at least in part on domestic cattle or buffalos for food. In certain heavily populated regions the tiger may rely on domestic stock for nearly *all* of its food, which does not endear the killer to villagers who themselves are always desperately hungry. Even in Kanha Park where, during the dry season, some 800 head of game are concentrated (and vulnerable to predators) in the five square miles near the only available water, Schaller estimates that ten percent of all cattle grazing on the fringes of the park are eaten by tigers each year.

A mature tiger needs between fifteen and twenty pounds of meat per day (or about three and one-half tons per year) to stay in prime condition. Since about a third of each prey animal is composed of large bones, stomach contents, and other inedible matter, a tiger must kill about four and one-half tons of live animals annually to survive. Theoretically each tiger must kill either seventy adult chital (the most common wild deer), thirty domestic cattle, or some equivalent combination. The kill might have to run even higher than that; for instance, a female may have the great burden to kill for and feed as many as three or four cubs besides herself. And in some places, natives who find a kill drive the cat away and eat the meat themselves. These kill statistics are most important to the tiger's future, and we will refer to them later.

In common with most big-game animals, the dimensions of tigers have been grossly exaggerated. Old accounts speak of large specimens which measured thirteen feet and more from nose to tip of tail. But the official Indian Field Shikar Book lists fewer than twenty trophies slightly exceeding ten feet long. The average large male will measure nine feet six inches long and weigh about 425 pounds. Females average smaller. An especially large prime male might tip the scales at as much as 600 pounds after feeding heavily. Tigers are figured to reach prime at five years and remain so for ten more, after which a rapid decline begins. But in open hunting areas during the past decades, few ever reach a ripe old age.

George Schaller was surprised to find that tigers are not as solitary as many authorities have claimed them to be. On many occasions he noticed that after a tigress would make a kill, others (not necessarily members of the family) would show up to share it. And cubs normally travel with their mother until nearly full grown, at which point they are still unable to fend for themselves. Some cubs may depend on their mother for as long as two years, or until she comes into estrus again and drives them away. That means there is a long period with every litter when a female's ability as a hunter is sorely tested.

There is evidence that the strong pressure to feed a family of demanding cubs has driven some females to become man-eaters, the logic being that unarmed human beings are a lot easier to catch and kill than wild animals. But the old hunter of man-eaters, Jim Corbett, did not buy that theory intact. He agreed that man-eaters had to adopt an unnatural diet due to circumstances beyond their control. However, the circumstances Corbett found were festering or disabling wounds in nine out of ten cases, and in the tenth case, old age. The wounds may have been gunshot wounds from a careless hunter or injuries from the infected and imbedded quills of a porcupine.

A number of the man-eaters Corbett tracked down became famous far beyond the borders of India. One tigress known as the Champawat Man-Eater made 434 known human kills in Nepal and Kumaon during a four-year period. When Corbett finally caught up with the animal, he found that both her upper and lower jaws had been smashed by a bullet, making it almost impossible for her to kill natural prey.

Another tiger known as the Mohan Man-Eater, which Corbett killed in 1926, had had an early encounter with a porcupine. The hunter extracted more than twenty-five quills, some five inches long, from one leg and the chest of the tiger. That leg was virtually useless, and Corbett wrote that the flesh under the skin from the chest to the paw was dark yellow in color and soapy to the touch. The Mohan cat, which was slowly wasting away, actually moaned in pain when it walked.

Though Corbett had far more than one man's share of close calls with man-eaters, some of which stalked *him*, he had a tremendous regard for the species. He considered tigers gentle and harmless to man except in those cases when strange circumstances transformed them into man-killers. In the latter years of his life, the great old woodsman believed that tigers were doomed. He often wrote that they should not be hunted except with a camera. Corbett himself photographed some of the best motion picture footage ever taken of wild tigers in their natural habitat.

What exactly has happened to the species? Why is the Indian tiger in such serious trouble today? Why do the most educated current estimates place India's total population at less than 3,000? Just before World War II it was figured to be between 40,000 and 50,000, and perhaps the figure ran to 150,000 when the

Whether lying in a copse or slipping up a stream, tigers have proven adaptable to a variety of forestial environments. Tigers of tropical climates comprise one of the few cat groups with no fear of water; in fact, they use streams and lakes—and even oceans—to cool themselves.

country was first invaded by Europeans.

Shooting—hunting for sport—always appears to be the most obvious answer, and there is much in Indian history to support this. It is difficult for today's outdoorsmen to comprehend the vast shoots held as recently as a century ago. These were organized by Indian royalty for royal guests and other VIPs. A single operation often employed thousands of beaters on foot and hundreds of elephants, which drove game of all sorts past hunters and whole batteries of guns. The toll was terrible, and thirty or more tigers might be slaughtered in a single hunt during which many square miles of real estate were scoured.

A few years ago the Maharaja of Surguja modestly noted that his own total bag of tigers was (up to that writing) 1,150. Tiger hunting naturally became a great pastime for rich nawabs and bored British colonial officials. During one typical four-year tour of duty between 1850 and 1854, one Major Rice, an army officer, wrote home that he "shot or wounded 158 tigers in Rajasthan state in his spare time." The Maharani of Jaipur at the time of this writing told an interviewer that she had shot twenty-five tigers before she was twenty-five years old. On a recent visit to the palace of the Maharaja of Wankaner in Gujarat, I found the vast, princely trophy rooms carpeted almost wall-to-wall with tiger skins, not all of them from trophy-size animals. Britain's King George V killed thirty-nine tigers on a single hunt in 1911.

Some of the early tiger shikars produced by Maharajahs and the other princes of India were more elaborate, colorful and expensive than even modern millionaire sportsmen can imagine. Near the selected hunting area, a huge camp containing hundreds of tents pitched on cleared ground and encircled by a canvas fence

was erected for honored guests. Oriental tapestry rugs covered the floors of the tents. Silk curtains hung inside. Outside the camp compound a fragrant, smoky bazaar soon sprang up to provide for the hundreds (sometimes thousands) of beaters, camp helpers, and followers.

A simple shikar banquet, probably served with sitar music under a vast open shamiyama, included curried wild boar, young peacock breasts, broiled partridges and venison pilau. If there were Europeans among the guests, the best champagne and brandy would flow freely. Ice was reportedly transported by bullock cart from the Himalayas to cool the champagne and sweets.

Perhaps the last of the splendid shikar extravaganzas was put on for Queen Elizabeth II, exactly one half-century after her grandfather's big shoot in 1911. The government of Nepal spent a fortune just to clear a two-mile square campsite, to exterminate all insects and snakes from the clearing, and to install electric generators and a sprinkling system. The Queen rode into the field astride the lead elephant, perched between the mahout and a servant holding a purple parasol over her head. Behind followed eighteen other hunting elephants carrying members of the entourage. And behind the tuskers, one observer counted twenty-five lorries and assorted motor transport, regal flags flying.

On her fourth try the Queen, it was reported, shot a small tigress, for which a good many of her majesty's subjects at home were not overjoyed. It was one of the rare occasions when humans showed any concern for tigers.

Within the past decade, it has been possible to arrange a mini-version of the elephant-back tiger shikar. A few maharajahs down on their finances went into the business commercially. But these hunts were extremely costly and most recent hunting by Europeans and North Americans used simpler methods. The most popular and productive technique was to tether a young buffalo to a tree in tiger territory, then wait nearby and overnight in a machan or blind. When a cat approached the buff to kill it, someone flashed a light on the spot and shot the tiger. Whether or not that proved exciting to the hunter, no sportsman ever forgets the tedious hours of darkness spent in the machan. It is roughly like spending the night in an upper berth of an old Pullman with a swarm of mosquitoes. Still, a hunter couldn't expect his tiger (if he scored) to cost less than $3,000 (in addition to air fare to and from India).

During the peaceful 1930s British administrators in India had time to become concerned about rapidly dwindling wildlife populations. Here and there sanctuaries were established and shooting restrictions were published, although these were not always rigidly enforced. Give the British credit everywhere for being the most concerned of all colonialists about wildlife conservation. This new concern gave the tigers a fresh lease on life, and for a time most of the cats killed were those collected on legal hunting trips for trophies by serious big-game hunters from North America and Europe. The total bag for a couple of decades wasn't terribly high.

When India gained independence in 1947, a disastrous time for the nation's wildlife began, particularly for the tiger. Any of the refuges and shooting regulations installed by the British were considered a form of detested colonial repression and ignored. Because this was a serious famine period (famines had already become chronic in India), the new gov-ernment issued arms and ammunition freely to farmers ostensibly to protect their crops from wild animals. However, most of the same Hindu farmers would not protect the same crops from their own sacred cattle. Any wildlife near cultivation was doomed, and for the next half-decade the slaughter of game continued unchecked.

Many old-timers will remember when India contained one of the richest and most varied wildlife communities on the face of the earth. Vast herds of hooved animals rivaled the number and variety on east and south African plains today. Included were many beautiful and unique species found nowhere else on earth. There was the antelope with four horns, for example, and the rhino with only one. By contrast, consider the tragic state of India's wildlife today.

Already extinct are the Indian cheetah, pygmy hog, hispid hare and pink-headed duck. Either extinct or nearly so are the great Indian bustard, the Nilghiri tahr, and the red goral. The list of very rare and very endangered species is long; it includes the barasinga (a swamp deer, about 150 remaining), the dhole or wild dog, brow-antlered deer (only about fifty survive), the onager or wild ass (about 700 left), snow leopard, clouded leopard, Asian lion (less than 150 left), Kashmir stag (about 200 surviving), chinkara or Indian gazelle, blackbuck, wild buffalo (few of pure wild stock remain), the great Indian one-horned rhino (300 survive in India and another 200 in Nepal) and, of course, *Panthera tigris tigris*.

It is easy to blame the deplorable situation on excessive shooting, because it *has* been excessive. But for the *real* cause, it's necessary to search elsewhere.

Wildlife biologists know that shooting alone,

particularly regulated trophy hunting as we now know it in America, seldom decimates a species. Birds and animals are renewable resources. Given a suitable habitat plus protection, they quickly bounce back to the carrying capacity of that habitat. Tigers especially will prosper and multiply where there is suitable cover and enough food to eat.

But there is neither cover nor food. The plight of the tiger is a direct result of India's frightening overpopulation, which all the time grows worse, and the total apathy of Indians towards their deteriorating environment.

To date, only token effort has been made to stem the human population rise, and it has been notably unsuccessful. Population densities average about 1,150 people per square mile on the Ganges Basin and are figured to double by the year 2000, when life there will be intolerable. An equal number of cattle wander about unmolested, eating everything that is green yet spared from slaughter by religious beliefs. Very little forest remains, and most of that is overgrazed and degraded. Erosion and the great western desert are moving inexorably eastward from West Pakistan, itself an impoverished country. Neither tigers nor human beings will be able to survive on such land.

There has been some belated sentiment in favor of setting up wildlife sanctuaries or national parks, and of enlarging the pitiful few which already exist. The Indian tiger would greatly benefit from this, although the motivation is perhaps more to promote tourism from abroad and a more favorable balance of payments at home than genuine interest in wildlife. Just the same, more wildlife sanctuaries are unpopular with both the mass of Indian people and with the politicians they elect to office. Even when a small wildlife area is set aside, there is massive protest. The timber cutting, cattle grazing and poaching continue as before. As a result the deer, antelope, boars and other animals which tigers require in large numbers are driven out. The tigers are thereby forced to kill native livestock, for which they are quickly sentenced to death.

If anything, tigers have fared even worse elsewhere than in India. In India the great cat is a victim of apathy and conflict with human interests. But in other areas the species is persecuted, hunted, and trapped just because it is believed capable of curing man's ills. The meat is in immense demand as a remedy for various kinds of stomach disorders; the pelt is valuable for ladies' garments.

Consider the following sixteenth-century Moslem treatise which lists the tiger pharmacopoeia: use brain and tiger "oil" to cure laziness and pimples; eat the gallstones for better vision; add dried tail to the bath as a skin balm; make pills from the eyes to stop convulsions; mix fat with roses for a face cream which will bring honor to the wearer; wear fangs, claws and whiskers as love charms or amulets to guard against danger. Not much is wasted. Although the treatise is 400 years old, its content is still, in this space age, believed valid by many Asians. It helps explain why the tiger is doing so poorly on that continent. Let's check to see exactly how the six other subspecies are doing in other parts of Asia.

Once the Chinese tiger, *P. t. amoyensis,* had a wide distribution in eastern, southern and central China, particularly in the large river basins and as far west as Szechwan and Kansu. Today this race is very scarce, if not actually extinct. No tigers here have ever been considered a serious menace to the vast human population, but tiger bones ground into powder are considered valuable medicine to give strength, courage and fertility.

Until World War II, the comparatively small Sumatran tiger, *P. t. sumatrae,* was not regarded as endangered. But after Indonesian independence, the big cats were hunted and trapped without restriction. If any survive, and there is no current information that they do, the survivors would exist in the more remote mountainous regions of the northern and southwestern parts of the island.

The Caspian tiger, *P. t. virgata,* is a medium to smallish dark colored cat with a range which once stretched from Transcaucasia and northern Iran, through Afghanistan to the Aral Sea and Lake Balkhash in the U.S.S.R. They are very rare in most of this area, and there have been few reports of tigers at all during the past twenty years. An estimated ten to fifteen animals are believed to survive in northeastern Iran and east of the Caspian Sea, although none have been seen since 1959. More than that are believed to exist in northern Afghanistan, but an expanded cotton agriculture and land clearing have eliminated much essential cover. It was earlier pointed out that each tiger needs a great number of prey animals on which to exist, and these prey animals (except possibly wild boars) have been almost eliminated in much of the Caspian tiger's original range. The outlook is grim.

The Siberian tiger, *P. t. altaica,* is the largest of all the races, occasionally measuring thirteen feet long and weighing almost 600 pounds. It is long-haired and nomadic. As recently as the turn of the century, it ranged over much of eastern Siberia, into Manchuria and Korea. Today an estimated one hundred survive in Siberia, mostly in the vicinity of the Ussuri

River, where the species now is fully protected. Two large reserves totaling 600,000 acres have been set aside for protection. But it is ominous to note that only two sets of tracks of wandering tigers were observed there since 1964. No tigers have been seen in South Korea since 1960, and only about forty are figured to survive in the highlands surrounding Mt. Baekdu in North Korea.

The status of the Javan tiger, *P. t. sondaica,* isn't at all clear. The race may now be extinct, but as many as twenty may still exist on the Udjong Kulon and Betiri reserves, where poaching has always been a problem.

Authorities cannot agree on whether the Bali tiger, *P. t. balica,* was long ago introduced by man to that island from Java or whether it reached there unaided in prehistory. Its racial characteristics are quite different from the Javan subspecies. Very possibly it is extinct, although a few could survive in two national parks in extreme west Bali, where hunters from Java continue to poach.

The species appears to have its best chance for survival in the Soviet Union, where all at once there is serious and growing concern for the Siberian tiger and all wildlife. In fact, there is a vastly more enlightened attitude towards the whole environment in Russia today than in many parts of the world, particularly in comparison to Asia. It might be possible to save the Caspian tigers in Iran, where a North American-style fish and game department (staffed with two U.S. wildlife biologists) is doing a competent job with that country's wildlife resources.

Enough tigers still roam the Indian hill and forest country and Nepal's Terai to save the species. But that will require a turnabout of human attitudes. It will necessitate increasing

Sensing imminent danger, a rare white tiger arcs his tail and rumbles a warning growl. Males such as this one grow to nine-and-a-half feet in length and weigh more than 400 pounds.

the size of existing sanctuaries to encompass whole wildlife communities, and keeping them from human use. That means no timbering, no cattle grazing, no farming, and no poaching within the sanctuary borders. Admittedly, such regulations will not be popular in countries already impoverished and getting worse.

However, nothing else can save the tiger, except for the few specimens pacing behind bars in the world's zoological gardens. For my money, that isn't saving the species at all.

Asian Lion

LATE IN THE afternoon several times each week, game scouts of the Gir Wildlife Sanctuary in northwest India lead an old or emaciated domestic buffalo into a woodland clearing and tether it to a tree. Not long afterward a pride of lions appears to kill the buffalo. Then while tourists and visitors from the nearby rest house at Sasan watch and take pictures, the big yellow cats feed on the carcass, noisily as lions always do. They are often very quarrelsome, and it is quite a popular show. The lions pay little notice, even when the photographers approach near enough for close-ups.

Thus it is easily possible for anyone to see *Panthera leo persica,* the Indian or Asian lion, now one of the rarest animals on the face of the earth.

Normally it is far more difficult—sometimes virtually impossible—to see the world's rare or endangered species. If you want a glimpse of the mountain gorilla, for example, it means a back-packing expedition high into Uganda's Mountains of the Moon. To see a walia ibex or mountain nyala you go far on foot (your mule's or your own) into the most formidable mountain massif of Ethiopia. It is difficult to see a tiger anywhere, as already stated.

Recently the attention of most conservationists has focused on those endangered species which live in very remote places or for other reasons are very hard to see. There have been polar bear symposia and international conferences on how to save the Atlantic salmon, as there should be. The tiger also has been in the news; belatedly, hunting *Panthera tigris* is being banned everywhere and there is legislation designed to curtail traffic in the valuable striped pelts.

But perhaps because it is so easily visible and

295

obliging, little thought has been directed to the Asian lion, an equally magnificent mammal which now numbers far less than only a few of the world's large carnivores. And all of these 150 or so survivors are concentrated in the 500 square mile Gir Forest of Gujarat state, India, where their future is desperately precarious.

Perhaps we do not think of the lion as anything but an African animal. Therefore it is surprising to learn that the range of an Asian subspecies once stretched in a wide arc from the Bosphorus and most of Asia Minor all the way to northern India. They were abundant enough in Syria, Lebanon, present-day Israel and the Jordan Valley during the Old Testament period to be mentioned at least 150 times in the Bible. The species existed in some portions of Arabia and was common in Mesopotamia and eastward into present-day Iran. Excavators of the ruins of ancient Nineveh were at times harassed by lions, and Sir Henry Layard wrote in 1849 that they were common along the Tigris River near Bagdad. Even at the beginning of this century, some lions survived in Iraq as well as in Arabia and Iran. But 1900 can be considered as the beginning of the end.

A few years previously, in 1891, the well-traveled big-game hunter Sir Alfred Pease had reported: "The lion does not occur any more in Asia Minor." The last specimens from Iraq were captured in 1914 on the Khabur River and lions vanished from Arabia at about the same time. There is no record to commemorate Afghanistan's or modern West Pakistan's last lion, but the species is gone from there forever.

In 1941 R. N. Champion-Jones, who was a competent observer, saw a lion along the Kharki River in wild and mountainous country of southwest Iran. Since then there have been scattered reports of cattle killed by lions in this still sparsely settled region of the Zagros Mountains. An American oil geologist in 1966 claimed to have seen a lion in the same general area. But this is leopard country as well, and the reports could have been mistaken identity. And if a few lions—miraculously—survive here, the only possible chance for long-time survival of the animal is still in India's Gir Forest, which is about 1/10,000th of its original range. The last lion killed in India outside the Gir area, incidentally, was shot in 1884.

In size, habits, and general appearance, there isn't much to differentiate Asian lions from their African cousins. Observers who have studied both closely believe that the Asian variety has a thicker coat, a longer tail tassel, and more hair on the belly fringe and elbows. Full-grown Asian males are said to grow scantier manes. But all these points may not be too important when the great variation in color and mane lengths among the African cats is considered. I personally could never detect any difference, although the number of Indian lions I have seen is only a fraction of the many hundreds I viewed wandering across Africa. But apparently taxonomists have found enough skull and structural differences to list the Asian lion as a separate subspecies.

There is also remarkable similarity between the Asian lion and tiger, whose ranges once overlapped in India. An average adult male of either would weigh 425 to 450 pounds and measure nine feet and six inches from nose to tip of tail. The main difference between lion and tiger was in outer appearance and habitat preference. Tigers tended to stay in jungles and deep shade. Lions lived more in the open, in drier bush country. It was only where these conditions adjoined that the two cats encountered each other, and there is no reliable evidence or reason to believe there was ever conflict between them.

Another interesting comparison between tigers and lions is worth pondering. In the past there have been many man-eating lions in Africa, and the exploits of some (such as the Tsavo Man-eaters already mentioned) became well-known around the world. Many books have been written about man-eating tigers in India, as by Ken Anderson and Jim Corbett whose *Man-eaters of the Kumaon* became a bestseller. The Champawat tiger made 434 human kills. But now they depend heavily on livestock and there are almost no records which can be authenticated of man-eating lions in India. The subspecies definitely cannot be considered dangerous to man, even where it lives daily in such extremely close contact as in the Gir Forest.

Asian and African lions live in very much the same way. The gregarious nature and family life of African lions have often been described. Indian lions behave in the same manner. While all of the other great cats of the world tend to be solitary, even furtive creatures, lions live, hunt and travel in prides. These prides are composed of one, two, or parts of several families and may contain animals of all ages, from many very young cubs to a prime male or two. The older they grow, however, the more solitary Asian males tend to be. That may be because the younger, breeding males will not tolerate them in the group.

There appears to be no definite breeding season. In the Gir Forest most activity occurs in October and November, when pairs of animals leave the prides to mate frequently and noisily for the duration of the female's estrus. Vicious fights occur among males during the breeding season, but only a few end in bloodshed. Gestation requires about 116 days and therefore the most Indian lion cubs are whelped in January and February, when Gir weather averages the coolest and driest of the year. Cubs stay with their parents until old enough to hunt on their own, and that may be well into their second year.

There are two cubs in the typical litter, sometimes three, and occasionally as many as five. But it is a very rare thing when more than two survive, and the average is lower than that. Disease, starvation, predation, abandonment and perhaps other factors still unrecognized by biologists take a considerable toll.

Not many qualified wildlife biologists have ever been able to see, let alone study, the Indian lion, probably because the profession is relatively new and the best men in the field to date have been more profitably employed elsewhere. However, during the early 1970s, a thorough study of the species was undertaken by a young Canadian Ph.D. student, Paul Joslin. His work has been underwritten by the World Wildlife Fund and the Smithsonian Institution, and he almost certainly knows more about the Indian lion than anyone else living today.

At the present time, the lion is completely protected by law. Only individual man-eaters can be legally eliminated and anyway, as pointed out, lions in India have never been troublesome. Why, then, given an absolute sanctuary of 500 square miles, is the species now estimated at only 150 and dwindling?

Overseeing the feast, a lioness watches one of her half-grown cubs rip into a buffalo that she has just killed. Cubs first participate in hunts when they are about ten months old, but do not become fully independent until the age of two.

What has hastened the decline of the Indian lion?

In the past, excessive hunting for sport was probably a factor. The toll of all kinds of animals shot by Indian princes and their royal guests during organized shoots, which resembled major military maneuvers, is beyond estimation. Because they prefer open country (as compared to forest-jungle preference of tigers), lions were especially easy targets and dozens might have been taken in a single drive put on by hundreds of beaters. Meanwhile, the hunters sat comfortably in large, attack-proof shooting "boxes" and fired until they couldn't tolerate the rifle recoil any longer. This wasn't really hunting, but slaughter. The emphasis was never on managed trophy hunting, which we know today is not destructive to big game. Even for a long time after India became a reluctant colony of Great Britain, the picture didn't change a great deal. Hunting became the number one diversion of colonial officials. One English Army officer claimed to have shot over 300 lions, fifty of these in the neighborhood of New Delhi. A cavalry officer wrote in his memoirs that in three years he killed eighty lions from on horseback. At least this hunter exposed himself to some risk: a good many horseback hunters did not survive encounters with lions. It isn't any wonder that by the tag end of the nineteenth century all the lions left in India were confined to the Gir Forest.

Even in Gir the number of lions dwindled to just a dozen or so by 1900, and there is an often quoted figure that at one low point only eight remained. About that time, luckily, the Viceroy of India, Lord Curzon, suggested to the Nawab of Junagadh (who owned the entire Gir Forest) that he would earn the gratitude of his countrymen and all posterity if he strictly protected the lion. The Nawab agreed, but reserved the right for his family and guests to hunt if they so chose.

Evidently hunting was kept to a minimum or limited to trophy males, because a rough count in 1950 estimated the population at 240 lions. Another census in 1955 claimed 290 survivors. But rumors of poaching and poisoning by disgruntled villagers whose cattle had been killed resulted in a hurried census in 1963 which reported the number of lions at "a little over 280." Remember that these tabulations were made by diligent and well-meaning persons rather than by biologists with up-to-date wildlife census methods. All these figures could have been much too high, or too low. What counts now is the present population, and during a visit in February 1970, Paul Joslin told me there were definitely no more than 170, most probably fewer. But the low number wasn't what alarmed him most.

As a renewable resource, any kind of wildlife, including lions, will prosper and increase under protection and given the proper conditions, in other words a suitable environment, to do so. To understand the Indian lion's plight, it is necessary to consider its environment. And that is a sad, sad story.

An untrained visitor to the Gir Forest in midwinter might very well marvel at its beauty and wonder why lions aren't running all over the place. Flame of the forest trees are everywhere in bloom, forming a scarlet canopy overhead. The days are bright and cool, and flocks of gorgeous peafowl scurry along forest trails. That is deceptive, because most of the Gir is not really forest but rather at best, semi-desert scrub brush. About half of the area is teak from which any commercially valuable timber has been taken. The rest, even the secondary growth and brush, is constantly hacked up for firewood and grazed on by domestic animals. Under the thorn and acacia scrub the ground lies bare, except where the brush is interspersed with cultivated patches which can be irrigated. The only good cover for lions exists in the thin strips along waterways, and these now dry up so often that water is chronically in short supply.

The Gir could grow back and become green again, except for the fundamental obstacle that is destroying all forests and wild fauna of the Indian subcontinent today. That is the frightening increase in human population and livestock during the past century. In certain areas once inhabited by lions, there is a human density of more than 1,800 persons per square mile.

In 1970 more than 7,000 people and about 57,000 cattle lived in and badly abused the Gir Forest. Most of the cattle are domestic buffalos (each of which consumes twice as much forage as a Zebu cow) plus Zebus, work oxen, camels and goats. The aggregate totals more than twice the optimum number possible for the range. Overgrazing has naturally eliminated undergrowth and seedling trees so that the forest is no longer able to sustain itself. The overall result is that the nearby Gir Thar Desert is advancing at a speed of one-half mile per year. At this rate, even if cattle and people do not increase, the Gir has only two more decades of existence. Then it will be uninhabitable for humans and livestock, as well as for the lions.

The cattle overgrazing has the more immediate effect of driving out or infecting with disease such wild species as the chital, nilgae, sambar and wild boars on which lions would normally prey. It has been estimated that a full-grown lion needs between four and four and one-half tons of meat during a year to subsist. That means it must kill about seventy chital if restricted to a wild diet, otherwise about thirty domestic buffalos. When the wild deer are gone, the only alternative is to feed on livestock. Gir lions are figured to kill between ten and twenty cattle every day, or about 5,000 per year. Actually this is a great conservation service, but cattle owners do not see it that way and there are constant attempts to poison the cats, no matter what the law or their sanctuary status.

There is no way to calculate the toll the poisoners take, because a buffalo can easily be placed in the woods and impregnated with poison. No poisoner would take the trouble to count how many lions or other carnivores and birds die slow deaths because of it. But poison is not selective, and occasionally it backfires.

Many of the Hindu residents of Gir neither eat nor kill bovines for any reason. But there are Moslems thereabouts who *do* eat beef. One day in 1969 a party of them out for timber-cutting found several lions dining on what seemed to be a fresh buffalo kill. Immediately they drove away the lions and carried home the buffalo meat. Next day nine people were dead, since the carcass had been laced with insecticides and deliberately set for the lions. The incident very nearly precipitated a major religious conflict.

As if this picture is not grim enough, there is more. The Indian lion has become a political football. No candidate for office in or from Gujarat state is likely to be elected if his platform does not promise more grazing and cultivation rights from the central government in the Gir Forest. And there are many politicians today holding office who stand firmly for solving the sticky controversy once and for all by eliminating all lions from the area. That attitude is gaining more strength than a handful of dedicated conservationists can counteract.

One point indeed is certain: this *is* the twilight of the Indian lion. Whether it passes over the brink or survives may not matter immediately to humans living on earth today. But the passing of any species, be it a magnificent big cat or a frail mayfly, is surely another warning signal that human beings are fast approaching their own twilight.

 Asian Rhinos

For several hundred yards the mahout had prodded our elephant through a swamp almost impenetrable to smaller animals or humans, where grass grew twenty feet tall. Visibility was zero. When we finally emerged into a clearing, we could hear the excited shouts of other mahouts coming from another direction, for this was a big-game drive. Next we heard the angry snort of the animals being driven toward us.

An instant later a huge female one-horned rhino broke out of the swamp grass, followed closely by a small calf. The two stopped and stood facing us, the female on the verge of charging. Even safely atop an elephant that was a chilling confrontation, because the cow was furious. Her huge body quivered.

My first instinct as a wildlife photographer was to focus a motor-driven Nikon on the pair and shoot. But our elephant had other ideas; it sensed that a mother rhino is nothing to trifle with. An instant later the elephant fled and the rhinos bolted back into the swamp. Later, the elephant pulled up trembling.

Ram Krishna, the young mahout, apologized for the animal's nervous behavior, explaining that at only twenty-one it was very young. "Don't worry," he said in accented English, "we soon see more rhinos."

Before that morning ended we flushed out three more and had a very close look at one large bull as it lumbered across a shallow stream. In succeeding days I had good opportunity to observe still other rhinos, as well as the lush environment in which they live.

Watching rhinos is no big deal nowadays. Anyone who joins a photo safari to eastern or southern Africa is certain to see many of both the black and white varieties. A black rhino might charge the safari car and give everyone a thrill. White rhinos even roam freely in the new "safari parks" being established in the United States. But the Great Indian or one-horn rhino, *Rhinoceros unicornis,* is one of three members of the family Rhinocerotidae which is not easy to see. Probably less than 400 still survive on earth. For just brief glimpses of them, it is necessary to travel to Asia where 250 to 300 exist in the Kaziranga and Manas sanctuaries of troubled Assam state, India. The rest occur in the Terai, a portion of southern Nepal which few outside travelers have yet visited but which is now Mahendra National Park. Today it is high among the best places on the entire continent to see rare Asian wildlife, with emphasis on the one-horn rhino. The park, with its unique new accommodation for visitors, is certain to become very popular.

It is easy to think of Nepal in terms of picture postcard scenes of the high Himalayas and the mysterious city of Kathmandu. Indeed the 54,363 square mile kingdom includes nine of the eleven highest mountain peaks on earth and many more over 20,000 feet elevation. Less than one hundred miles as the crow flies from Everest or Annapurna, Nepal's most visible pinnacles, there is a lowland jungle, or Terai, not far above sea level. It contains about 1,200 square miles of uncut hardwood timber, and is probably the largest virgin forest left in Asia south of Siberia. This is fringed by the swamp habitat of the rhino, and the whole region is laced by clear cool streams which are headwaters of the Ganges River. Wildlife is wonderfully varied and abundant.

Until 1965 when the region was declared a wildlife sanctuary, poaching rhinos just to secure the horns was common. But that was stopped. At the same time, with an eye toward improving Nepal's balance of payments overseas, a facility was built to attract tourists to see the Terai wildlife. Completed in 1968 and called Tigertops, it is a good destination for anyone who enjoys the outdoors and watching big game.

Tigertops was modeled after Treetops in Kenya. It consists of twin lodges built on mahogany stilts at treetop level, with rattan walls and thatched roofs to best blend into the leafy environment. The showers are cold water and the illumination is courtesy of vintage Coleman kerosene lamps, but otherwise the place has everything—no telephones, no radio, no television, not even a portable power plant. A small concession to luxury is a circular dining room and bar, built of native stone and thatch beside a large fireplace. Surrounded by sal forest, it is a happy place to spend evenings, to listen to night sounds outside and to wait up for a tiger or leopard to visit baits placed nearby.

Just getting to Tigertops can be an adventure. It is first necessary to fly to Kathmandu from New Delhi or Bangkok, either way offering a breathtaking view of the main range of the Himalayas during the trip. From Kathmandu it is a forty-minute hop via Royal Nepal Airlines DC-3 to Meghauli "airport," which is nothing more than a level cow pasture at the edge of the jungle. Elephants are waiting at Meghauli to carry travelers and luggage to Tigertops, which is eight miles away. During the ride the first rhinos and several species of deer are likely to be seen.

All travel and rhino viewing out of Tigertops is done on elephant back for two good reasons. It is the best way to approach close to rhinos, which are far less suspicious of the tuskers than of four-wheel drive jeeps. And in some places it is the *only* way. Vehicles are impractical without extensive road building, and that would destroy the wilderness atmosphere.

The riding elephants, most of which have been captured from the wild herds which still range in the Terai, are fascinating beasts. Most are very tractable (to the mahouts who must virtually live with them) and staunch when encountering any kind of game. The riding qualities vary a good deal from one to another; some give a very smooth ride, while others seem to be traveling on only three stiff legs. On the average, females prove easier to train and handle than bulls. Evidently the mahouts are very romantic fellows, having given the Tigertops elephants Nepalese names which translate into Pearl of God, Handsome Prince, Flower of Destruction, Mysterious Goddess, Rose Goddess and (no originality here) Elephant of Rajasthan, which is a state in India.

I was "aboard" Rose Goddess during the closest encounter with a rhino. We were travelling along a well-beaten game path which paralleled a shallow water course when tall grass alongside us began to waver closer and closer. Then a loud snort, which was more of a snarl, and a rhino poked its ugly snout out of the grass barely twenty feet away. Just as quickly it vanished, only to reappear behind us. Apparently the mahout (this one couldn't speak English) was puzzled by that rhino behavior, because we turned and without explanation hurried away from that general area.

The Indian one-horned rhino is even more grotesque and intimidating in outward appearance than his African cousins. The skin of this massive animal folds and seems to overlap on its neck, shoulders and thighs. Its skin is entirely studded with masses of convex tubercles which resemble steel rivets. Except for the horn, the large head and face are piglike; the eyes are small, and the upper lip is prehensile. But the low-slung armored body and short legs are deceptive, because the rhino is more agile than it appears.

One-horns are solitary, sedentary and almost entirely grazers. Mating takes place in late winter and gestation is about nineteen months. One newborn calf weighed 120 pounds, which probably is average. The average weight of an adult is less than the larger African white rhino's and greater than the black rhino's. Females mate only every third year, and maybe not that frequently.

Even in densest cover, rhinos are not too hard to find. They bathe or wallow daily in the same place as long as the water supply remains. Tramped-down trails lead from all around to these wallows. One-horns also defecate in the same place until a large pile of dung accumulates. When approaching these deposits, the rhino walks backward and so is a very easy mark for poachers-in-waiting.

Before the European arrival in India, the one-horn rhino was abundant, ranging from Kashmir and Peshawar in the west, all along the Himalayan foothills, the Ganges and Brahmaputra headwaters to the Burma border. On the edges of the Terai, teams of farmers once used gongs, firecrackers, and other noisemakers to drive rhinos from their fields. At one time a bounty was levied on the beasts in Bengal. Today there is only the relict population already described in Nepal and India, and the rhinos of India's Kaziranga are by no means secure. Domestic stock still is permitted to compete for available food, and the small sanctuary staff cannot cope with the continuous poaching on the fringes. In 1966 thirteen rhinos were victims of poachers. And the toll continues. In 1971 there was talk of relocating

ASIAN RHINOS

A rare one-horned rhinoceros, browsing as it moves, trundles slowly across an Asian plain. In profile, this animal's resemblance to an armored vehicle is startling: its plates of tough hide seem riveted together by nodules called tubercles.

refugees from the East Bengal (Bangladesh) revolution in Assam near the sanctuary. That would be the beginning of the end for the rhinos and other wildlife.

Compared to that of the Javan (or smaller one-horn) rhino, *Rhinoceros sondaicus*, and the Asiatic two-horned (or Sumatran) rhino, the future of the Great Indian species is positively bright. The Javan once ranged widely across southeast Asia from Bengal, the Sikkim Terai, and Assam across Burma and the Malay Peninsula to Sumatra. As recently as World War I, the species was hunting in the Mekong Delta and in marshes near Saigon. The dozen or so left are all on the Udjong Kulon Reserve, a peninsular area of extreme western Java. During the last century alone, the human population has multiplied at least tenfold so that the rest of the island naturally is devoted to intense agriculture and thus the end of Javan rhinos.

Udjong Kulon is 117 square miles of undisturbed jungle (also containing the Javan tiger, probably the world's rarest predator) and should be a suitable stronghold for the rhinos. But the very density of the sanctuary's cover makes it difficult to keep out poachers, and they continue hunting the rhino for its horn. At one time rhino horn was valuable enough in southeast Asia to supply the annual tribute from princes and kings to more powerful Chinese emperors. It is still a valuable enough dowry to assure a rich husband for a poor girl in parts of Indonesia.

The Javan rhino is very similar to the Indian except that it is smaller and has a smaller horn. The cows have no horns (or almost none) and are the only females of the five rhino species which do not. The reproductive rate of the species is low because calves suckle for two years or more, and females are not believed capable of mating more frequently than every fourth or fifth year. Only stringent, unrelenting protection in Udjong Kulon can save the Javan rhinoceros from oblivion.

The one-ton Sumatran rhinoceros which stands only four to four and one-half feet at the shoulder is the smallest of all living rhinos. *Didermocerus sumatrensis* is also the only Asiatic species with two horns, the front horn always many times longer than the other. The skin folds of the Sumatran rhino are also less noticeable than those of the Javan and Indian.

The Sumatran rhino once ranged from wooded hill country of East Pakistan and Assam, throughout Burma, Thailand, Cambodia, Laos, Vietnam, Malaysia, Sumatra and Borneo, where in areas it was fairly numerous. As late as the 1920s, good numbers were present in Cambodia and along the Mekong River. But except for very small and isolated populations which may or may not survive in remotest Burma, Thailand, Malaysia, Borneo and Sumatra, the species has been wiped out. The same senseless hunting for horn and the rapid pace of rural development have reduced the species to 100 to 120 animals, as estimated by the International Union for Conservation and Natural Resources in a report that the organization issued in 1969.

Dwarfed in a field of tall reeds, an Indian rhino listens for danger. And danger abounds; only some 600 animals of this species survive today. They have fallen victim to man's encroachments on open grasslands and to poachers who sell horns—considered to be an aphrodisiac—for upwards of $200 per ounce.

Asiatic Deer

ANY HONEST REPORT on the status of wild deer in Asia would amount to a lengthy obituary. Many species are dead and gone or almost so. It is a tragedy difficult to comprehend, but the disappearance of the deer closely parallels the increase of the human population, the declining standard of living, and the quality of human life on that continent.

Consider the strange case of one Asiatic deer which still survives on earth, but which has been extinct in the wild for more than 2,000 years. Its existence wasn't even known until 1865 when the French naturalist-missionary Abbé Armand David peered over the wall of a strongly guarded imperial hunting park near Peking, which was off limits to Europeans. He saw that the herd of deer inside was different than any known. Later, he contrived to have a few live specimens shipped to zoological gar-

dens in Europe, and the species was designated Père David's deer, *Elaphurus davidianus*, after the discoverer.

In 1894 a flood of the Hun Ho River breached the hunting park wall and the enclosed deer escaped, only to be slaughtered by peasants just then suffering from one of the famines which became chronic in China. Only a few Père David's deer survived the 1900 Boxer Rebellion, and by 1921 the last one died in a Peking zoo. However, the deer which had been sent to England by Père David prospered, and in 1964 four animals were shipped back to Peking and their home country, where they might have the best chance to survive.

Perhaps the most abundant deer continent-wide in Asia is the same red deer of Europe, *Cervus elaphus,* which includes a number of widely scattered races. The exact range in Asia isn't too well defined, but red deer probably live in suitable woodlands east of Russia into Siberia. During late February and early March of 1969 while hunting wild boars in Iran's eastern Elburz Mountains, I saw several red deer, here called maral stags, on the wooded slopes. And I was surprised to see that most (if not all) of the bulls were still carrying their antlers at that late date.

The red deer and in fact all wildlife have a brighter future in Iran than in any other Asian country, with the possible exception of the Soviet Union, at least as long as Prince Abdorreza Pahlavi, brother of the Shah, is able to exercise his considerable influence as a conservationist. Abdorreza is best known as an international big-game hunter and may have the largest collection of big-game trophies in the world. But more important, he has organized a game and fish department after North American models to manage game scientifically. In the department is a capable ranger or warden corps to enforce the conservation laws.

One important race of the red deer is *C. e. hanglu,* the Kashmir stag or hangul. Only a few hundred are left in the Valley of Kashmir, India. The hangul is essentially a forest animal and since the forests are rapidly being eliminated, so is the deer. After antlers are shed in March or April, hanguls begin to follow the receding snowline upward to a summer range between 9,000 and 12,000 feet where they gather in large herds. The antlers of stags harden by September, the velvet is shed, and a month later both the fighting for harems and the downward migration begin. The deer spend winters at lower elevations where browse is most available.

Not much is known about another race of red deer, the shou, *C. e. wallichi,* except that it

Displaying its characteristic sweeping rack, a brow-antlered thamin stag rests at the edge of a pond. Once a deer common throughout much of Asia, the status of various subspecies in India and Southeast Asia is now in grave doubt.

lives in the Chumbi Valley in Tibet and certain adjacent valleys of Bhutan. The shou is said to have a larger body and larger antlers than the hangul.

The various races of thamin, or brow-antlered deer, have a wide distribution from India eastward to Indochina. One, *Cervus eldi siamensis,* was formerly abundant in Thailand, Cambodia and Laos. It still lives in scattered plains within forest-edge habitats of Thailand, but because of the long, ugly war elsewhere in its range, its status isn't well known at this writing in 1971. A subspecies of Burma, *C. e. thamin,* is in no danger. But the brow-antlered deer of India, or Manipur, *C. e. eldi,* is one of those unfortunate species whose survival hangs in the balance from day to day. There may be as many as 200 alive in the wild, but there also may be none at all.

All of the thamins are distinguished by coarse, sparse, dark brown hair; the females are lighter in color. The antlers, distinctive to this species, somewhat resemble the curved base of a rocking chair tipped forward. Twin curved beams extend from beyond the nose of male deer up and back over the shoulder. Unlike the other two, the hooves of the Manipur race have adapted to the swampy habitat, the pasterns being horny and elongated rather than hairy. This makes it possible to travel over the *phumdi,* which is a dense mat of floating vegetation in Logtak Lake, Manipur, the last refuge in India of the thamin.

Rapidly withdrawing to preserves in India and Nepal, the barasingha (above and right) face extinction. This resplendently reddish-haired species needs a swampy environment to survive.

Two races of the highly gregarious swamp deer, or barasingha, exist in India and Nepal. *Cervus duvauceli duvauceli* belongs to the Assam and Uttar Pradesh states in India, and in Nepal's Terai. It is not abundant anywhere outside the protection of sanctuaries but manages to hang on where habitat is suitable. In Assam (particularly Kaziranga sanctuary) this attractive, very reddish deer lives on high ground but always in proximity to water. In the Terai it keeps closer to water and may even spend much time in it. Swamp deer exist in very large herds of up to fifty or more head. When not heavily hunted, they are more diurnal than most other deer. When alarmed, the entire herd quickly departs into dense cover, baying shrilly all the way.

The fate of the other barasingha, *C. d. branderi*, is also in grave doubt. During the winter of 1970, part of which I spent in Kanha National Park, Madya Pradesh, central India, I saw a herd of about forty-two barasinghas, and that was about one-third of the total surviving population. It was a thrill to see such striking animals, one of which was a massive master stag. But it was also sad to realize that only about 130 animals then existed, all in the maidans—meadows—of one small park.

The sambar, *Cervus unicolor*, is a large forest deer which has fared fairly well in its forest habitat of southeast Asia. It is a very furtive, distrustful animal which tends to be nocturnal and therefore not easy to see. The sambar's coat is coarse and shaggy, various shades of

The stag on the opposite page boasts a stunning set of multi-tined, asymmetrical antlers that are branched on the right and palmated on the left.

314

dark brown in color. Males are darkest of all, and they carry long manes on the neck and throat.

My best opportunities to observe sambars have occurred in the national parks of Ceylon. But even here where no hunting has been permitted for several decades, they are the most difficult of the large animals to photograph. At Ruhunu National Park, stags emerge onto the high sand dunes of the Indian Ocean coast and prance in the last golden rays of the setting sun. It is always an exquisite sight, but when so exposed the deer never permit a close approach. The best time and place to see sambars is soon after daybreak when they are wading or wallowing around the edges of small ponds, at times in the company of buffalos.

Three races of sambars have been identified. The Indian deer is *C. u. niger*; *C. u. unicolor* is confined to Ceylon; *C. u. equinus* ranges from Assam westward to Malaysia and the Philippines.

The most beautiful deer of Asia or perhaps of the world is *Axis axis,* the chital or spotted deer. Its coat is bright rufous-fawn, liberally spotted with white at all ages. Bucks are darker than does. In forest shade the coat blends well into natural camouflage and the deer is not easy to spot. But in open sunlight the coat fairly glistens. Males grow graceful antlers, each usually with three tines and very long main beam.

Not only is this a very elegant animal, but it is the one I associate with the most beautiful settings—the green grassy glades at the edge of a jungle, clear streams, and cool, still mornings. The sights of India which I will remember longest are not the Taj Mahal, the crumbling and dismal antiquities, or the pink palaces of Jaipur, but rather the large herds of chital grazing at daybreak in Kanha Park.

Although spotted deer today are few in number compared to only a few decades ago, the species is in no danger. It is most abundant in the Himalayan foothills, in the Terai, and in moist (rather than dry) forest land interspersed with meadows. In the national parks of Ceylon where spotted deer abound, they are the principal prey species of leopards, as they are for both leopards and tigers in Indian sanctuaries. Chital are very prolific and fawns appear at any season. Apparently does are able to mate more than once in a year. In Ceylon I noticed that bucks at any one time carried antlers in every stage of development, from velvet nubbins to huge polished racks ready to be dropped. This indicates that there is no one specific rutting time.

A close, inelegant relative of the chital is the hog deer, *Axis porcinus*. The name derives from its squat, furtive and hoglike movements. Hog deer run with heads held low rather than erect, and without bounding as do most species of deer. A large hog male may reach 125 to 150 pounds, while a chital buck might weigh 190 to 200 pounds.

Hog deer prefer a grassy habitat, most often along watersheds or on delta islands. They are most abundant in the alluvial grass plains across northern India and Burma. Hog deer are much more solitary than chital, are nocturnal, and not often surprised far from dense grass cover. The best way to see them is from elephant back very early or late in the day. Hog deer also populate parts of Ceylon.

The muntjac or barking deer, *Muntiacus muntjak,* is far more often heard than seen, although its bark, which resembles a dog's is not always correctly identified. This small, red deer seldom weighs more than fifty

Its regal rack held high, a chital stag pauses in a forest clearing. The stunning white spots that freckle this species' glossy coat afford it excellent protective coloring.

Deep in a thicket, a hog deer finds a daytime refuge. These squat-bodied animals, which feed nocturnally, are among the most ungainly of all deer. They move through their grassland habitat not in bounding gallops but in hoglike lumbers.

pounds and is distributed from India and Ceylon eastward over most of southeast Asia and northward into China. Unique to this species are the small antlers (on males) which consist of short brow tines on unbranched beams. These are set on bony, hair-covered pedicels which extend down each side of the face as bony ridges. This feature is responsible for the common name of rib-faced deer normally used in Europe.

The musk deer, *Moschus moschiferus,* is a small antelope-like deer with wide distribution from Kashmir, Nepal and Sikkim across central and northeastern Asia. It is unique in that it has no antlers or horns but has a gall bladder which is absent in all other deer. The musk deer has a musk gland which produces a secretion very unpleasant to humans, but which is used as a base in perfumes. Its pointed hooves give the species firm footing on slippery rocks or snowy slopes. The absence of horns is believed to be compensated for by long, usually protruding, canine teeth of the males.

The water deer, *Hydropotes inermis,* of eastern China also lacks antlers. Instead the males have long, tusklike canine teeth. This species is small, reddish-brown in color, and a dweller of grassy river bottomlands. It is unique among all deer in bearing four or five fawns (and as many as seven) as compared to the usual one or two. A tufted deer of western China, *Elaphodus cephalophus,* is closely related to the muntjac. Its unbranched antlers are barely visible. Neither the tufted, water nor musk deer can be considered as very game.

Almost certainly extinct and probably never even seen alive by Europeans or Americans is Schomburgk's deer, *Rucervus schomburgki,* a species of Thailand jungles. It is known only by skull specimens brought by natives to Thai markets. It was probably medium to large with brow tines growing far above the faces of stags. Some biologists consider this as another race, now lost, of the thamin or brow-antlered deer.

A species which rivals the chital in beauty is the Persian fallow deer, *Dama mesopotamica,* which is now hovering on the brink of oblivion. It is known to exist only in two small riverine thickets along the Dez and Karkeh rivers of Iran, although its range once included most of the Middle East. It has disappeared everywhere because of inability to compete with domestic stock, especially goats, which have already destroyed much of the cover in that part of the world.

The Persian deer is larger than the common fallow, and males do not have the palmated or flattened antlers. The Persian deer is rich reddish with white spots on the face, neck, shoulders, back and flanks, but is white or gray below. On each side the white spots blend into an unbroken white dorsal stripe which is a distinctive marking.

If it is possible to save the Persian fallow deer, credit must go to the Game Council of Iran. They established a Dasht-e-Naz Reserve on the southeastern shore of the Caspian Sea, where live-trapped animals have been introduced in an area free of livestock. Hopefully this will become a nucleus for reestablishing the species to parts of its former range.

At one time the sika deer, *Cervus nippon,* was widely distributed across eastern Siberia, Manchuria, parts of China, most of the Japan-

At maturity no bigger than a German shepherd, the muntjac is also referred to as the barking deer, after their distinctive yaps. The stag above displays a typical muntjac antler configuration: short brow tines and hair-covered pedicels that descend to appear on the face as ridges.

ese islands, Formosa, and the Ryukyus. Most authorities agree that there are seven races of sikas which differ in size and general appearance. In the wild all are forest dwellers, mostly dark in color with conspicuous erectile rump patches edged in black. In summer coat they are at least faintly spotted with white, and in winter there is a distinct throat and neck mane. Five of the seven subspecies are now considered as gravely endangered in their own lands. Only *C. n. nippon* of the Japanese archipelago and *C. n. hortulorum* of Russian Ussuriland, Manchuria, eastern China and Korea are considered as secure.

Typical is the predicament of the Formosan sika, whose critical status does not concern the government. The animals have always been trapped, snared and shot without restriction. Probably the only Formosan sikas which sur-

vive in 1971 are in a herd of 100 to 200 head maintained on Lutao, an island where they are farmed for venison. Much smaller herds live in the Taipei zoo and at Woburn and Whipsnade in England. The Formosan is considered the handsomest, although not the largest, of all the sikas.

The last Shansi sika, *C. n. grassianus,* was known to have been shot and killed in 1920. Formerly widespread in the magnificent mountain forests of the Shansi region, this large sika (males reached 200-220 pounds) was diligently hunted without controls not only for meat, but for the antlers. These were dried, shredded and boiled in soup to make those who drank it more fertile. Perhaps it worked. In any case, it would be a miracle if Shansi sikas survived anywhere.

Even in 1929, sika antlers brought up to $300 on the Chinese market for use as an aphrodisiac. The velvet before shedding was particularly desirable. No wonder anyone who could dig a pitfall, fashion a snare, or rig a set gun went out after deer. And no wonder also that both the north China sika, *C. n. mandarinus,* and the south China race, *C. n. kopschi,* were finally exterminated in the turmoil of World War II.

In January, 1955 the Ryukyu sika, *C. n. keramae,* was officially designated a "National Monument," perhaps the first big-game species to attain such status anywhere. However, that is meaningless now because there are only about thirty Ryukyu sikas left on earth (at last count in 1971) on three small islands, each about one-half square mile in size, where the limited low quality forage must be shared with goats. It is not known if plans to eliminate the goats have been carried out.

Unfortunately, the future of Asia's deer is not bright.

Prominent white rump patches rimmed in black are characteristic of sikas, Asian deer whose numbers are rapidly diminishing. Only in heavily forested areas along the Chinese-Russian border and in Korea and the outer Japanese islands do subspecies remain unthreatened.

Wild Sheep and Goats

OF ALL ASIA's big-game animals, the wild sheep and goats have the best chance to survive the twentieth century. Although their numbers today are greatly reduced—only a few species are endangered—they are safe mostly because of their environment. Sheep particularly inhabit the most remote and most rugged mountains of the continent—regions inhospitable to humans where the animals are safest from human persecution.

Because of their inaccessibility, Asiatic sheep have never been examined scientifically as have other big-game species, and it is no wonder that great confusion exists over their proper classification. The various sheep will intergrade, and from one limited range close to another the sheep will exhibit minor but baffling differences in structure and appearance.

The sheep of Asia live in a broad S-shaped band which begins in Asia Minor and curves generally to the northeast, covering most of the major mountain ranges to the Bering Sea. For the sake of simplicity, let's say that urials inhabit the western portion (as far east as Afghanistan and India), that argalis inhabit the eastern part, and that there is some overlapping.

All wild sheep have thick, hairy (rather than woolly) coats. Both sexes have horns, but in rams these are more massive. The urials are lower altitude animals, usually confined to pastures below 10,000 feet; argalis range above that height. Urials have redder coats and thinner horns which grow outward rather than curve in circular shape close to the head. Most urial males are also characterized by long, lighter ruffs on the throat and chest. Authorities differ on whether urials and argalis are separate species or races of the same species.

323

Iran is the outdoorsman's best bet for hunting or photographing urials. The country is more politically stable than most, and there are presently three races of urials, all but one fairly abundant. The Armenian or western red sheep, *Ovis ammon orientalis* (or *O. orientalis* according to some), is a small animal of the Elburz Mountains south of the Caspian Sea. Individuals seldom weigh more than sixty or seventy pounds. They prefer fairly dry, unwooded, steep mountain slopes.

I have hunted the red sheep in two widely separated areas and their behavior was sharply contrasting. In the Elburz Mountains only forty miles or so northeast of Teheran, the sheep were nearly as wild and spooky as any North American bighorn rams. The country was open and steep enough that small bands of rams could easily stay beyond sensible rifle range of hunters. The result was a challenging hunt, typical of sheep hunts anywhere.

During the winter of 1969, Jack Antrim and I also hunted Armenian sheep on an island of Lake Rezaiyeh near the Turkish border in northwestern Iran. The island was about 850 acres, mostly dry, steep, and rocky. It is not known whether the sheep are indigenous to the island or whether they were once introduced as on a private royal hunting preserve. No matter, though, because the sheep were indistinguishable from red sheep we had encountered earlier.

Either because of their long isolation or the lack of hunting pressure on the uninhabited island, these urials were less wary than any sheep I've ever seen except the Dalls and bighorns in North American national parks. On several occasions I was able to stalk close enough for good photographs. The only trouble was a constant drizzle which damp-

ened the scene (cameraman's luck!) until a rusty old Russian cattle boat came to carry us back to the mainland. Only then did the sun break out, and our last view was of several fine rams bedded on a cliff overlooking deep, blue Lake Rezaiyeh.

Iran's largest sheep is the eastern Elburz urial, or shapo, *O. a. vignei,* a classification of the Iranian Conservation Council which is not accepted by other authorities. Other races of this urial are found in Turkestan, Afghanistan and as far east as Kashmir, Punjab and western Tibet. In Iran it is most abundant in the Mohammed Reza Shah National Park in the extreme northeastern part of the country. During each of several days in late February of 1969 I saw more than a hundred urials, most in large herds of ewes and lambs. The rams were segregated into small groups of three or four head. All of the sheep were then at a very low elevation, having been driven down by deep winter snows.

Little is known of Iran's rarest sheep, the Laristan urial, *Ovis laristanica,* a resident of the furnace-hot south central mountains. It is small, less than two and a half feet at the shoulder, and probably should be on the endangered species list. Reports persist that oil explorations crews hunt the animals without restriction.

Not many of the world's big-game animals have excited the imagination as much as the argalis, the largest wild sheep on earth. They have the most massive horns and therefore rate near the top of any big-game trophy list. Heads measuring sixty inches each have already been taken in Mongolia, and there are rumors and reports of horns measuring as much as seventy-five inches on the curve. It is

Clambering up a rocky mountainside in the Elburz range, a pair of shapo rams searches for browse. This nimble animal is the largest wild sheep in Iran.

hard to determine where fact ends and fiction begins.

Adding to the great argali mystery is the fact that most argali country still remains remote and secure behind the Iron Curtain. Although a few American hunters began filtering into Mongolia and Russia in 1970 and 1971, relatively few outsiders have ever seen an argali. Nor are many likely to see them, because the cost of a trip is immense, even when it is possible to obtain an entry visa and a hunting permit.

James Clark, whose book *Great Arc of the Wild Sheep* is required reading for anyone addicted to sheep hunting, lists no less than a dozen races of argalis and/or Asiatic bighorns. But few scientists today agree with that number or with Clark's nomenclature. In any case, the two argalis of most interest to outdoorsmen are *Ovis ammon poli*, the Marco Polo sheep, and *O. a. ammon,* the largest of the argalis.

Perhaps during his long trip from Venice across Asia in the thirteenth century, Marco Polo saw the salvaged skull and horns of the sheep later named after him, but he did not encounter the animal alive. The first European to see and describe a Marco Polo sheep was a Franciscan friar, in 1253, but the animal wasn't scientifically named until 1758. In the United States, existence of this sheep with the huge widely flaring horns was almost unknown until 1926, when Kermit and Theodore Roosevelt, Jr. made an expedition into the Russian Pamirs to collect the group of five animals still on view in Chicago's Natural History Museum.

The range of *O. a. poli* today is not large, being restricted to the high, desolate Pamirs of the extreme southeastern Caucasus and

Afghanistan, Turkestan, possibly of China's western Sinkiang Province and bordering Hunza (India). An expedition after Marco Polo sheep requires considerable financing, determination, excellent physical condition for hunting at 15,000-feet-plus altitudes, and an aptitude for stripping red tape.

The exact range of *O. a. ammon* isn't too clear, but probably most if not all are confined to the Altai Mountains of Outer Mongolia. Their horns average both heavier and longer than the Marco Polo sheep's. Hunting this magnificent argali is expensive and complicated to arrange, but this is the king of all wild sheep and to a serious sheep hunter, the great curving horns may be worth any ordeal or expense.

Another large argali, or nayan, is mostly confined to Tibet, but it isn't very well known. Clark called it *O. a. hodgsoni*, but it may be identical to the Mongolian race.

At one time the bharal or blue sheep of western Tibet and China was considered a true sheep (*Ovis*), but recently it has been classified as *Pseudois nayaur*. It is a sure-footed dweller of very high places, seldom venturing below 9,000 feet and usually found on grasslands between the tree and snow lines. This is a stocky animal standing about three feet at the shoulder and weighing up to 150 pounds. Horns are shorter than in true sheep and flare backwards. Not many blue sheep hang in hunters' trophy rooms.

A number of true wild goats are native to Asia. Most widespread is *Capra hircus*, a goat of cliffs, rockpiles, and precipitous ridges from Asia Minor to Iran (where it is called Persian ibex) to Afghanistan and Kashmir. These animals stand about three feet at the shoulder and males have sweeping, scimitar-shaped horns which are laterally com-

pressed and have large knobs on the inner front edge. Male horns may exceed four feet in length. Where the species is hunted—and that is virtually everywhere—wild goats become wary in the extreme, and hunting them can become a combination of hard climbing and disappointment. This species has a reddish-brown coat in summer which becomes grayish-brown in winter. Males have darker faces and beards.

A similar species is the Eurasian ibex, *Capra ibex*, which occurs in most mountain ranges of central Asia from the Himalayas to the Altais. It is a sturdy and thickset animal able to withstand intense cold of mountain winters because of soft and dense underfur. The outer coat is coarse hair in varying shades of brown.

Ibex prefer higher elevations than wild goats, almost always far above timberline, but never far from nearly vertical cliffs which offer escape cover. These goats live in herds from a dozen or so to forty or fifty and when anyone gives a shrill whistle, all take flight. And even the very small kids can negotiate the sheerest rock faces almost with ease. The largest of several poorly defined races is the Siberian ibex, *C. i. sibirica*, of Outer Mongolia, western China and eastern Siberia. Occasionally it shares habitat with argalis, and at present is being considered for experimental release in mountainous areas of New Mexico.

The markhor, *Capra falconeri*, is the largest, most spectacular, and most sturdily built of all the wild goats. Males stand three and one-half feet at the shoulder and have long, pointed, spiraling horns which may reach five feet in length. The markhor's coat is long and silky. Billies have long beards which hang down to the chest. These goats of the mountain forests move up and down with the seasons but are never far from steep rocky ridges and cliff

Hunkered against the fierce mountain winds, a Persian ibex ram gazes down from a spectacular aerie. This ibex is considered the top trophy goat in Iran, and for good reason. In the dramatic silhouette above, the animal's horns cleave the dusk like scimitars.

faces. They are never found above the snow line and seldom venture into the meadows below timberline.

Markhors have always been very coveted trophies, but increasing invasion of their habitat and hunting for the valuable hair, rather than trophy hunting, have forced the species into a precarious status. They inhabit certain of the wooded mountain ranges from extreme eastern Iran along the Afghanistan-West Pakistan border, extending into southern U.S.S.R. and the western Himalayas. There are six living races and all are today in short supply, although only one, *C. f. jerdoni*, of Punjab, India, is rated in the ultra-rare category.

The various races differ mainly in the size and shape of horns. Horns of *C. f. jerdoni* have a tight corkscrew twist of up to three full turns in a full-grown male. The more widespread horns of the Astor markhor of Kashmir and Baltistan seldom complete more than one and a half turns. Not much is known of the Kabul markhor, *C. f. megaceros,* of northern Afghanistan; of *C. f. cashmiriensis* of Pir Panjal; or of *C. f. chialtanensis* of the Chialtan range near Quetta.

Three species of goatlike tahrs inhabit Asia. These animals have much shorter horns than the goats or ibex, but the relationship is evident. Most abundant is the Himalayan tahr, *Hemitragus jemlahicus,* which has a

327

Arcing articulated horns are a trademark of the Siberian ibex (below). Hunting this and other ibex subspecies can be an expensive, time-consuming proposition, for these sure-footed goats favor the snow-line regions of craggy mountainsides.

With characteristic corkscrew horns and silky coat, the markhor (above) is a much-hunted Asian goat. Interestingly, the species is prized more for the commercial value of its hair than for its superb horns.

328

rusty red-brown coat of long, coarse hair. Perhaps of all wild goats, this one lives on the most inaccessible ground. It never wanders above tree line, above 10,000 or 12,000 feet, but seeks out towering cliffs and vertical rocks surrounded by tangled forest or dense scrub. Tahrs are herd animals which rut in winter. Then billies fight savagely on the faces of cliffs, where few other animals could even maintain a foothold, for dominance of a herd. These contests sometimes end when one combatant goes crashing down into the crags below. Habitat is the tahr's best defense. The species has been stocked in New Zealand, where it thrives.

Larger than the Himalayan and standing more than three feet at the shoulder, the Nilgiri tahr is characterized by shorter, stiffer hair and conspicuous, white, saddle-shaped patches on the backs of males. Males possess a very strong odor. This species, *Hemitragus hylocrius,* is confined to 4,000 to 6,000 foot elevations towering over the jungles of southern India, from the Nilgiri Hills southward along the Western Ghats. The Nilgiri tahr is extremely shy and difficult to approach. Today it is very rare, but not because of leopard and dhole (wild dog) predation as is commonly believed. Its dire straits arose mostly from unrelenting poaching by the hungry humans who live in the region. An estimated 800 Nilgiri tahr survive, but the number dwindles annually.

Rarer still is the Arabian tahr, *Hemitragus jayakari.* Except that it once existed in fair numbers in mountainous portions of southeast Arabia, little is known about this goat. Thorough library research on the species reveals little, and it may already be extinct.

Antelopes

NOT ALL OF THE world's antelopes live in Africa. Many species, some very unusual, are distributed across Asia, although in pitifully small numbers as compared to only a short time ago. Probably the best known is the blackbuck, *Antilope cervicapra,* which is native only to India and Pakistan. Once it occurred in herds of twenty to thirty and sometimes hundreds, wherever there were open plains.

The most striking feature of the blackbuck is its set of spiral horns which can grow as high (thirty to thirty-two inches) as the male stands at the shoulder. Not all of the blackbucks are

Tugging on a tasty shoot, a blackbuck—one of Asia's rarest antelopes—displays its striking characteristic spiral horns.

black; the predominant color is yellowish-fawn. But beginning at three or four years of age bucks gradually grow darker until the dominant male in any herd is either a very dark brown or black. A male's position in a herd appears to have more bearing than age on the darkness of its coat: the boss of a herd will be darker in color than an older buck which is only a contender.

The species breeds at any time of year and there seems to be continual quarreling among the pugnacious males. Whenever a herd female comes into estrus, bucks strut about with a comical mincing gait, head tossed upward and horns flattened along the back. Sometimes superiority is determined by challenging and grunting alone, but at other times a fight may result that drives one of the contenders away.

Many authorities believe that except for the

cheetah, the blackbuck is the fastest of all animals. Swiftness, however, has not been enough to save the species from the edge of extinction in its native land. Today blackbucks are far more abundant on Texas and Argentina ranches than in India and Pakistan where, except for a few scattered sanctuaries, they have ceased to exist. The disappearance of the blackbuck also sealed the doom of the Indian cheetah, which depended on it for food and which has been gone for several decades.

In a slightly less precarious position is India's largest antelope, the nilgai or blue bull, *Boselaphus tragocamelus*. In contrast to the blackbuck, this is an ungainly animal, somewhat horselike in build, with high withers and low rump. Males stand about four and one-half feet at the shoulder, have coarse, iron-gray coats (females are fawn-colored), and carry short horns which never exceed a foot. The average horn is about eight inches. This species is found only on the Indian peninsula from Mysore to the base of the Himalayas.

Nilgai have never been highly regarded as trophies. However, they are not really as clumsy and unattractive as they seem on first impression. All senses are well-developed, and a nilgai can outrun most other animals over rough, brushy ground. Although the animals often cause crop damage, nilgai enjoy immunity in some parts of India, being cousins of the cow and therefore sacred.

A most unusual antelope of India is the chowsinga or four-horned antelope, *Tetracerus quadricornis*, which is more deerlike than any other antelope. It is small, about twenty-four inches at the shoulder, and a dweller of jungle or tall grass never far from a permanent source of water. Also unlike antelopes, chowsingas do not gather in herds but

Though it lacks the graceful appearance of most antelopes, the nilgai (above and right) is a deceptively agile animal that thrives in the scrublands of southwestern India. Its distinctive markings include a white throat patch, underlined by a black tuft among bulls; a small neck mane; and white blazes on the ears, nose and legs.

prefer a solitary existence. They escape by skulking rather than running at high speed. Light brown in color, the chowsinga male is the only antelope with two pairs of horns, the front pair shorter than the others. In some areas, the front horns do not develop.

The great desert of northern Tibet is the home of another strange species, *Pantholops hodgsoni*, the chiru or Tibetan antelope. It is stockier than the average antelope, with dense

Peering from a forest clearing, a diminutive chowsinga (above) prepares to slink away. This is the only antelope in the world with four horns. Because of its small size—at maturity, it is little bigger than a pet dog—and its habitat amidst tall, clotted grass, the chowsinga uses stealth instead of speed to evade its enemies.

wool of a light fawn color. The chiru is remarkable for its swollen snout. Each nostril is equipped inside with a lateral chamber or sac which assists in breathing the rarefied atmosphere at high altitudes of up to 18,000 feet.

Chiru scrape out pits in soft or sandy earth and there lie motionless in partial concealment and possibly as protection from bitter winds. The horns of males grow to twenty-four inches or slightly more, and these may be the only visible sign that a whole herd is hunkered down out of sight. Since the Chinese occupation of Tibet, not much is known of the chiru's fate. Most likely there is increasing competition with domestic animals for available grasses.

Not long ago another unique antelope, the saiga, *Saiga tatarica*, was considered a certain candidate for extinction. This species has an inflated trunklike nose with widely separated nostrils opening downward. It was hunted for centuries for its short, lyre-shaped, amber-colored horns which are still believed to have certain curative and restorative properties in China. The result was almost fatal to the saigas, which have been eliminated from most of their range in the Soviet Union from the Don River to the China frontier.

Nearly too late, the saiga was given complete protection in Russia and poachers, when caught, were severely dealt with. The results have been astounding. In 1966 the population was estimated at 500,000, and in 1971 *Pravda* reported one million animals, most concen-

Once common throughout India, the chinkara (right) is a gazelle now found mainly on the arid plains near the India-Pakistan border. Males of this sturdy species have, in profile, S-shaped horns.

trated in the Bet Pak Dala desert region north of Tashkent and east of the Aral Sea in Kazakh. There was even fear of a massive winter kill because of overuse of the range (severe winters always take a toll of the species), and a systematic harvest of 250,000 to 300,000 was planned for the fall of 1971. The meat, considered tasty, was scheduled to be sold in Moscow stores.

A number of gazelles are native to India and several are very widespread in distribution. The chinkara or Indian gazelle, *Ga-zella gazella bennetti*, inhabits the dry plains and sandhill country of India and Pakistan. Often the range overlapped with that of the blackbucks, and there may have been competition between the two. Chinkara are more durable, can get along with less water, and probably can withstand more intense heat. Males have slightly S-shaped, curving horns which appear straight when viewed head-on. The species is no longer abundant anywhere.

The range of *Gazella subgutturosa*, the goitered or Persian gazelle, extends over suitable dry plains areas from Iraq to Mongolia. In Old

Senses aquiver, a Persian gazelle stands vulnerably on an open plain in northeastern Iran. This animal's interesting nickname—the goitered gazelle—derives from its characteristic neck inflammation during the mating season.

Testament times it was superabundant, and vast herds were described, but today the small herds are scattered and receive protection only in Iran. Goitered gazelles are distinguished by inflated throats during the breeding season.

I observed several herds of goitered gazelles in Mohammed Reza Shah National Park of northeastern Iran, but even here they were extremely wild. It was impossible to stalk or make an open approach within 500 to 600 yards of the animals. We could not even maneuver them past a camera by encircling and driving them on foot. Not many other animals are so unapproachable.

A few Arabian gazelles, *Gazella arabica*, may survive from Aden to the Sinai. Fairly large numbers of the zeren, or Mongolian gazelle, *Gazella gutturosa*, are reported to range across the steppes of central Asia from Tibet to China and eastern Siberia. Males of this species exhibit distended throats during the rut.

Not much is known of a Tibetan gazelle, *Procapra picticaudata*, or about its range and status behind the Bamboo Curtain today.

337

Other Asian Big Game

MANY YEARS have passed since the Asian elephant, *Elephus maximus,* was hunted for sport. Far more often elephants have been used (and still are) to carry hunters and drive game. One type of hunt unique to India and Nepal was called the "elephant ring," in which a hundred or more of the pachyderms encircled an area to herd all the big game inside—tigers, deer, forest antelope, everything —toward hunters waiting in blinds or on an elephant back in the center. But the scarcity of game and enough trained riding elephants has made the "ring" an event of the past, and probably it is just as well.

Trumpeting its pleasure, an Indian elephant splashes itself cool. This herbivore needs from thirty to fifty gallons of water daily to survive.

The original range of the Asian elephant was vast. It included most forest-clad portions of India, Ceylon, Burma, Thailand, Laos, Cambodia, Viet Nam, Malaysia, Borneo and Sumatra. The species has disappeared from most of these areas and exists now in scattered, isolated herds in India, Thailand and Ceylon, perhaps also in Borneo. The demand for tamed elephants to be used as beasts of burden has encouraged live capture and harassment everywhere in the wild, but the elephant's most important enemy now is expanding agriculture and the resultant jungle clearing.

This extremely adaptable animal thrives equally well in steaming, sea level jungles and cool, bamboo forest highlands. Elephant tracks have been found as high as 12,000 feet in Sikkim, and I have seen them on sand dunes along Ceylon's Indian Ocean coast.

Elephus maximus males have much smaller tusks than African bulls and females have none at all. Asian elephants are also smaller than the African species, although the difference is not nearly as great as often stated. Figure the African animals to average ten to fifteen percent heavier per individual of the same age. The longevity of Asian elephants is also exaggerated in most literature. Researchers of a Smithsonian Institution Elephant Survey of the Ceylon elephant (*E. m. maximus*) in 1968 could locate only one living elephant older than fifty years, plus the skull of another in a museum which was judged to be sixty. There is little reason to believe that other races would live substantially longer elsewhere.

The habits and breeding behavior of Asian tuskers are not greatly different than those of the African cousins described previously. In my limited experience of photographing in national parks of Nepal, India and Ceylon, the Asian elephant has been more aggressive, both toward its own species and toward humans who approach too near with cameras. That is inconsistent with the well-known fact that Asian elephants have been semi-domesticated and trained for twenty-five centuries. This has never been accomplished with African animals.

Nor are there authenticated records of African bulls engaging in serious, savage combat. But such events have been described in various places in Asia. Typical is an incident reported by Will Soysa in 1933 at Ruhunu National Park, Ceylon. The place was Buttawa Rock, a spot where today visitors often wait for glimpses of passing elephants, leopards and sloth bears. It was late afternoon when a tracker called Soysa's attention to a pair of animals in a forest clearing. On closer approach, the animals were identified as large bulls fighting.

According to Soysa, the animals would back off, always facing one another, as far as fifty yards apart. Suddenly both would charge forward to a loud, sickening thud of heads, followed by slugging with trunks and forefeet. "There were livid gashes on the faces and heads of both animals," Soysa wrote. "Teeth had been dislodged and the bodies of both were reddened with bloody saliva."

The contest lasted for at least forty-five minutes of repeated charges of skull-splitting force. One animal went down once on fore-knees, but he got up and resumed the battering. However, darkness fell, the fighting drifted away into dense cover, and Soysa did not learn the outcome.

Close behind the elephant and Asian rhinos in size is another huge animal, a handsome wild bovine, *Bos gaurus*, the gaur. It is a dark brown or blackish animal with white legs below the hocks and outward-curving, yellow-ivory horns. Bulls reach a ton in weight and are challenging game animals of formidable country which is no pleasure to hunt.

In his excellent *Book of Indian Animals*, S. H. Prater describes the gaur as "The embodiment of vigour and strength with its huge head, steep, massive body and sturdy limbs." Bulls may stand taller than six feet at the shoulder. The gaur is a herd animal native from India eastward to Burma and Malaysia. It was once abundant in the hill forests up to 6,000 feet of most of this range and still may exist in good numbers where enough suitable cover remains.

I had one brief and disappointing encounter with gaurs. After spending a week in India's Kanha National Park without taking a single

Standing sentry, a trio of gaur bulls protects one flank of a herd. Largest of all wild cattle, the gaur, which sometimes measures six feet high at the shoulders, is prized—and cursed—by game hunters for its elusiveness.

photograph, I finally found a meadow surrounded by thick forest to which a small herd came every morning. They traveled to and from the meadow on the same well-worn trail, arriving in darkness and leaving very soon after daybreak. My strategy was to wait beside the trail, at the edge of the forest, where I figured to certainly intercept the animals as they retreated to cover and shade for the day.

The strategy was good enough. At first light I spotted the herd, about eighteen head, grazing and drifting slowly, directly toward me. There was at least one very massive bull in the herd and he stayed near the center and in the fore. If all went well, the animals would reach perfect camera range at about the same time the first rays of sun flooded the meadow. I realized that bull gaurs can be very aggressive and

in some areas are considered very dangerous, but in this case I had no worries. I could let all come very close because the trees just behind me were easy to climb. I knew that because I had tested them.

The gaurs had reached seventy-five yards and were still entirely unaware of me when a most unbelievable thing occurred. A jeep carrying two men suddenly zoomed from the forest at the opposite side of the meadow and bore down directly on the gaurs. They bolted and that was that. The driver of the jeep was a government forestry officer just out for a little morning "fun," and I found his act typical of the average Indian's regard for wildlife. This also explained the extreme wariness of gaurs in Kanha Park, and probably elsewhere in Asia.

Another wild ox of Asia which is even warier than the gaur is *Bos banteng,* the banteng or tsaine. It is less impressive than the gaur in appearance, smaller in size, and has much shorter horns. Its range includes Indochina, Malaysia, Borneo and Java.

The kouprey, *Bos sauveli,* of Cambodia wasn't even known to science until just before World War II. In the intervening period, few outsiders have ever seen it and possibly no more ever will. The animal lives only in two localities 150 miles apart, separated by the Mekong River. It stands to six feet at the shoulder and of all wild cattle only the Indian buffalo has larger, more widespread horns. A few authorities have suggested that the kouprey is a hybrid of the gaur and banteng, but the majority believe it is a separate rare species. Uncontrolled hunting by military personnel living off the land is responsible for the animal's decline, and the Indochina war may have ended it.

The story of the Indian wild buffalo, *Bubalus bubalis,* is tragic because it soon will no longer exist. Some species of wildlife have been eliminated by shooting or other overharvest; most have vanished because of loss of habitat or the deadly introduction of alien species. But the wild buffalo is being diluted out of existence.

A purely wild Asian buffalo is dark gray to slate in color with whitish legs. It is sleek, powerful, and has a fine carriage with head held high. Males are aggressive and unpredictable enough to be splendid game animals, especially when found in the thick, tall grass that is their preferred habitat. Their charge is sudden, swift, and sometimes fatal. Wild cows with calves may be equally dangerous. Not even a tiger is a match for a mature wild buffalo.

The most impressive thing about a wild buffalo bull is its pair of wide, outward-curving scimitar horns. Taped from tip to tip across the forehead, male spreads have been measured at almost ten feet! One female was measured with a six and one-half foot spread. No other animal on earth has such widespread horns, but sadly they grow shorter and shorter each year because nowhere is the species safe or segregated from the scrubby domestic stock which exists (and with which it readily breeds) all across India and southeast Asia.

If any pure wild stock still exists, it is the herd in Kaziranga Sanctuary, Assam, India, or Mahendra National Park, Nepal. In the latter place recently there has been the threat of rinderpest, which could hasten the inevitable decline of this splendid big-game animal.

The largest endemic animal of the Philippines is the tamarau, *Anoa mindorensis,* a dwarf buffalo known only to Mindoro Island. Although it stands only three feet at the shoulder, it is among the most courageous of animals, never hesitating to defend itself from dogs and hunters. Tamaraus once ranged all over the island, but felling of the forests, increased domestic livestock grazing, and unrestricted hunting have had the obvious result. A few hundred, now mostly nocturnal, still survive in two sanctuaries where no one pays any attention to the laws designed to protect the resident wildlife.

The same is true of *Anoa depressicornis* of Celebes, Indonesia, the smallest of the world's wild cattle. There are three races, all ferocious when unduly disturbed and all in grave danger of extinction. Aboriginal people of Celebes lived in harmony with the anoa because they were afraid of it. But the introduction of guns and tractors has depleted the numbers of the mini-buffalo.

Wallowing in swampy ooze, a magnificently horned Indian wild buffalo seeks respite from insects. This species of bovine boasts the widest spread of any horned animal. Its ferocity and strength are legendary; even tigers keep their distance.

Several species of bears inhabit Asia, all similar to their North American counterparts except for two: the Malayan or sun bear, *Helarctos malayanus,* and the sloth bear, *Melursus ursinus.* Seldom measuring more than four feet long, the sun bear is the smallest of all bruins. It has short, smooth fur and is very retiring. Though omnivorous, it depends on finding wild honey for much of its diet. Natural range includes Burma, Thailand, Malaysia, Borneo and Sumatra.

The sloth bear of India and Ceylon is greatly feared in some regions and the cause of curious superstitions in others, perhaps because there were isolated records long ago of man-eaters. Nowadays the shaggy, short-legged bruin with mane-like hair on the neck is either rare or so nocturnal and retiring in habits that it is seldom seen. The sloth bear is also omnivorous but specializes in wild fruits (often traveling far to reach a ripened crop) and termites. The bears dig out termites with very long claws and after the dust is blown away, suck them up with mobile lips. Sloth bears are excellent tree climbers but do not hang upside down from limbs when at rest. When traveling, young cubs may ride on the mother's back.

The Eurasian brown bear, *Ursus arctos,* is distributed widely across Asia to Hokkaido, Japan, where numbers are low but where the animal apparently is not in danger. Little of the current status of the Syrian bear, *U. a. syriacus,* is known. It is a small, ashy-brown bruin of Asia Minor and the Syrian mountains. The Isabelline brown bear, *U. a. isabellinus,* of Kashmir and the western Himalayas has a pale coat said to resemble the silvertip coloring of the U.S. grizzly. Similarly frosted is the blue or snow bear, *U. a. pruinosus,* of western China and Tibet.

An Asiatic black bear, *Selenarctos thibetanus,* lives in most of the mountain and foothill ranges of central Asia from Iran across the lower Himalayas to China. This cousin of the North American black bear, which has a fairly thick black coat and a prominent white V-patch on the throat, is not popular with herdsmen, who wage constant war on it. At times the species is aggressive, and there are records of its driving leopards away from their kills. Black bears may range as high as 12,000 feet in summer and either hibernate or descend to lower, warmer elevations during the winter.

Much of the black bear's range is shared with an exquisite, little known cat, *Panthera uncia,* the snow leopard or ounce. The ounce reaches seven feet long, including three feet of tail. The long, almost woolly fur is whitish-gray to pale olive, spotted with irregular dark rosettes. There is a black stripe down the back and the underparts are pure white. Except that the animal ranges from 6,000 to 18,000 feet in central Asia, the Altai Mountains and Himalayas, almost nothing is known about the snow leopard in its wild state.

Even less information exists about the clouded leopard, *Neofelis nebulosa,* which is slightly smaller than the ounce and a resident of the lower, more forested parts of its range. The precise range of the clouded leopard can only be guessed, but it is known to live from Nepal eastward through mountainous China to Malaysia and Borneo. There are also scattered records from Formosa.

A splendid animal which has managed to survive remarkably well and cope with expanding human civilization is the Asiatic leopard. It is not exactly abundant in much of its original range but somehow manages to hang

Messy in appearance, clumsy afoot and a noisy eater to boot, the sloth bear, which inhabits South Indian and Ceylonese forests, seems a most inefficient animal. But its distinctive snout is ideally suited for slurping up its favorite diet of such social insects as bees and termites.

on, and here and there even prospers just as its African counterpart has done. The Asian leopard survives in many places where the tiger was long ago wiped out.

During the winter of 1971, I had good opportunity to study one race of leopard, *Panthera pardus fusca*, in Wilpattu National Park, Ceylon, where the cat remains very numerous.

I have never seen a park or sanctuary exactly like Wilpattu. It is 377 square miles of virgin forest—classified as "dry" jungle—punctuated only by twenty-six ponds (or wilus) which vary in size from five to eighty acres. Encircling each pond is either a strip of parklike grass, swamp, or low brush beyond which extends the unbroken jungle of palu, satinwood, kum-

buk, dan, and ebony trees. To accommodate visitors, the park service built rest houses at park headquarters and bungalows beside six of the wilus. These accommodations are tidy, blend well into the environment, and have just enough amenities (example: a small gas refrigerator and flush toilet, but no electricity) to make jungle living comfortable. None of the bungalows is closer than four miles to another, and each is staffed by a cook and a housekeeper. Altogether, living in a jungle bungalow is a rich wilderness experience. Our cottage was known as Kali Vilu.

While I gulped breakfast the first day at Kali, the cook, P. H. Siremoies, explained his theory about the Kali Vilu leopard, whose coarse coughing just outside the window had awakened me at daybreak. Simon Gamage,

Warming itself in the late afternoon sun, a brown bear pauses on its rounds. These bruins are highly territorial, staking out for themselves ten-square-mile areas which they patrol regularly. They are omnivorous eaters, killing smaller mammals with cuffs of their clawed forelimbs.

guide and jeep driver who could speak English, translated from the Sinhalese something like this: "There is a pit near this bungalow in which we bury kitchen refuse. Wild boars have discovered the pit and come at night to dig there. That's why the same leopard comes each morning in search of a boar for its own breakfast. It is very tame. Several days before it had caught a shoat which it devoured in view of several guests at the bungalow."

The sunlight had not yet filtered down into the jungles when after breakfast we headed away from camp in a jeep. Accompanying us was H. H. A. Bandara, a young tracker on the park staff. At his direction we headed for Borupan Vilu, which is about seven miles away and where much game had been seen of late, including a large male leopard.

Driving on the thin track completely canopied by jungle, dripping with dew, was a novel experience. A red, barking deer darted out ahead of the vehicle and paused to look at us, but not long enough for me to focus a tele-photo lens. Ceylon jungle fowl were every-where; the males resembled barnyard roosters (most of the world's domestic chickens were de-rived from these and three other species of wild Asian jungle cocks). Rounding a bend in the track we suddenly emerged from the deep purple shade into bright sunlight reflected on the surface of Borupan Vilu.

My spirits fell, however, because except for a pair of whistling teal, no wildlife was in sight anywhere near the pond. The tracker wasn't disappointed, and he instructed Simon to park in the shadows at the edge of the jungle.

"We'll wait awhile here," he whispered, "and see what happens."

An egret circled the pond and dropped down to a soft landing. For awhile nothing else stirred. The tracker lit a cigarette. Simon pro-duced a betel nut and several betel leaves from a pouch, all of which he stuffed under his lip with one forefinger. Idly I brushed the dust from my camera lenses, and then all at once I had the strange feeling we were no longer alone at the wilu. At that instant the tracker touched me gently on the shoulder and pointed to the left.

There a leopard crouched, regarding us with cold lemon eyes. Its outstretched tail flicked ever so slightly. It was only about fifteen feet away.

For the second time that morning, I felt a cold chill, but the instincts of a photographer won out and I turned as slowly as possible to face the cat with a camera. At the same time a second larger leopard materialized from no-where, purred and rubbed against the first one. Then both strolled out into the sunlight toward water's edge where side by side they drank. It was a wildlife scene of tremendous beauty.

During the next hour or so we watched a remarkable show. The two leopards were a mating pair which cavorted about like small domestic kittens. They climbed trees and am-bushed one another, dropping down from overhead. Once both ventured far enough out onto the same limb that it broke under the weight. Obviously, both were very hungry (their ribs showed through the sleek coats) and constantly watched the shores of the wilu for a meal to appear.

A monitor ventured out from its burrow and the more agile female made a short stalk fol-lowed by a blinding rush to try to catch it. The lizard barely escaped underground in time. Far more exciting was the unsuccessful chase by the male of a mongoose which some-how managed to duck into a hollow tree trunk. Both leopards then tried to dig it out, but soon gave up. Perhaps it was a bad morn-ing for the cats, because they were even unable to catch a nightjar which fluttered about on the jungle floor just out of reach of the cats.

"Love and hunting," Simon winked at me, "do not mix."

He probably was right.

Wilpattu Park must contain the greatest concentration of the spotted cats any-where on earth. At least here they are the most visible and obliging to wildlife watchers. Dur-ing the course of many trips through leopard country in Africa and Asia, I had always con-sidered myself extremely lucky to have seen a dozen individuals. Two of them I shot long ago. Two were on snow-covered slopes of a mountain in northeast Iran. Most of the rest were either fleeting glimpses or at very long range. But I saw exactly that many more—a dozen—in just one week at Wilpattu. Most of these were near enough to photograph. Each encounter was exciting and a good illustration of leopard behavior.

One strong impression I formed was that leopards are not nearly as solitary as generally believed. A day after the first encounter, we found three (the third was a second male) cats together in the vicinity of Borupan Vilu and there seemed to be no conflict between the males. Later, Chief Park Ranger Percy de Alwis revealed that he had at times seen five and once six in a group. Threesomes are not at all uncommon. De Alwis also noted that there has never been a single incident between leopards and humans in the park, and he has never known of a man-eater in Ceylon as they have been reported in India and elsewhere. Man-eating leopards in India are considered greater terrors than tigers.

The most abundant big game in Wilpattu Park are the beautiful spotted deer which are concentrated around the wilus in fairly large herds. Late one morning while returning to camp, we came upon a dead buck at the edge of the jungle. After close inspection, we concluded that it had been attacked by a leopard (perhaps a young one) but had managed to escape due to its size and strength. The wounds to the throat and head were too severe, however, and it died of them. When we left the buck, it was already beginning to bloat under the hot sun. Bandara the tracker suggested that we return to the spot in the afternoon to watch the carcass.

By three o'clock, Simon had parked the jeep in the shadows nearby and we did not have long to wait. How they sensed from underwater the presence of the carcass is impossible to say, but soon a pair of crocodiles emerged from the wilu and walked directly toward the deer as if guided by radar. They did not start soon enough, because a large leopard appeared from dense cover (from where it might have been watching) on the opposite side of the wilu and hurried straightaway toward the carcass, which it dragged part way into the jungle before tearing into the paunch. Then unaccountably the cat dragged it even farther away where we could not follow. But there was evidence that the Ceylon leopard will utilize dead, even ripe, meat in addition to making its own kills.

One evening a herd of about fifty spotted deer plus a number of buffalos and boars were feeding near water's edge, just opposite Kali Vilu from our own bungalow. According to the cook (I had not yet returned to camp) it was a very peaceful scene, exactly like a postcard, until all scattered when the Kali Vilu leopard suddenly killed a deer and dragged it away. The cat had appeared twelve hours earlier than normal, said the cook, and that plainly revealed how intelligent leopards really can be. Or how hungry. Either way, I'm sorry I missed that bit of action because the sun still had been high enough for photography. I didn't miss an equally exciting incident later on, although this time it was too dark for using a camera.

We were returning from another session of watching the trio of leopards at Borupan make an unsuccessful attack on a sambar hind. Although it seemed to be surrounded and doomed, the large deer simply splashed out across the knee-deep water of the wilu where it easily outdistanced the closest pursuer. From there we turned campward and en route passed a small wilu beside which a band of about fifteen buffalos were grazing. We stopped and put the glasses on the animals to see if any bulls were in the herd. By now it was twilight, but we could see two very young calves, probably only several days old, among the buffs.

As we focused the binoculars, a leopard was suddenly in the center of the herd and had one of the young ones by the throat and flipped on its back. This happened with indescribable suddenness.

Next, the cat began dragging the calf away while the older buffs kept harassing it and trying to hook it with heavy black horns. One buff, perhaps the mother, became far too bold, and for that boldness the leopard raked its face with one paw and blood gushed out around the nose and eyes.

As suddenly as the attack had been made, the incident ended when the leopard evaporated into the forest, still in possession of the small buffalo. I'm not certain, but I doubt if the whole encounter lasted more than twenty seconds.

"More proof," Simon grinned, "that a leopard not in love is a better hunter."

I hated the day we had to leave Wilpattu and Ceylon and the leopards. Nowadays there are too few opportunities to watch wildlife and hunt with a camera in Asia, as I did.

South America

THE CONTINENT OF South America equals any other continent in the beauty of its landscapes and diversity of its geography. Between cold, storm-lashed Cape Horn on the south and the tropical Caribbean on the north are great savannas and grasslands, vast jungles and unexplored highlands, swamps, deserts, the world's longest major mountain chain, the largest of all rivers, and the greatest continuous tropical rain forest on earth. It is no wonder that South American flora and fauna are among the richest known anywhere and among the most unique.

But on the entire continent there are very few large mammals in the big-game category. The short list includes several varieties of deer, the spectacled bear, and two of the world's great cats, the mountain lion and the jaguar.

Because of the scarcity of large mammals, South America has never been a popular destination of sportsmen; nor is it a good place to see and photograph wildlife. Most federal governments have been oblivious to wildlife conservation as well as to conservation of any natural resources. There are no national or wildlife parks of the types set aside elsewhere around the world. Many areas designated as parks in Argentina and Brazil are populated with people, poorly policed or too small to be of value. There is no place, for example, where a visitor has even a remote chance of seeing a jaguar in the wild today.

El tigre, *Panthera onca,* is the largest and most impressive of all New World cats, resembling superficially the leopard of Africa

Slipping sleekly through water, a jaguar searches for prey. The jaguar, largest of all South American cats, inhabits rain forests, particularly areas near rivers and estuaries. Unlike most cats, it takes readily to water; in fact, it is a nearly invincible opponent when afloat.

and Asia. Both are marked with dark rosettes on a lighter yellowish hide, but the jaguar grows to slightly larger size, has a shorter tail, and is stockier and more muscular of build. Overall, it gives the impression of power as opposed to the grace and speed evident in the leopard.

Much less is known about the jaguar than any of the other big cats, not only because it lives in the least accessible environment but also because of the lack of interest, either sentimental or scientific, in wildlife of Latin American lands. Wherever the species shares its habitat with man, it is considered a potential nuisance to be eliminated by any means as quickly as possible. That kind of attitude neither stimulates study into what makes the jaguar tick nor extends the jaguar's longevity.

Tigre's approximate original range covers a great variety of environments from central Argentina and Chile northward to the United States border. The jaguars occupy (or once occupied) most of this vast region, except the deserts or cold bare elevations above timberline. Lowlands, particularly lowland jungles, are the most favored areas. The preference is for heavy cover rather than open spaces, although that may not have been true before the animal came under heavy hunting pressure. Jaguars once roamed slightly north of the border in our own Southwest, and as recently as 1964 they were seen by hunters and hounds who were chasing cougars.

Mature males may reach 200 or even 250 pounds; mature females considerably less. The biggest animals are found in northern South America below the Isthmus of Panama. I have in my possession a skull which would qualify for seventh place in the Boone and Crockett 1964 record books of North American game, but which was only a very good animal in Colombia where it was taken. South American trophies do not qualify for Boone and Crockett recognition.

Hunting jaguars can be an unrewarding pastime, and persistence or endurance are necessary ingredients for bagging one of the cats. Hunting conditions are seldom very pleasant, combining heat, humidity, and dense cover with a quarry which knows how to take advantage of its surroundings. Add the unfortunate fact that a good many fly-by-night or downright unscrupulous individuals are in the business of outfitting jaguar hunters—and the chances of a successful hunt are very low. It was not until my fourth hunt and a total of twenty-seven days in the field that I finally saw a jaguar, and that one by accident.

El tigre can be hunted in a number of ways. Calling is favored by natives who cannot afford to feed packs of good hounds, or who have unlimited time to spend in the woods. The mature cats are very vocal and do a good bit of coughing and grunting at night, which in the distance sounds like a muffled roar. Once heard close up, it isn't soon forgotten.

The caller uses a large earthen jug or gourd and tries to imitate the roar by blowing into it. Some callers can do this extremely well. An alternative is to spend nighttimes out in the jungle listening for a jaguar and answering it, hoping it will be curious enough to get shot. Another is to build a tree blind in a territory known to contain cats and wait there, blowing at intervals in hopes of reaching the ears of a passer-by. But sitting in a jungle blind all night, night after night, is not very pleasant; I don't enjoy sitting in blinds even when there are no insects and the humidity is less than ninety percent.

In places it is possible to put out live or dead baits (goats, cattle, even dogs) for jaguars, and this may work where an animal has been preying on livestock. When tigre comes to the bait, he is shot at from a nearby blind or hounds are turned loose on him.

No method of hunting is nearly as effective as using trailing dogs. The object is to find a fresh jaguar kill, very fresh tracks in soft earth, or otherwise get the hounds started on a fresh spoor. What may follow has all the excitement and action a person can wish for.

There are drawbacks to hunting with hounds, however. To begin, good cat dogs are very rare and naturally very valuable. The best usually are proven cougar and bear dogs from the North, but too many of these cannot stand the unaccustomed heat or soon succumb to heart worm and other tropical diseases which affect imported canines. The attrition in hounds is high because instead of treeing, as a cougar will do, a jaguar will stop often and fight. A really angry cat—for example, a female trying to protect kittens—can cause terrible damage to a pack of dogs and maybe even wipe it out. And the best, most aggressive dogs are the ones which sustain the damage.

In much of its natural range, a jaguar's habitat is all in its favor against dogs and even more so against hunters who cannot keep up with both. No type of terrain is more formidable than the edge of South American jungles, or cutover wet jungle laced with swamps and rivers. Once the animal reaches sanctuary in a swamp or across a large river, pursuit by the best hounds is almost impossible.

Unlike other cats which swim only of dire necessity, jaguars readily hit the water and are completely at home in it. Woe to the animal, including a dog, which the big cat catches in the water. That's the end of the game.

Because tigre does a good bit of hunting and living along waterways, there is another way to hunt the species. This is to travel jungle rivers at night by boat or canoe while scanning both banks with the beam of a powerful searchlight. For reasons not easy to explain, the jaguar is not greatly bothered by the drone of an approaching outboard motor and may pause long enough in the light beam (perhaps temporarily blinded by it) to allow a hunter to try a shot.

Many of the jaguar's most important prey species are concentrated near or must come occasionally to water. Among these are deer, capybara, agoutis, peccaries, anteaters and even the large South American tapirs. In some regions peccaries comprise nearly all of the diet. Elsewhere jaguars may become good fishermen, scooping out turtles and fish which they find close to banks or exposed on shallow riffles.

Years ago during a hunting trip by houseboat up Colombia's Magdalena River to Cienega de Zapatosa, an Indian woodsman who had killed many jaguars told me that the cats often capture caimans along the rivers. These are small members of the crocodile family. He also claimed that he once found a large anaconda rendered almost inert from swallowing an unidentified large animal. The Indian killed the snake with a machete and inside of it, he said, was a jaguar about half grown. The

snake itself showed little damage from the encounter, which no doubt took place in the water.

Mating may take place at any time of the year, and this seems to be the only period when adults are found together. Most of their lives are spent wandering and hunting alone. We can only guess at the size of the territories which individuals cover but may assume that it is similar to the mountain lion's range described previously. In captivity, female jaguars begin to breed at two and one-half to three years, and that may also be true in the wild. The litter of from two to four kittens is born in a cave or similar secure place. The survival rate of young born to other species of cats is low, and there is no reason to believe that it is any different with young jaguars.

El tigre has known considerable conflict with man, but never more than when humans have chopped clearings in the jungle to create pasturage for livestock. In many parts of Latin America, a cow represents a meal too easy for a cat to ignore. There is a reported case of a cat swimming out to an anchored cattle boat to attack a steer on board. Individual jaguars have become cattle killers too clever to control by any means, despite their operating in the same area for several years. The Brazilian government once estimated that in a single year the spotted cats accounted for 6,000 head of livestock.

The cattle-cat conflict has created the job of professional hunter in many South American frontier communities. Best known (because of his lecture tours in the U.S.) of these men was Sasha Siemel, who claimed to have killed 250 in the Mato Grosso with spear or bow-and-arrow alone. His technique was to track a jaguar with dogs, corner it, encourage a charge, and impale the cat on a spear.

355

Poised to pounce, an ocelot crouches in ambush. This cat usually hunts at dawn and at dusk.

All of the big cats have inspired legends, myths, and curious beliefs around the world, and el tigre is no exception. To many ancient Mexicans the beast was considered sacred, and the most important relic of Mayan civilization remaining today at Tikal, Guatemala, is the Temple of the Jaguar. In some remote jungle areas jaguars are considered reincarnations, perhaps of mothers or other beloved relatives, and elsewhere as avenging spirits. Most likely to hasten the demise of *Panthera onca* is the relatively recent discovery that when dead, the animal can be converted into an elegant fur coat. This is causing even the most religious natives from the Amazon to the Andes to revise their thinking. With cash prices for pelts so high, maybe they're not reincarnations of cousins after all.

Recently great attention has been focused on the decline of the tiger and leopard and how the fur industry has contributed to it. Meanwhile, European fur dealers have invaded South America where, by comparison, jaguars seem to exist in inexhaustible numbers. As a result, the traffic from the tiniest jungle communities all the way to Frankfort, West Germany, center of fur processing operation, has been terrific. It is difficult to say how long el tigre can survive the pressure.

The other big cat of South America is *Felis concolor,* the cougar which has been described before. Though its exact range on the continent is not precisely known, it is at least as widespread as the jaguar and probably lives as far south as Tierra del Fuego and at higher altitudes than its spotted cousins. The cougar has rarely been troublesome as a cattle killer; it is more furtive and satisfied to survive on wild fare.

Hunters pursuing jaguars with hounds in south or central America may encounter other smaller cats not really in the big-game category. These are the ocelot (*Felis pardalis*), margay (*F. wiedi*), and pampas cat (*F. colocolo*). The ocelot or tigrillo is the largest of these and is also spotted. Unfortunately, its fur is in great demand. The best way to hunt it is with packs of hounds.

Only one bear lives in South America and it is also the only bruin found in the Southern Hemisphere. The spectacled bear, *Tremarctos ornatus,* is named for the characteristic marking around the eyes. Also known as the Andean bear, its natural range includes most of the cooler foothill forests of Pacific

Nestled in a savanna clearing, a herd of marsh deer rests from a foraging expedition. These cervids are about the size of their North American cousins. In South America, though, deer are rarely hunted as trophies; rather, they are killed for meat.

slopes of the Andes, from northern Chile on to Colombia.

Spectacled bears seldom exceed two feet at the shoulder and are not very abundant anywhere. They are blackish and shaggy, but the hair is less dense than on bears from North America. They are largely herbivorous, but whatever else is known about the species comes from specimens confined in zoos. No one has ever made a scientific study of the species.

Eight species of deer—Cervidae—inhabit South America, but none are really well known and none have been paid much attention by trophy hunters. Most are hunted for meat alone. The largest species is the South American marsh deer, *Blastocerus dichotomus,* which is reddish in color and black below the hocks and knees. The horns are multi-forked and not unlike those of the North American mule deer. Marsh deer are found from the Guianas southward through Brazil to northern Argentina.

A common deer of the Guiana savannas, Venezuela and the Amazon valley is *Odocoileus virginianus gynmotis,* a relative of the whitetail. A small, reddish-brown resident of the dry open plains of Brazil, Paraguay, Uruguay and Argentina is the pampas deer, *Ozotocerus bezoarticus,* which in places is fairly common. The antlers of the male are normally thin, and the main beam is forked.

The Peruvian guemal, *Hippocamelus antisensis,* is speckled brown and the coat is coarse and brittle. Mature antlers have only a single fork. This animal lives in the Andes of Ecuador, Peru, Bolivia and northern Chile. Another (Chilean) guemal, *H. bisculcus,* is smaller and the coarse hair is a fine-speckled yellowish-brown. This one inhabits the mountains of southwestern Argentina, central and southern Chile.

The brown brocket deer, *Mazama gouazoubira,* with spiked horns on the male, is native to the region of the Amazon basin south to northern Argentina. The red brocket deer, *M. americana,* is a most attractive animal, bright reddish-brown in color and larger than the brocket. It is found from Colombia, Venezuela and the Guianas across Brazil to northern Argentina.

Smallest of all South American deer is the Chilean pudu, *Pudu pudu,* which lives from the south central Chile forests southward almost to the Straits of Magellan and on the island of Chiloe. Its simple spike horns seldom exceed three inches in length. Two other forms of pudu, Ecuadorian and Colombian, exist in northwestern South America. They are extremely shy and hard to see, let alone to collect.

Hunters in South America are rarely burdened with bag limits, closed seasons or other restrictions, except for transporting firearms (which is usually difficult). This has not helped wildlife populations. Several species of exotic big game have been introduced and have greatly spread. Most significant are the red deer from Europe and blackbuck of India, both of which are now more abundant in Argentina than in the places of their origin.

Europe

THE STATUS OF Europe's big-game animals is exactly what might be expected in a part of the world so densely populated and so intensively developed for industry and agriculture. Some animals have long been extinct or are nearly so now. Nowhere, with the possible exception of the Soviet Union, is there an abundance of big game.

The most widely distributed animal is *Sus scrofa,* the wild boar. It exists in all countries, at least in small numbers, except Scandinavia and the British Isles. Boars are most numerous in the forests and forest edges of eastern Europe where the hunting is usually to eliminate a nuisance rather than for sport. Except in the most remote areas, however, the pure wild boar no longer exists, having too long been exposed to domestic swine.

In Russia male boars have reached weights of 400 pounds and more. They are dark, powerfully built, bristly animals, surprisingly agile afoot. Their agility and large, upward-pointing tusks make the animals dangerous when cornered or wounded. As often as not the species is hunted with packs of dogs.

A formerly very widespread native of Europe was the red deer, *Cervus elaphus,* which is the cousin of the North American elk, or wapiti. The red deer exists on estates or government forest lands in most countries but is genuinely wild only in isolated regions (usually in highlands) of Scotland, Spain, Yugoslavia, Poland and western Russia. It is a woodland dweller everywhere except in Scotland, where it has adapted to living in open moorlands.

It is difficult to distinguish a European red

Pausing in a frigid Finnish pond, part of a reindeer herd rests from its migratory trek. This animal thrives on subarctic tundra. Reindeer and caribou are the only deer species in which both sexes are antlered.

deer from a Montana elk, except that the former may be more reddish (rather than dark brown) in color. They live in herds, sexes separated, until the beginning of the autumn rut when the intense competition between bulls to collect harems begins. The challenge of a red bull is a drawn-out roar or bellow rather than the elk's shrill and penetrating whistle. It is an exciting sound nonetheless.

Alces alces, the European moose (which is most commonly called elk) is also almost indistinguishable from the Canadian moose. It is gray-brown to black, lighter on the legs, with the same, huge, downward-curving snout. A bull may reach a half-ton in weight. The moose is confined to forests, especially in lake regions, of Scandinavia and northern Russia. Its behavior is very similar to that of its Canadian counterpart.

The reindeer, *Rangifer tarandus*, is Europe's most abundant deer. It still occurs in vast herds in Lapland and northern Russia. Herds also are present in southern Norway, Iceland, Spitzbergen, and Novaya Zemyla. They are animals of the sub-Arctic mountains, tundra, and taiga, or woodland laced with numerous waterways as is most of northern Russia. Except that its wanderings and migrations are more directed by man, the reindeer differs little from the North American caribou. In fact, the two readily interbreed. Reindeer never travel as far, because their range is more restricted than the vast northern slopes of Alaska and Canada.

An animal which has managed to survive fairly well with civilization is the roe deer, *Capreolus capreolus*. This very attractive deer is bright red-brown in summer and turns to gray in winter. Bucks seldom exceed fifty-five or sixty pounds. An adult male grows branched, six-point antlers, three per side.

A pair of fallow deer bucks displays the palmated antlers unique to this species. Fallow deer originated in the Mediterranean countries; today, however, they are common in parks and forests throughout both western and eastern Europe.

Roe deer do not migrate or even travel far, but in a given area they move about both day and night to feed. Favorite habitat consists of cutover woods, dense undergrowth, copses, wetlands, and open fields which are encircled by good escape cover. This is a lowland species as well as a mountain dweller. The roe deer is very compatible with a variety of environments and many kinds of agriculture. It is at least present in all European countries except Ireland, and its range extends into Asia as far as Iran as well.

Time has virtually obliterated the exact origin of the fallow deer, *Dama dama*. Probably a Mediterranean species, its range extended eastward through the Middle East, where it no longer exists. It was always such a handsome deer that it was widely distributed over the continent, by accident and design. Fallow deer found their way onto royal estates from Surrey to St. Petersburg, and gamekeepers commonly bred pure white or very dark strains from the wild color of reddish-brown with faint white spots.

Most fallow deer today are still estate animals, but they also exist ferally, especially in eastern Europe. In the wild they tend to be nocturnal and very shy. Similar in size to whitetails, they differ from other deer in the unique palmated antlers of the bucks.

The North American whitetail lives ferally in Finland. A few Chinese water deer (*Hydropotes inermis*) and muntjacs, or barking deer (*Muntiacus muntjak*), live wild in England and France, probably having escaped from estate deer collections. The Japanese sika deer

The sturdy Spanish sheep (left), which once roamed freely through the Pyrenees range, now survives only in several wild Iberian mountain areas. The mouflon (below) was a species indigenous to many Mediterranean islands; today, only a small herd remains on Cyprus.

(*Cervus nippon*) has also escaped to roam free in several areas.

A remnant herd of between 300 and 400 wisent, or European bison, *Bishon bonasus,* survive in Poland's Bialowieza Forest. Those pitiful few are remarkable, considering that the animals once existed in the millions from Lithuania to the Caucasus and eastward into Siberia, and that the world's total wild population was a dozen or less after World War II.

The wisent is the Eurasian counterpart of the North American bison. It is more slender of structure and prefers woodland to plains habitat. Hunting the species is out of the question.

Originally the mouflon or wild sheep (*Ovis aries musimon* or *Ovis orientalis musimon*) was native to Sardinia and Corsica, and another race (*O. a. ophion*) was confined to Cyprus. Centuries ago the sheep probably inhabited most areas of those islands, but they were gradually driven higher and higher into woodlands by increasing human pressure. During the past few decades, conservationists have been busy trying to save just a few. Hopefully there are one hundred or so still on Cyprus.

The Sardinian and Corsican sheep, probably extinct on their native islands, were widely stocked in mountain areas of central and eastern Europe where small herds may survive. The original strain has been diluted with domestic stock. Males of all these Mediterranean sheep are extremely elegant animals, with the heavy curving horns characteristic of all the world's wild sheep.

A number of races of ibex or wild goats still survive in several of Europe's highest, craggiest mountain ranges. In scattered portions of the Alps, the race is *Capra hircus ibex,* a fairly large species whose males occasionally reach 200 pounds. The Spanish goat of the Pyrenees, *Capra hircus pyrenaica,* is smaller. The Portugese and Balkan races disappeared in the 1890s. Some authorities believe that the wild goat surviving on Crete, *Capra hircus cretensis,* is not really a wild species.

An animal which might be confused with the goats is the goatlike chamois *Rupicapra rupicapra,* which shares some of the same lofty range in the Alps and Pyrenees. Chamois have only short, forward-curving horns, and the white on their faces is distinctive. Originally the chamois may have been a woodland animal, at least a dweller of mixed deciduous-coniferous mountain slopes. But for centuries it has been pressed upward to a last stronghold in the highest, rocky places where it is difficult to follow, almost always above 5,000 feet. Chamois are agile, effortless climbers. When surprised or aware of danger, the species hisses, whistles and heads for still higher elevations. Altogether, the chamois is a splendid game species, probably most abundant today in the Carpathian Mountains and in New Zealand, where it was long ago introduced and is thriving.

Recently the muskox, *Ovibos moschatus,* has been reintroduced as a wild animal in Norway and Spitzbergen, where its habits are virtually the same as the Greenland or North American varieties.

Except for the white bear, Europe's largest carnivore is the brown bear, *Ursus arctos.* When Roman legions were fanning out across the continent, the brown bear had a wide distribution and was abundant in a variety of habitats. Today it is found only in remote woodland or mountain areas of the Soviet Union, northern Scandinavia and Yugoslavia.

Scattered individuals may also survive in Spain and Rumania.

The European brown bear most resembles the grizzly in appearance, behavior and habits, sleeping away part of the winter and feeding on anything that is edible. However, the Old World bruin has more successfully avoided conflict with man than has the grizzly, and it may be a more sedentary animal. European brownies have been more amenable to training than silvertips, as witness the "Russian bears" which skate and ride motorbikes in circuses. These are deplorable ends for such magnificent animals.

Summed up, the best place to see European big-game animals is in zoos.

Hunting Big Game With a Camera

FOR THE past quarter-century I have been professionally hunting wildlife, especially big game, with a camera. Not too many years ago that was a unique profession. But nowadays, with expanding interest both in photography and wildlife conservation, it seems that everyone who owns a camera is getting into the act. And it's no wonder. More and more Americans, sportsmen and non-sportsmen alike, are discovering that wildlife photography is a most fascinating and rewarding pastime. Entire vacations can become photo safaris at any time of the year. There are unlimited opportunities to photograph the beautiful animals of our country, occasionally as close to home as the shy deer in our own gardens or pastures or as far off as the most remote national parks.

Hunting big game with a camera has a good many advantages over hunting with a gun. It can be far more challenging because the hunter must approach much closer to his target: even with the greatest lenses ever developed, shots at 200 and 300 yards are out of the question.

Furthermore, the cameraman is never burdened with closed seasons, bag limits or similar restrictions. He can hunt any time of year and photograph endangered species as well as common big game. Hunting in sanctuaries is permitted, even invited, and there are no expensive licenses to buy. Make no mistake about the satisfactions and rewards of camera hunting; I am as proud (probably more so) of the photos in my files as of the heads on my wall. And I've had my share of exciting moments shooting some of those pictures.

From a good, high vantage point, I scan the savanna for wildlife during a photographic safari in Tanzania.

Serious big-game photography carries no guarantees against physical discomfort, such as sudden dunkings in cold water or suffering through blazing heat. One dunking I recall must be blamed on my enthusiastic friend Bill Browning. He thought we could photograph elk and mule deer if we ran through a certain canyon of the Madison River in Montana called the Beartrap, via rubber raft, emerging intact at the other end. It seemed like a good idea to me too, until we approached the first rapids. But by then it was too late to turn back, and my lingering impression is that we were violently sucked the complete distance through the Beartrap. Somehow en route, before one camera was doused, I managed to take pictures of the ducking. But no elk or deer.

At least the Beartrap trip taught me a few things about keeping photo equipment dry in similar situations later on. It was an expensive but very valuable lesson.

Thanks to big-game photography, I know what it's like to be lost. Once in Tanzania I had been trying to photograph a fine greater kudu bull by following the animal through dense thornbush. I didn't get many pictures of value and by late afternoon of the very cloudy day, when the kudu finally spooked for good, I suddenly realized I hadn't the slightest idea where I was. Rather than walk and stray even farther, I sat down to think it out.

There are better places to be stranded overnight than the Tanzania bush. An hour or two later a savage face, grinning hungrily, peeked through the bush and said: "Jambo." Fortunately *jambo* means hello, and the face belonged to a remarkable Nderobo tracker who was a member of our party. He had tracked me to the spot with all the skill and keen senses of the best bloodhound.

369

I have also been lost on the opposite end of the earth, in Alaska's inhospitable Chugach Mountains. On this sheep venture, a camp and supplies which were to be air-dropped at a certain destination in sheep country were somehow dropped in the wrong place. Temporarily, I lost myself trying to find the gear. Completely without shelter, Lew Baker and I managed through three days of almost continual sleet or drizzle. It seemed that the only conclusion of the trip would be an insurance claim on waterlogged cameras.

But discomfort can be quickly forgotten when things suddenly break right. Next morning, after locating the thin trail which led to our supplies, I felt tremendously exhilarated as I looked at four white Dall rams in my ground glass viewer. And the sheep looked back at me just long enough for the photos I wanted. Then and there I forgot the earlier hardships of the expedition.

Although any kind of photography may appear bewildering at first, taking good big-game pictures is not difficult. You need a certain amount of equipment, and some pros carry prodigious amounts of it, but extraordinary wildlife photos have come from cameras which are neither costly nor complicated. Photography experience is valuable, as is some prior knowledge of wildlife behavior. Gun hunting experience is helpful. But even starting from scratch, good big-game animal photos are very soon possible.

The best camera for wildlife photography is the single lens reflex 35mm, which is most convenient to handle and takes either color or black-and-white film. (I do not always use the 35mm and at times prefer the 2¼″ x 2¼″, but for reproduction reasons rather than convenience.) Most of the 35mm models on the market today are so virtually foolproof that you simply aim and snap to get a perfect exposure. Which model to buy or use depends more on budget than anything else. Details on how to select cameras and equipment can be found in my book, *Outdoor Photography*, published by Outdoor Life Books. Often the only difference between expensive and inexpensive models is the small variation in quality of the lens (which few but the experts will be able to detect), or the feature of being able to interchange lenses.

Because all big game is shy to some degree and will not allow humans to approach as close as they would like, one accessory—the telephoto lens—is particularly important to nearly all wildlife photography. The so-called normal lens that comes with every 35mm camera has a focal length of 50mm, the distance between lens glass and film inside the cameras, and produces a picture exactly as the eye sees it. But a telephoto lens with a longer than normal focal length increases the size of the animal's image on film and therefore makes it seem much closer. Telephotos for 35mm cameras are manufactured up to 600mm, which magnifies the subject 12 times, but 200mm or 300mm, which magnify the subject four or six times, are far more practical for the amateur.

It is absolutely necessary to hold *any* telephoto lens perfectly still when shooting, using the fastest possible shutter speed—up to 1/1000 second if the exposure permits it. This is because the longer the telephoto lens, the greater the magnification of any camera motion, resulting in fuzzy pictures. Whenever possible, use either a rest (the car door or a tree limb will do) or a tripod for the most sharpness and detail in the finished picture. Try to avoid ugly or unnatural backgrounds

A reliable camera that can take some punishment —and a secure case to lessen that punishment—are essential for a photographic safari. My favorite camera for all-purpose wildlife shooting is a Nikon F, shown at right with a 500 mm reflex lens. I pack it in a dustproof, waterproof aluminum case (bottom) that is roomy enough to hold an ample supply of film.

such as fences, buildings, or wires. Telephoto lenses with small depths of focus will help accomplish this by blurring everything but the subject. The best method is to adjust your camera angle and correctly approach the subject to eliminate the unwanted background.

Let's consider the types of telephoto lens now available and suitable for hunting big game. Most common, usually least expensive, and obtainable in focal lengths up to 300mm are those telephotos which are focused by turning a focusing ring, exactly as are shorter lenses. A major disadvantage is that they are slow to operate, and the cameraman needs some field experience before he can quickly find his subject and then focus on it sharply. Most of the popular 35mm systems offer several different telephotos of this type. Most also offer a more recent development—the zoom lens—which may offer a range of focal lengths (depending on the model) from 90mm or 100mm to 200mm or 250mm. These are heavier and more expensive than the telephotos of a single focal length.

Another type of telephoto is known as the follow-focus lens. This is manufactured by Novoflex in 450mm (with an optional extension tube to make it 600mm), features a pistol grip midway out on the lens, and is focused by squeezing and relaxing the grip. Adapters will fit this lens onto most of the better 35mm cameras.

Newest development is the mirror or reflex telephoto. The advantage of this is that it is shorter and lighter, and therefore far more convenient and faster to use than normal or follow-focus telephotos of the same focal length. In other words, the tube or actual distance between glass and camera connection of a 500mm mirror lens may be half the length and weight of any other type of 500mm lens.

However, there are drawbacks. The f-stop of mirror lenses is fixed at one place—say f8 on a 500mm lens or f11 on a 1000mm lens—and the correct exposure is obtained by changing shutter speeds. In spite of this handicap, my favorite and most frequently used of all big-game lenses is a 500mm mirror mounted on a Nikon F with motor drive.

Many big-game hunters like to mount their camera and telephoto combinations on gunstocks or something similar for faster shooting. Some commercial stocks are available, but most like to custom-build and design their own. I do not prefer these stocks and regard them as only an added weight to lug around. But excellent big-game photos have been made by gunstock fans.

Although expensive and sometimes temperamental, motor drives can be extremely valuable. They can shoot as many as three or four frames per second and are excellent for sequences and for following animals in motion. More important, a motor drive permits a cameraman to concentrate more on his subject, without having to bother with advancing the film. For the serious big-game shooter, that one advantage more than justifies the considerable expense of the drive.

It is easy to overemphasize the importance of equipment. The most frequent comment a professional photographer hears about an especially good photograph is: "You must have an expensive camera." But no camera or lens combination is ever any better than the cameraman himself. Vastly more important than cost and quality is familiarity with whatever equipment is being used. And familiarity, which means fast, accurate handling and focusing, comes only with plenty of practice, even when there is no film in the camera.

The practice can begin at home. Take the family pet outdoors and photograph it in action—running, jumping, retrieving a stick, doing anything. This is good training for staying on a target and for more rapid camera handling. Use black-and-white for these initial exercises, because it is much less expensive than color. For more advanced practice go to the local zoo, to racehorse farms, ranches, rodeos or even livestock shows. Many modern zoos exhibit wild animals in completely natural surroundings. No matter where you shoot, your goal should be to shoot automatically— to follow and focus without having to think about it.

An exposure meter can be helpful, in fact indispensable when the light is very poor or constantly changing. But often it is only a downright nuisance which finds the cameraman taking a light reading when he should actually be photographing a subject which isn't predictable.

Every big-game hunter should know before going afield the correct exposure for over-the-shoulder or front-light sunlit subjects, for whatever film is in his camera. He should also be able to judge and estimate with fair accuracy amid normal changes in light. All this comes from practice and experience. Later, if he has time and is shooting a trophy which is fairly tame and in no hurry to escape, he can check his own first exposure with a meter. He can also check the exposure information which comes inside every package of film.

More and more cameras are being produced with built-in exposure meters, and these are excellent. But they do not accurately measure back-lit subjects or scenes very early and late in the day. The best meter for big-game photography is the spot sensor, which measures the light of a small, restricted surface—for instance an animal's hide—rather than the light in the entire scene.

Another important part of camera gear is the container in which to carry it. The usual leather camera cases and equipment bags are almost worthless to someone spending much time afield searching for big game. A plastic freezer or garbage bag is much better, as it can be both waterproof and dustproof. Moisture and dust are genuine bugaboos, both to getting good pictures and to smooth operation of the equipment.

When traveling, I carry my gear in sealed aluminum luggage lined inside with polyurethane to spare shock and rough handling. In the field, I carry each piece in individual plastic bags, and I take along plenty of spare bags.

Although freezing temperatures have no real effect on film or equipment (if it is clean and dry), pictures taken under those conditions may require slightly greater exposures than the same shots in summertime. A notable exception is a marine or snow-covered scene in bright sunlight. If you do not have an exposure meter, consult the exposure data sheet which comes with every roll of film. Do not bring cold cameras suddenly into warm rooms. Condensation will occur, especially inside the lens, and that can cause trouble.

I use two different techniques to photograph wild creatures. I either stalk or play the waiting game. The same techniques apply to motion pictures as well as still photography.

Most stalking is done on foot and is not unlike hunting with a gun. You must spot the target and then try to walk as close as possible, slowly, cautiously, never directly toward the subject, and never making sudden moves or loud noises. In some parks and sanctuaries where wildlife is accustomed to people, the animals often become tolerant of humans with cameras. Elsewhere, "stalking" can be done by car; in many national parks, animals allow a vehicle to approach very closely but bolt the instant a person steps outside.

Let's assume that we have spotted a herd of whitetail deer while driving through a state park. First, remember that the deer have seen the car, even if the car did not stop at the road's edge and even if the deer did not look up in recognition. Since the animals are fairly distant, our only chance for a photo is to walk closer. In this case, the best bet is to stay in full view during the approach rather than attempt a stealthy stalk unseen, and avoid staring directly at the animals. It's wise to make exposures at regular intervals in the event you never get any closer. Watch for signs of nervousness (which all animals exhibit) such as stomping, drifting away, flicking ears, snorting, raising a tail—and stop short when you see them. One anxious animal can spook the whole herd. If the animal does appear nervous, stop the stalk for a few moments and try to appear completely disinterested in the target. If the camera happens to be a reflex model, it is possible to continue shooting and focusing even while looking in another direction.

Virtually all big-game animals are most active very early and very late in the day, which means that these are the best times to be afield. I've found a very early breakfast far more important for better wildlife photos than an expensive camera. I use the middle of the day to clean lenses and load film, especially during very hot periods of summer.

The waiting game—sitting in a fixed blind —works best in a baited area or in the vicinity of a game trail or waterhole which wildlife are known to frequent. The blind might actually

For the on-the-go wildlife photographer, few pieces of equipment are as useful as a portable blind. This lightweight model is made of camouflaged fabric stretched over a tubular aluminum frame. It can also be carried on a packboard.

374

be your own kitchen from which you photograph the deer at bait or feeding station just outside. Farther afield, blinds can be anything from a small tent or camouflaged packing crate to a mere screen of natural foliage. Many animals never expect danger from above and seldom look up. A tree or platform blind is good for these. Professional photographers use lightweight, collapsible blinds of aluminum tube framing covered with burlap, weathered canvas, or artificial turf material. If the structures are left standing long enough, many animals become so used to them that they pay no attention.

The best places to take pictures are those where wildlife is given some protection or to which it is deliberately attracted. A list of these would include all National Parks, most National Wildlife Refuges, many state parks and refuges, wintering grounds, municipal or private game sanctuaries. Not all of these have populations of unsophisticated big-game animals, nor are all accessible in winter. But these are easy matters to check by writing to various park superintendents or naturalists.

For hunting American big game, the National Parks of both U.S. and Canada deserve the most attention. There are deer herds in nearly all of them. Don't overlook Custer State Park in South Dakota's Black Hills (for antelope, bison) and the National Bison Range near Moiese, Montana (elk, antelope, goats, mule deer, bighorn sheep, as well as bison). See the attached list for other good possibilities. Most visitors to Banff, Alberta, Canada are interested in the skiing, but the perimeter of town is a snow-covered bonanza where a wildlife photographer could spend the whole season. There roam elk, deer, moose, and herds of mountain sheep, all easily visible from the Trans-Canadian Highway. As in so many other places, winter hunting is great here.

The two million or more visitors to Yellowstone National Park in summertime see only a fraction of the animals which a handful of travelers see during the dead of winter. With deep snows smothering the high country, huge herds of elk, mule deer, and bison collect around the Firehole and Madison Rivers, which are kept free of ice by water from hot springs and geysers. The areas around Mammoth and Old Faithful become vast big-game pastures. It is an extraordinary spectacle. No wonder stalking winter wildlife with a color camera is becoming very popular there. West Yellowstone, Gardiner, and Cooke are in fact turning into winter as well as summer resorts. Cross-country skiers are able to approach within a few feet of some animals here.

The average sportsman may already own nearly all of the non-photo gear he needs for winter wildlife photography in America: a station wagon (with snow tires for northern latitudes) or a Jeep with four-wheel drive, warm clothing, and either a still or movie camera. In some cases, snowmobiles can be used, but winter-weakened wildlife must *never* be harassed by them. A light rucksack will carry plenty of equipment for walking, and saddlebags are fine when horseback riding. A pocket hand-warmer can be extremely welcome for handling cameras on very cold days.

East and South Africa are still the camera hunter's best bet on earth for photographing big game. Nowadays such camera safaris have become possible for outdoorsmen of average means, as well as for more wealthy sportsmen.

A very typical, modern photo safari I made

with John Moxley recently began in Nairobi, Kenya's capital, where we rented a Jeep and driver for three weeks. We didn't really need the driver but figured he would give us a better chance to concentrate on the photography. Our first destination was the Samburu Game Reserve in the dry and lonely Northern Frontier. Here we photographed gerenuk, Grevy's zebras, oryx and especially the elephant herd which daily comes to loll and drink in the Uaso Nyiro River. These tuskers are so regular in their ablutions that clocks can almost be set on their arrival at water's edge.

Our second destination was the Masai-Mara Game Reserve in the southern part of Kenya. Here we photographed the black rhino, lions, topis and waterbuck. We surprised a lioness trying to stalk a pair of fighting topi bucks, and we also "bagged" our first Cape buffalos.

Just across the Tanzania border and adjoining Masai-Mara is the 5,600 square mile Serengeti National Park. This region contains the greatest and most spectacular concentration of game animals remaining anywhere on the globe. It is possible to stand in one place (as we often did), aim a camera in any or all directions, and *always* see herds of big game in the view finder.

At Serengeti we completed our "Big Five" for the trip. Leopards are not the hardest of the five for gun hunters to collect, but they are by far the most difficult trophy for photographers. In one day, John and I were lucky enough to see three spotted cats along the Seronera River, but only the third was not too shy to be photographed.

Elephants replace Land Rovers as the mode of transportation in India's Kanha National Park. Here, I captured a nicely antlered barasingha stag from an interesting camera angle.

Ngorongoro came next, but this time I had no close encounters with lions. Instead we "shot" three of the Big Five (rhinos, lions, elephants) all at once! Then Manyara National Park, sixty miles east of Ngorongoro and deep in the Rift Valley which bisects a big chunk of Africa. Manyara is best known for its lions which live in trees and its immense flock of pink flamingos. But we also photographed the most massive buffs an· outdoorsman is ever likely to see and a most exciting incident in which they treed two lions which were hunting *them*.

From Manyara we passed through the newly established Arusha National Park on the way northward, again to Kenya and the Masai-Amboseli Game Reserve. Arusha is not an important park for wildlife photography, but it contains some animals (elephants, rhinos, bushbucks, buffs), Ngurdoto Crater, the Momella Lakes full of waterfowl, and the greatest possible sunset views of Mt. Kilimanjaro.

Although Amboseli is not my favorite photography area (the government permits excessive grazing by domestic livestock which at certain seasons reduces the place to a dust bowl), we did have a couple of wonderfully productive days of photographing. Our bag included cheetahs, both elephants and zebras in the shadow of Kilimanjaro, black rhinos, Grant's gazelle bucks in a savage head-to-head fight, and more lions.

The last stop was Nairobi National Park, where the large carnivores—lions, leopards and cheetahs—live within four miles of the center of one of Africa's largest cities. For this reason it may be the world's most unique big-game sanctuary.

Maybe the most amazing fact about the three weeks' trip was that it then cost the two of us under $3800, or less than $1900 apiece! In 1973, the figure probably is ten percent higher. That includes economy air fare New York to Nairobi and return and American plan accommodations at safari lodges and camps along the way. The only items *not* included are cameras and film, bar bills, and tips. With a larger group than just two, and by cutting a few corners, the same safari might be made for somewhat less per person. A check of several safari and transportation companies assured me that in 1972 parties of from six to eight could practically duplicate our trip for as little as $1800 apiece. That is a bargain any way you look at it. In fact, the photo safari may be the greatest bargain available to the serious outdoorsman today.

Let's compare regular hunting safaris. Nowadays a sportsman cannot expect to enjoy a shooting trip with a first-class outfitter for less than $7500. That figure represents a total investment which includes all expenses from air fares to trophy handling. But elsewhere than East Africa, the minimum figure might be as much as $8500 to $10,000. There are a few outfitters offering "economy safaris" here and there, but these are seldom successful or satisfactory. The "economy" is usually in the poor results.

A decade or so ago, the goal of every hunter leaving on safari was to shoot the so-called dangerous "Big Five"—elephant, lion, buffalo, leopard, rhino. That is still possible today, but it is very, very unlikely during a single trip. Most reputable white hunters advise their cli-

Close-ups can be shot through telephoto lenses— or by stalking up close. In Zululand, I maneuvered to within ten downwind yards of a white rhino, a docile species, to get a striking picture.

ents that to shoot two of the five is par for the course. No matter what has been written in the past, or advertised currently, trophy lions are not numerous anywhere anymore except in reserves. They belong in the category of rare animals. And the shooting of rhinos is not even permitted anymore in very many places.

Remember that John Moxley and I "shot" the Big Five in just a few days. And except for the one leopard, we photographed several "Big Fours."

Nor is hunting with a camera any less exciting than shooting to kill. You pick out your trophies in the same way and then get even more intimate glimpses of them. In fact, you try to get as close as possible and you have more opportunities. Daily you can be in action photographing, while even the best shooting safaris have empty days. No closed seasons or bag limits are ever a bother. The truth is that many of my pictures were far harder to obtain than mounted heads because I *had* to get closer, often with such headaches as poor available light versus slow film speeds working against me.

Many kinds of photo safaris are practical. It is possible to engage a white hunter with the traditional mobile camp and safari crew, but this is only slightly less expensive than a regular hunting trip. The *least* costly alternative is to take a two- or three-week group trip as I have outlined above. The smaller the group, the more it will cost per person. But a smaller group is more flexible and gives each individual more opportunity for serious photography.

Costs also depend on what type of vehicle is used. The most popular nowadays is the minibus which can carry up to seven passengers, plus the driver-guide, and all their luggage. Four or five passengers plus the driver is closer to ideal. These cars have either convertible roofs or roof hatches for taking pictures but do not have four-wheel drive. The last is a limitation in rough country or bad weather. The roof hatch is important because getting outside the car to shoot is not permitted in most East African parks and reserves.

is to contact a good travel agent who specializes in these, or one of the international airlines which serve East Africa. It is possible to combine photo trips with hunting and fishing, but at increased expense. There is a gradual trend in which hunting outfitters are catering more and more to photographers alone. A number of today's best known white hunters have made the changeover completely.

During the busiest season, which is wintertime in the U.S. and summer in the southern hemisphere, it is necessary to make safari reservations far in advance. The main reason is that photo safaris have become immensely popular with Europeans as well as Americans during the past decade, and so the safari lodges and camps are booked far ahead. These accommodations, incidentally, range from first-class hotels or motels to tent camps which are quite adequate. All are extremely well-located to take advantage of the surroundings and natural beauty. Usually herds of game are always within sight of the lounges and dining rooms. Safari bonfires are built every night, the meals are good, and the bars are great places to brag about what you bagged on film earlier in the day. Life on the photo safari circuit is pure pleasure and high adventure.

It is possible to rent a late model salon car or sedan, complete with air-conditioning, but these are not suitable for serious cameramen. At the other extreme are the popular four-wheel drive Jeeps, land rovers, and land cruisers, which will go almost anywhere. They are the most versatile for the really keen photographer, but they are also less comfortable than the mini-buses. Only four-wheel drive vehicles, however, can make the trip into Ngorongoro, for instance.

The way to plan or organize a photo safari

Another excellent photo safari area is Uganda, where unique photographing opportunities are available. Kenya and Uganda both offer a chance to film from boats, through Kazinga Channel at Queen Elizabeth and up the Nile from Paraa at Murchison. The amount of wildlife anyone sees any day on either of these film-burning trips is absolutely bewildering. Remote and lonely Kidepo Park is in Uganda, on the Sudan border. This one is made to order for the cameraman who really wants to escape into unspoiled wilderness Africa.

East Africa is not the only place to enjoy a photo safari. There are also unlimited opportunities in both South and Southwest Africa.

The big attraction in Southwest Africa is the Etosha Game Park, which is the largest game reserve in the world. Hides, or blinds, are built around many of the more important waterholes here to give photographers an even more intimate glimpse of wildlife than they can obtain from cars. The greater kudus are larger here than in any other game park, and there are such unusual antelopes as the gemsbok, springbok and Damara dik-dik. A trip to Kalahari Gemsbok National Park to the south can be combined with an Etosha safari.

The best known area in South Africa is Kruger National Park. This one is so vast and the terrain and wildlife so varied that a photographer could spend weeks here and never see the same region twice. Herds of impalas wander at will through the safari camps. Elephants are abundant in Kruger. Sable and roan antelope can also be photographed.

From my own experience, Zululand is South Africa's most exciting and fascinating photo safari country. The twin game reserves of Umfolozi and Hluhluwe are the best (and practically the last) remaining places to photograph the rare white rhino. These reserves also contain black rhinos, nyalas, kudus, buffalos and cheetahs. Within easy driving range in other directions are Nkumu, Mkuzi, and St. Lucia reserves, all of which can be included on a single photographic trip. Blinds for visitors have been erected at some of these.

A South African safari can be arranged for slightly less than a similar trip in East Africa. Because the road network is better and well-marked, and because there is no language or security barrier, it is also possible to rent a vehicle (perhaps even with a camping trailer) and to go photographing without a guide. But the round-trip air fare to South Africa averages $400 more expensive than to Nairobi.

The photo safari is never a time to be conservative with film. A good deal of time and money is already invested in the trip, and it is false economy not to shoot whenever an opportunity occurs.

I have had more than a normal share of excitement and have witnessed some strange spectacles of nature on photo safaris. One morning on the Nile several years ago, I was outboarding alone downstream when I spotted several elephants cavorting and splashing at water's edge several hundred yards ahead. Immediately I cut the motor, figuring to drift silently into close-up camera range.

Before I'd traveled very far, my boat was suddenly thrust upward and came within inches of being overturned. One film magazine *was* tossed overboard. By accident I'd drifted right on top of a hippo which was hiding in the murky water.

Later that day, and not far from the near disaster, I saw two Uganda kobs (local antelope which weigh about 120 pounds) try to swim the river. Only one made the far bank; crocodiles accounted for the other.

Each year there are incidents when elephants overturn safari vehicles or rhinos give chase to them, but these are isolated encounters caused by cameramen molesting the animals or trying to get too close. Wildlife photography is still a much safer activity than driving on busy highways.

Where to Photograph North American Animals

North America

ONLY THE big-game animals of east and south Africa are easier to see and photograph than those in North America. Fortunately, our matchless system of National Parks and National Wildlife Refuges, along with a number of state parks and sanctuaries, has made it possible to observe all but a few big-game species at close range. Following is a list of the best places, most of which are in the West.

Yellowstone National Park, Wyoming: elk, mule deer, bighorn sheep, Shiras moose, black bear, grizzly bear, antelope, bison.

McKinley National Park, Central, Alaska: white sheep, Barren Ground caribou, Alaskan moose, grizzly bear, wolf.

Glacier National Park, northwestern Montana, and adjoining *Waterton Lakes National Park, Alberta:* mountain goat, bighorn sheep, black bear.

Banff and Jasper National Parks, Alberta: bighorn sheep, goat, grizzly bear, black bear, moose, elk.

Yosemite, Sequoia, Kings Canyon National Parks, southern California: mule deer.

Zion National Park, Utah: mule deer.

Olympic National Park, northwestern Washington: Roosevelt elk, blacktail deer.

National Desert Game Range, near Las Vegas, Nevada: desert bighorn sheep.

Joshua Tree National Monument, near 29 Palms, California: desert bighorn sheep.

Bandelier National Monument, New Mexico: mule deer.

National Bison Range, near Moiese, Montana: bighorn sheep, antelope, mule deer, elk, bison.

Saguaro National Monument, near Tucson, Arizona: mule deer.

Aransas National Wildlife Refuge, near Rockport, Texas: whitetail deer, javelina.

Rob and Bessie Welder Wildlife Foundation, near Sinton, Texas: whitetail deer.

Wichita Mountains National Wildlife Refuge, Oklahoma: elk, bison.

Elk Island National Park, east of Edmonton, Alberta: bison.

Wind Cave National Park and *Custer State Park, in the South Dakota, Black Hills:* bison, antelope, mule deer, mountain goat (at Rushmore and Harney Peak) .

Isle Royale National Park, Michigan in Lake Superior: moose.

Great Smoky Mountains National Park, Tennessee: whitetail deer, black bear.

Myakka River State Park, south central Florida: whitetail deer.

Katmai National Monument, Alaska: brown bear, Alaskan moose.

Tule Elk State Park, near Bakersfield, California: tule elk.

Land between the Lakes, western Kentucky: bison.

Grand Teton National Park and *National Elk Refuge, Wyoming:* elk, moose.

Mesa Verde National Park, southwest Colorado: mule deer.

Cedar Breaks National Monument, Utah: mule deer.

Africa

KENYA

Nairobi National Park: Small at only 44 square miles, but nowhere in the world is such a park located on the edge of a large and busy city (Nairobi). Most species of East African plains game, including lions, leopards, cheetahs.

Samburu-Isiolo Game Reserve, in the brooding scenic North Frontier, is the writer's favorite in Kenya. Elephants, Grevy's zebras, gerenuks, lions, other game of semi-arid and desert country.

Masai-Mara Game Reserve has 700 square miles and the largest population of lions left in Kenya, plus numerous antelope.

Amboseli-Masai Game Reserve in the shadow of Kilimanjaro, was once among the finest of all, but overgrazing by Masai cattle herdsmen has reduced much of it to a dust-bowl. Good for filming black rhinos.

Tsavo National Park. Man-eating lions originally made the name famous. Now covers 8,034 square miles of dry brush and hill country. Many elephants, buffalo. Hippos can be seen from underwater at Mzima Springs.

Shimba Hills Reserve, only place to see sable antelope in Kenya. Near Mombasa.

Meru Game Reserve northeast of Mt. Kenya is best known for Elsa the lioness and writer Joy Adamson, but is good for general game filming, especially for giraffes, lesser kudus, other antelope.

Marsabit National Reserve is a remote sanctuary in dry northern Kenya. Best known for greater kudus and very large elephants.

Aberdare National Park, and site of Treetops. Much of it is damp mountain forest. Slight chance to film such rarities as bongo, leopards, giant forest hogs.

TANZANIA

Ngorongoro Crater Conservation Area is a magnificent, high-country natural wonder inside of which big game and birds are superabundant. Many black rhinos, eland, hyenas, vast herds of zebras and wildebeests, gazelles, magnificent red- and black-maned lions. Among the world's greatest wildlife spectacles.

Serengeti National Park is 5,600 square miles of grassy plains full of antelope and gazelles. Large lion population, some cheetahs. One of the best places to see and film leopards.

Manyara National Park is a small but remarkable wildlife reserve. Elephants, Cape buffalo, antelope share the shores of Lake Manyara. Large flamingo flocks, but not easy to film.

Arusha National Park is in a forested, cratered mountain region. Very scenic, but wildlife not always in evidence. Look for bushbuck, elephants, buffs, rhinos in cover.

Mikumi National Park is fairly new, has elephants, many kinds of antelope including sable.

Ruaha National Park is a vast, remote, completely unspoiled wilderness with an amazing amount of bird and animal life, but a full-scale tent safari must be organized to visit this park.

UGANDA

Murchison Falls National Park. Main feature is the magnificent falls of the Nile, but the park is also a wildlife treasure. Largest crocodiles to be seen anywhere are below the falls. Many hippos, elephants, Uganda kobs, fishing eagles, many antelope and water birds. Daily filming by boat up the Nile River.

Queen Elizabeth National Park is at the base of Mountains of the Moon. Hippos, tree-climbing lions, hartebeests, topis, waterbuck, whale-headed storks.

Kidepo National Park is Uganda's most remote sanctuary, on the Sudan Border, and a favorite of the writer. Elephants, roan antelope, oribis, buffalo, hartebeests. Occasional security problems at the border.

ETHIOPIA

Awash National Park is a beautiful nature area with oryxes, Grevy's zebras, mountain reedbuck, lesser kudus, but is a stepchild of the government.

There are also wildlife parks or sanctuaries in Ivory Coast (*Réserve Totale de Faune de Bouna*), Ghana (*Mole* and *Kujani Game Reserves*), Dahomey (*Parc National Dahomey*) and Cameroons (*Parcs Nationaux de la Benoue et du Boubandijah*). These are not as rewarding to the wildlife cameraman as the East African areas above and the South African parks following.

REPUBLIC OF SOUTH AFRICA

Kruger National Park is the oldest on the continent and still among the most exciting to visit. Elephants, lions, antelope, impalas, kudus, sables, hunting dogs.

Umfolozi, Hluhluwe, St. Lucia, Mkuze and *Ndumu Game Reserves*, grouped close together in Zululand. Excellent viewing of white rhinos, nyalas, reedbuck, kudus.

Giant's Castle and other nearby nature reserves in mountains of Natal. High mountains with blesbok, vaal rhebok, white-tailed wildebeests, red hartebeests.

Cape Nature Reserve near Capetown. The rare bontebok antelope. Matchless scenery.

MOZAMBIQUE

Gorongosa National Park, on Rio Pungue, best known for large elephant herds, good mixture of brush country antelope.

RHODESIA

Wankie National Park between Victoria Falls and Bulawayo. Lions, large herds of common antelope, lechwes.

ZAMBIA

Luangwa National Park, long an excellent wildlife area, but recent attempts to crop game as a source of food supply leave the future in doubt.

Kafue National Park near the capital, Lusaka, has vast mixed wildlife herds and is worth visiting.

SOUTHWEST AFRICA

Etosha Game Reserve is the largest game park in the world. Located in dry open country surrounding Etosha Pan, it's the habitat of vast herds of springbok, gemsbok, zebras, elephants, cheetahs, lions, kudus. Wildlife photography here is completely unlimited. Permanent hides (blinds) have been built at waterholes.

Asia

INDIA

Kanha National Park is the country's best, in Madhya Pradesh state. Wildlife here is trustful when filmed from elephant back. Chital, rare barasinghas, gaurs, sambars, leopards are most common. A tiger may at times be baited.

Kaziranga Wildlife Sanctuary in Assam, a last stronghold of great Indian one-horned rhino which can be closely approached on an elephant. Also wild buffalo, swamp deer, hog deer, wild boars, an occasional tiger. Excellent place for filming all wildlife. Special permit required to visit Assam, a security area.

Gir Forest in Gujarat state, last stronghold for the only Asian lions (less than 150) left on earth. Lions are brought to tethered bait and are easy to film; other wildlife is shy and wild.

Corbett National Park in Uttar Pradesh. Very beautiful park at fringe of Himalayan foothills, but animals are wilder than is best for photography. Chital, muntjacs, black and sloth bears, sambars, occasional tigers.

Dachigam Sanctuary in Kashmir, northwest India, last stronghold of Kashmir stag. Also musk deer, Himalayan black and brown bears.

Shivpuri National Park in Mahdya Pradesh, for sambars, chital, nilgais and chinkaras.

Bandipur and *Mudumulai Sanctuaries* in south India, for photographing elephants, gaurs, sambars, chital, occasional leopards, sloth bears. Also a station for capture and training of wild elephants for domestic work.

Periyar Sanctuary, Madras, south India, for photographing elephants by boat; gaurs, sambars, sloth bears.

CEYLON

Ruhunu National Park. Only 112 square miles and touching the southeast coast, this park has a huge wildlife population for its size, most of it very trustful and easy to film. Elephants, sambars, barking deer, buffalo.

Wilpattu National Park on west coast of the island, is probably the best spot anywhere to film leopards, which pay little attention to photographers. Also chital, sloth bears, barking deer, sambars.

NEPAL

Mahendra National Park. Great one-horned rhino can be photographed from elephant back. Best place anywhere to see a tiger.

Bibliography

Adamson, George, *A Lifetime with Lions,* Doubleday and Co., New York, 1968.

Adamson, Joy, *The Spotted Sphinx,* Harcourt Brace Jovanovich Inc., New York, 1969.

Anderson, Kenneth, *Nine Man Eaters and The Rogue,* George Allen and Unwin Ltd., London, 1954.

————, *The Tiger Roars,* Welbright and Talley, Inc., New York, 1967.

————, *Black Panther of Sivanipalli,* George Allen and Unwin Ltd., London, 1959.

————, *Tales from the Indian Jungle,* George Allen and Unwin Ltd., London, 1970.

Arizona Wildlife Federation, *Arizona Wildlife Trophies.* Phoenix, Ariz., 1970.

Barrett, Peter, Editor, *A Treasury of African Hunting.* New York, Winchester Press, 1970.

Bauer, Erwin, *My Adventures with African Animals.* New York, W. W. Norton and Co., Inc., 1968.

————, *Outdoor Photography.* New York, Outdoor Life and Harper & Row, 1965.

Bere, Rennie, *The African Elephant.* London, Arthur Barker Ltd. and New York, Golden Press, 1966.

Boone and Crockett Club, *Records of North American Big Game,* 1964 Edition. New York, Holt, Rinehart, and Winston, 1964.

Brandborg, Stewart M., *Life History and Management of the Mountain Goat in Idaho.* Idaho Department of Fish and Game, 1955.

Brown, Leslie, *Ethiopian Episode.* London, Country Life Ltd., 1955.

Burt, William H. and Richard P. Grossenherder, *Field Guide to the Mammals,* Boston, Houghton Mifflin Co., 1952.

Burton, Maurice, *Systematic Dictionary of Mammals of the World.* New York, Thomas Y. Crowell Co., 1962.

Callison, I. P., *Wolf Predation in North Country,* Seattle, I. P. Callison, 1948.

Clark, James L., *The Great Arc of the Wild Sheep.* University of Oklahoma Press, 1964.

Corbett, Jim, *Man-Eaters of Kumaon.* Harmondsworth and Middlesex, England, Penguin Books, 1944.

Dahlberg, Burton L. and Ralph C. Guettinger, *The White-*

tailed Deer in Wisconsin. Wisconsin Conservation Department, 1956.

Dalrymple, Byron W., _Hunting Across North America,_ Outdoor Life and Harper & Row, New York and London, 1970.

de Alwis, Lyn, _The National Parks of Ceylon,_ Dept. of Wildlife, Colombo, 1969.

Dorst, Jean, and Pierre Dandelot, _Field Guide to Larger Mammals of Africa,_ Houghton Mifflin Co., Boston, 1970.

Dufresne, Frank, _No Room for Bears._ New York, Holt, Rinehart, and Winston, 1965.

Edminster, Frank C., _Hunting Whitetails._ New York, William Morrow and Co., 1954.

Erickson, Albert W., John Nellor, and George A. Petrides, _The Black Bear in Michigan._ Michigan State University Research Bulletin 4, 1964.

Fisher, James, Noel Simon, and Jack Vincent, _Wildlife in Danger._ New York, The Viking Press, 1969.

Gard, Wayne, _The Great Buffalo Hunt,_ New York. Alfred A. Knopf, 1959.

Gee, E. P., _The Wild Life of India._ New York, E. P. Dutton and Co., Inc., 1964.

Guggisberg, C. A. W., _Simba, The Life of a Lion._ Philadelphia, Chilton Books, 1961.

———, _Man and Wildlife,_ Arco Publishing Co., New York, 1970.

Haines, Francis, _The Buffalo._ New York, Thomas Y. Crowell Co., 1970.

Hoover, Robert R., C. E. Till, and Stanley Ogilive, _The Antelope of Colorado._ Colorado Department of Game and Fish, June, 1959.

Hunter, J. A., _Hunter._ New York, Harper and Brothers, 1952.

——— and Dan Mannix, _African Bush Adventures,_ Hamish Hamilton, London, 1954.

Ionides, C. P., _Mambas and Man-Eaters,_ Holt, Rinehart & Winston; New York, 1966.

Kemp, Peter Turnbull, _The Leopard._ San Francisco, Tri-Ocean Books, 1967.

Labuschagne, R. J. and N. J. van der Merwe, _Mammals of the Kruger and other National Parks._ National Parks Board of Trustees of the Republic of South Africa, 1966.

Lang, E. M. Mickey, _Deer of New Mexico._ New Mexico Department of Game and Fish, 1957.

Laycock, George, _The Alien Animals._ Garden City, N.Y., The Natural History Press, 1966.

———, _The Deer Hunter's Bible._ Garden City, N.Y. Doubleday and Co., Inc., 1963.

———, _The Sign of the Flying Goose,_ Natural History Press, Garden City, N.Y., 1965.

McCracken, Harold, _The Beast That Walks Like a Man._ Garden City, N.Y., Hanover House, 1955.

Maberly, C. T. Astley, _Animals of East Africa._ Nairobi, D. A. Hawkins Ltd., 1965.

Madson, John, _The Elk._ Winchester-Western Press, New York, 1966.

———, _The White-tailed Deer._ Winchester-Western Press, New York, 1961.

Mech, L. David, _The Wolf,_ Natural History Press, Garden City, New York, 1970.

Morris, Desmond, _The Mammals,_ New York and Evanston, Harper & Row Publishers, 1965.

Murie, Olaus J., _The Elk of North America._ Harrisburg, Pa., The Stackpole Co., and The Wildlife Management Institute, 1951.

Murie, Adolph, _The Wolves of Mount McKinley,_ Washington, D.C. United States Government Printing Office, 1944.

O'Connor, Jack, _Hunting Big Game in North America,_ Outdoor Life, New York, 1967.

———, _The Big Game Animals of North America,_ Outdoor Life, New York.

Palmer, Ralph S., _The Mammal Guide._ Garden City, N.Y., Doubleday and Co., Inc., 1954.

Perry, Richard, _Bears,_ Arthur Barker Ltd., London, and Arco Publishing Co., New York, 1970.

Prater, S. H., _The Book of Indian Animals._ Bombay Natural History Society, 1948.

Schuhmacher, Eugen, _The Last Paradises._ Doubleday & Co., Inc., Garden City, New York, 1967.

Shaha, Rishikesh, _Notes on Hunting and Wild Life Conservation in Nepal,_ Sangam Press, Kathmandu, 1970.

Smith, Dwight R., _The Bighorn Sheep in Idaho._ Idaho Department of Fish and Game, 1954.

Stracey, P. D., _Tigers,_ Arthur Barker Ltd., London, and Golden Press, New York, 1968.

Taylor, Walter P., Editor, _The Deer of North America._ Harrisburg, Pa., The Stackpole Co. and The Wildlife Management Institute, 1956.

Udall, Stewart L. and editors of Country Beautiful, _The National Parks of America,_ G. P. Putnam Sons, New York, 1966.

Van den Brink, F. H., _Field Guide to the Mammals of Britain and Europe,_ Houghton Mifflin Co., Boston, 1968.

BIBLIOGRAPHY

Waterman, Charles F., *The Hunter's World,* New York, Ridge Press and Random House, 1970.

Welles, Ralph E. and Welles, Florence B., *The Bighorn of Death Valley.* Washington D. C. United States Government Printing Office 1961.

Williams, John G., *Field Guide to the National Parks of East Africa,* London, Collins-St. James Place, 1967.

Young, Gordon, *Tracks of an Intruder,* Winchester Press, New York, 1970.

Young, Stanley P., *The Bobcat of North America,* Harrisburg, The Stackpole Co. and Wildlife Management Institute, 1958.

——— and Edward A. Goldman, *The Puma,* New York, Dover Publications, 1946.

——— and Hartley H. T. Jackson, *The Clever Coyote,* Harrisburg, The Stackpole Co. and Wildlife Management Institute, 1951.

Index